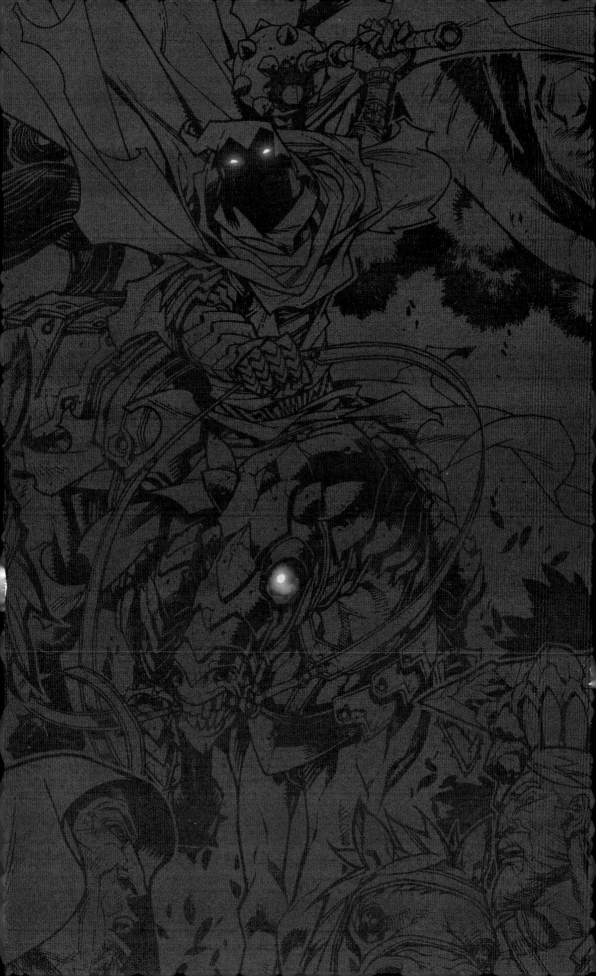

WRITER:
MIKE COSTA

ARTIST:
NEIL GOOGE

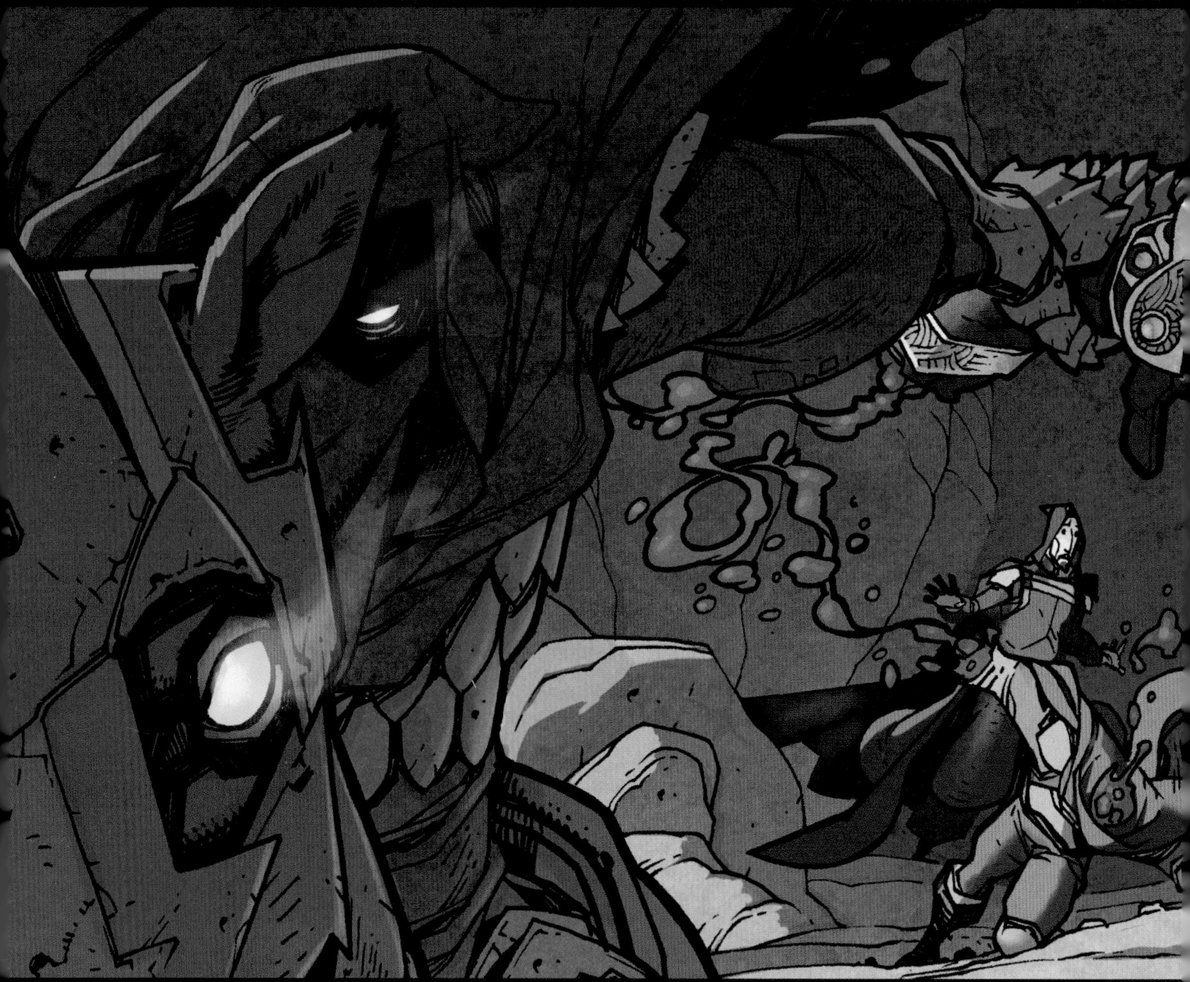

DC ENTERTAINMENT
SARAH GAYDOS & HANK KANALZ EDITORS
ROBBIN BROSTERMAN DESIGN DIRECTOR - BOOKS   SONIA CHOI PUBLICATION DESIGN

BOB HARRAS   VP - EDITOR-IN-CHIEF

DIANE NELSON PRESIDENT   DAN DIDIO & JIM LEE CO-PUBLISHERS   GEOFF JOHNS CHIEF CREATIVE OFFICER
JOHN ROOD EXECUTIVE VP - SALES, MARKETING AND BUSINESS DEVELOPMENT   AMY GENKINS SENIOR VP - BUSINESS AND LEGAL AFFAIRS   NAIRI GARDINER SENIOR
VP - FINANCE JEFF BOISON VP - PUBLISHING OPERATIONS   MARK CHIARELLO VP - ART DIRECTION AND DESIGN   JOHN CUNNINGHAM VP - MARKETING
TERRI CUNNINGHAM VP - TALENT RELATIONS AND SERVICES   ALISON GILL SENIOR VP - MANUFACTURING AND OPERATIONS   HANK KANALZ SENIOR VP -
DIGITAL JAY KOGAN VP - BUSINESS AND LEGAL AFFAIRS, PUBLISHING   JACK MAHAN   VP - BUSINESS AFFAIRS, TALENT   NICK NAPOLITANO
VP - MANUFACTURING ADMINISTRATION   SUE POHJA VP - BOOK SALES   COURTNEY SIMMONS SENIOR VP - PUBLICITY   BOB WAYNE SENIOR VP - SALES

COLORISTS: PIERRE MATTERNE, LEE LOUGHRIDGE & LEN O'GRADY

LETTERER: WES ABBOTT

STORY CONSULTANTS: CHRIS METZEN, ALEX AFRASIABI,
LUIS BARRIGA & MICKY NEILSON

COVER: ALEX HORLEY & SAMWISE DIDIER

SPECIAL THANKS TO JOSHUA HORST

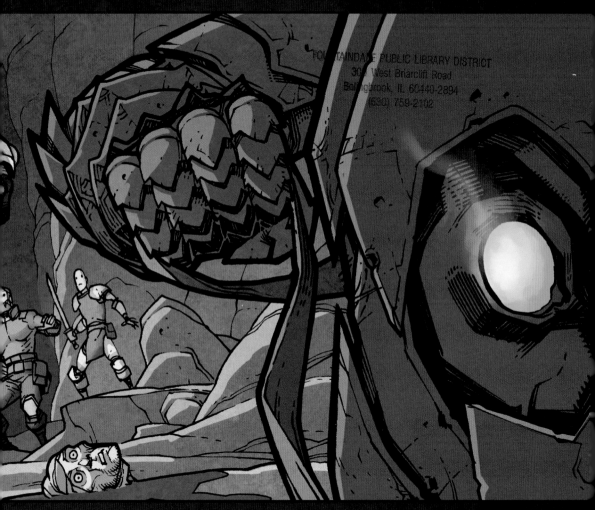

WORLD OF WARCRAFT: DARK RIDERS

WORLD OF WARCRAFT: Dark Riders, published by DC Comics, 1700 Broadway, New York, NY 10019.

© 2013 Blizzard Entertainment, Inc. All rights reserved. Warcraft, World of Warcraft and Blizzard Entertainment are trademarks and/or registered trademarks of Blizzard Entertainment, Inc., in the U.S. and/or other countries. All other trademarks referenced herein are the properties of their respective owners.

The stories, characters and incidents mentioned in this magazine are entirely fictional. Printed on recyclable paper. DC Comics does not read or accept unsolicited submissions of ideas, stories or artwork.

DC Comics, a Warner Bros. Entertainment Company.

Printed by RR Donnelley, Salem, VA, 3/26/13. First printing.

Library of Congress Cataloging-in-Publication Data

Costa, Mike, author.
World of Warcraft : Dark Riders / Mike Costa, Neil Googe.
pages cm
ISBN 978-1-4012-3027-2
1. Graphic novels. I. Googe, Neil, illustrator. II. Title. III. Title: Dark Riders.
PN6728.W69C67 2013
741.5'973--dc23
2012050101

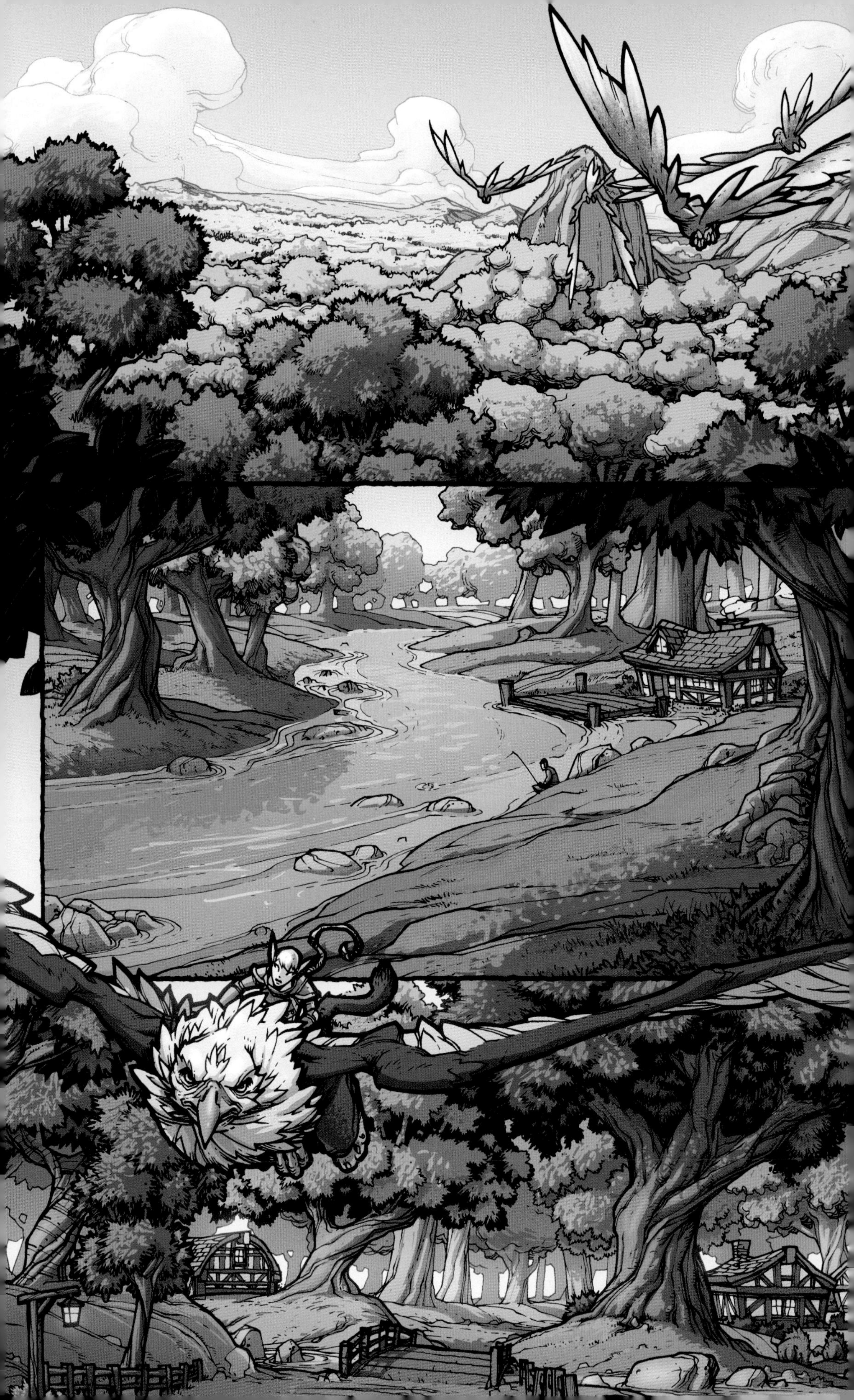

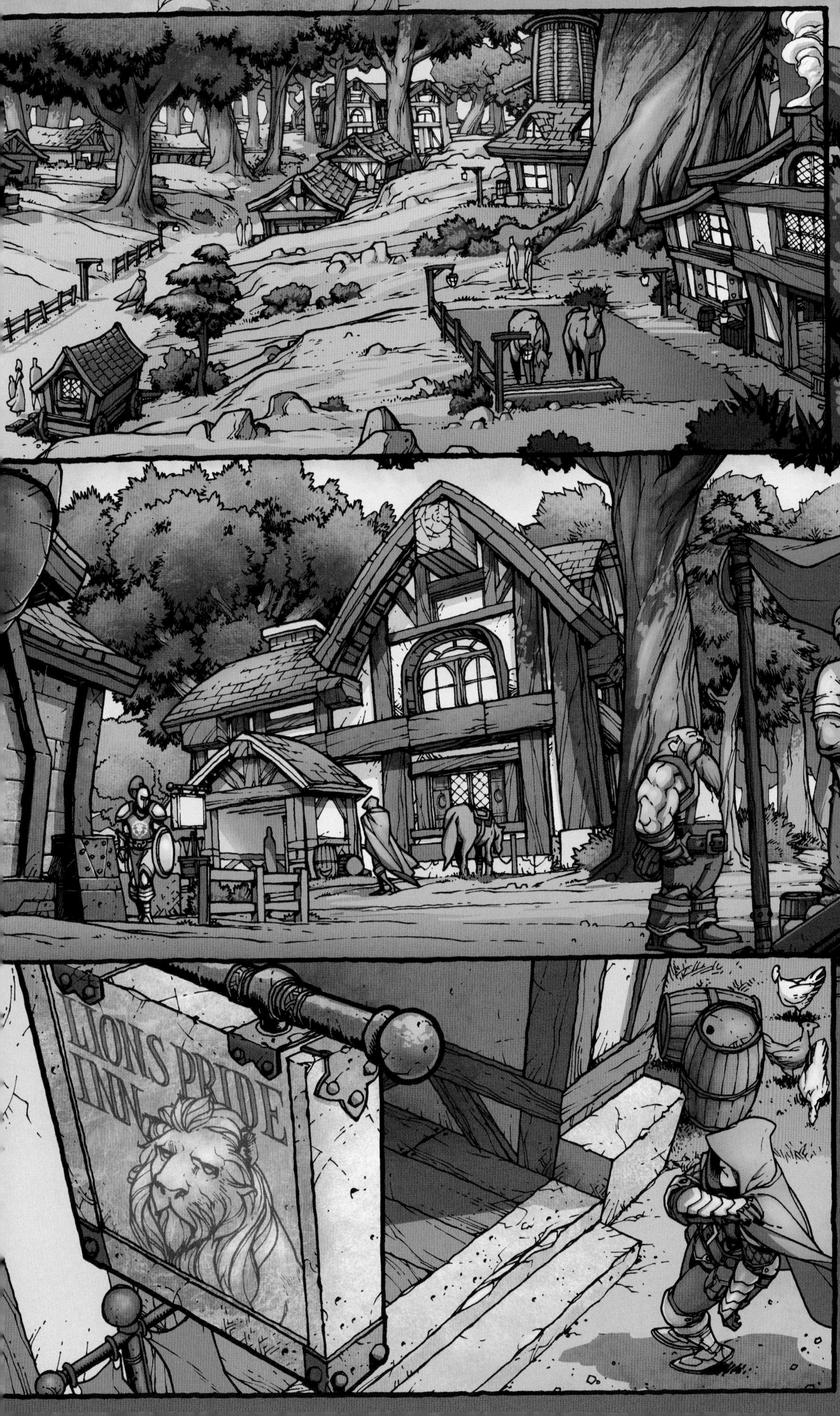
LIONS PRIDE
INN

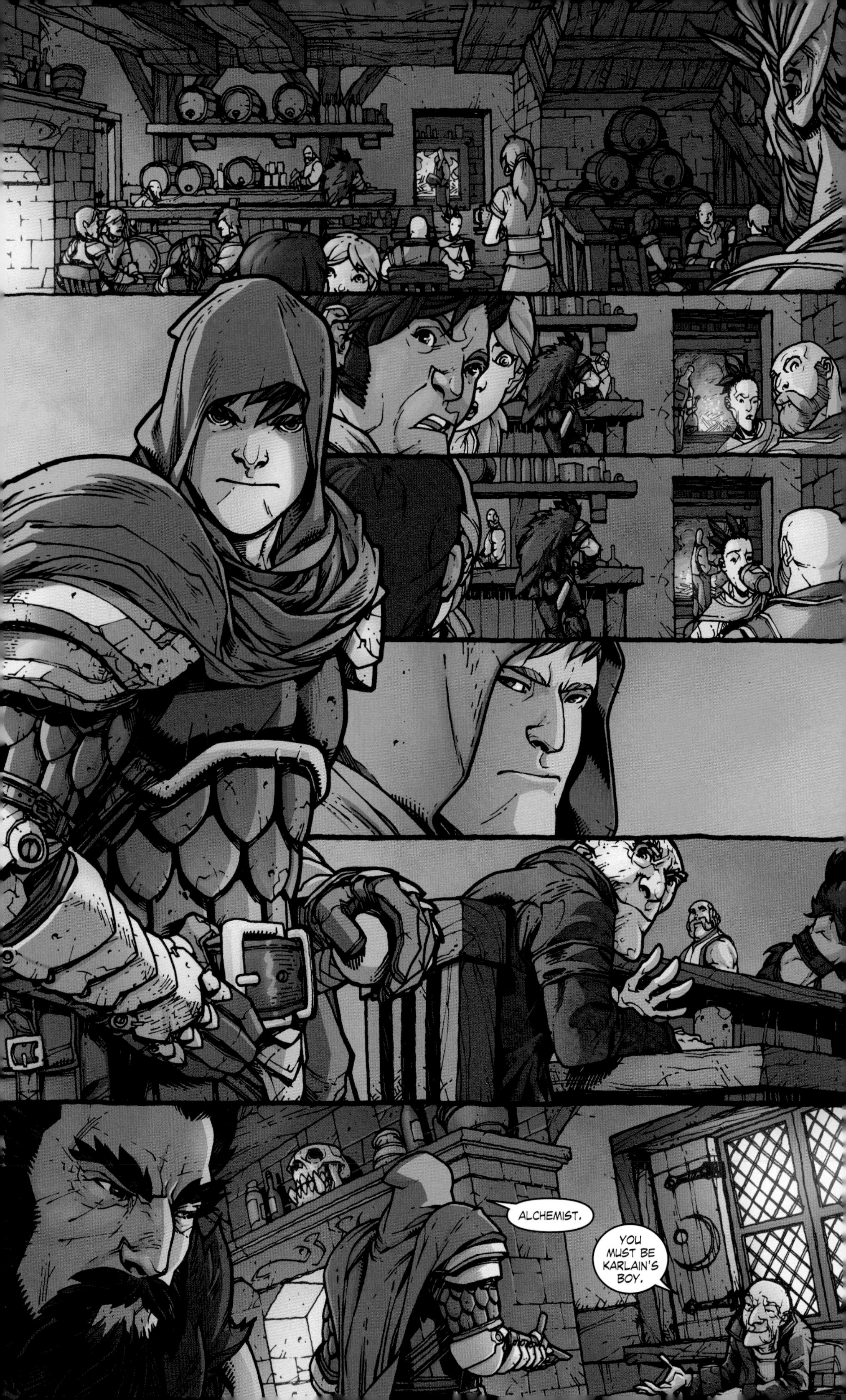
ALCHEMIST.
YOU MUST BE KARLAIN'S BOY.

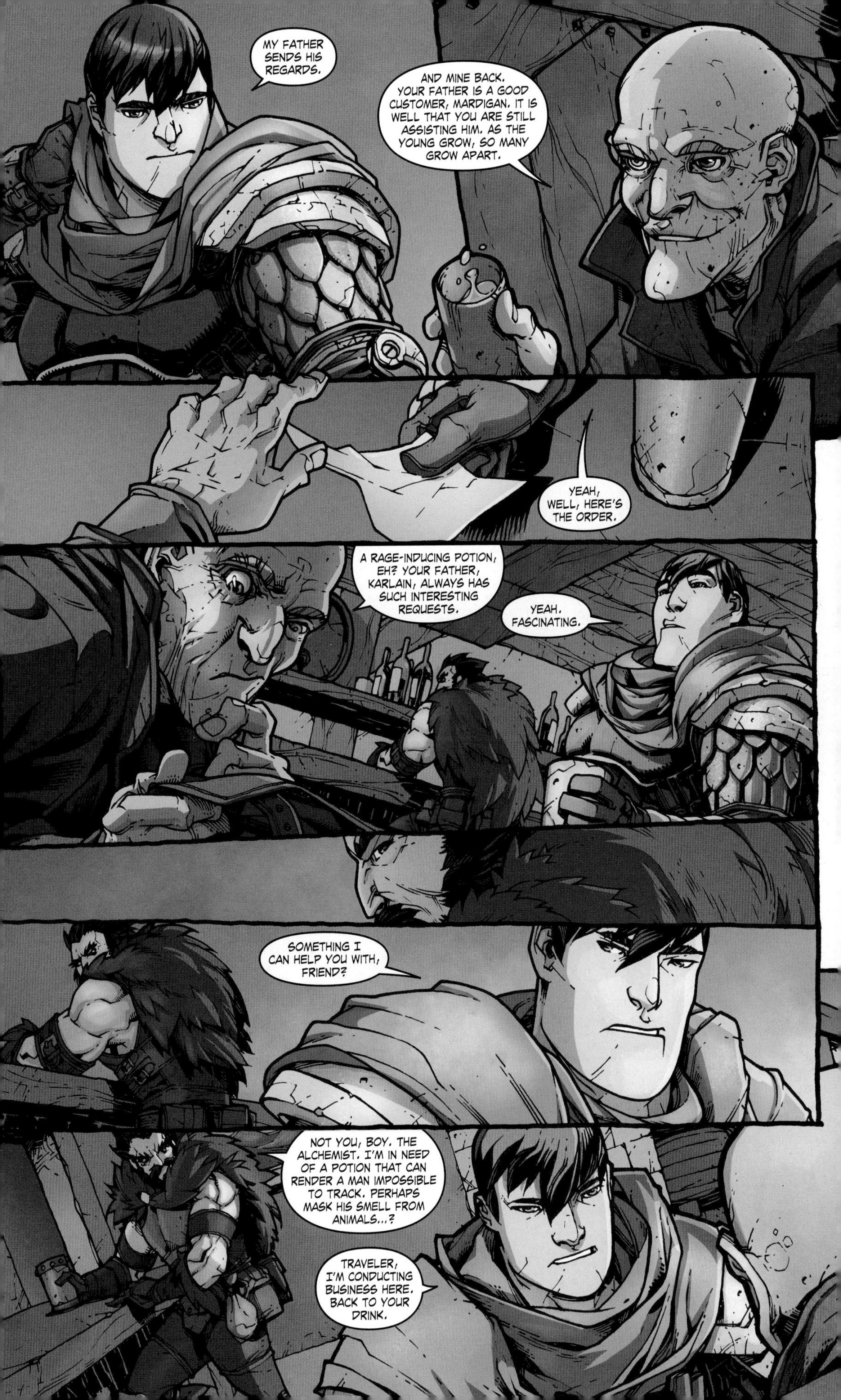
MY FATHER SENDS HIS REGARDS.
AND MINE BACK. YOUR FATHER IS A GOOD CUSTOMER, MARDIGAN. IT IS WELL THAT YOU ARE STILL ASSISTING HIM. AS THE YOUNG GROW, SO MANY GROW APART.
YEAH, WELL, HERE'S THE ORDER.
A RAGE-INDUCING POTION, EH? YOUR FATHER, KARLAIN, ALWAYS HAS SUCH INTERESTING REQUESTS.
YEAH. FASCINATING.
SOMETHING I CAN HELP YOU WITH, FRIEND?
NOT YOU, BOY. THE ALCHEMIST. I'M IN NEED OF A POTION THAT CAN RENDER A MAN IMPOSSIBLE TO TRACK. PERHAPS MASK HIS SMELL FROM ANIMALS...?
TRAVELER, I'M CONDUCTING BUSINESS HERE. BACK TO YOUR DRINK.

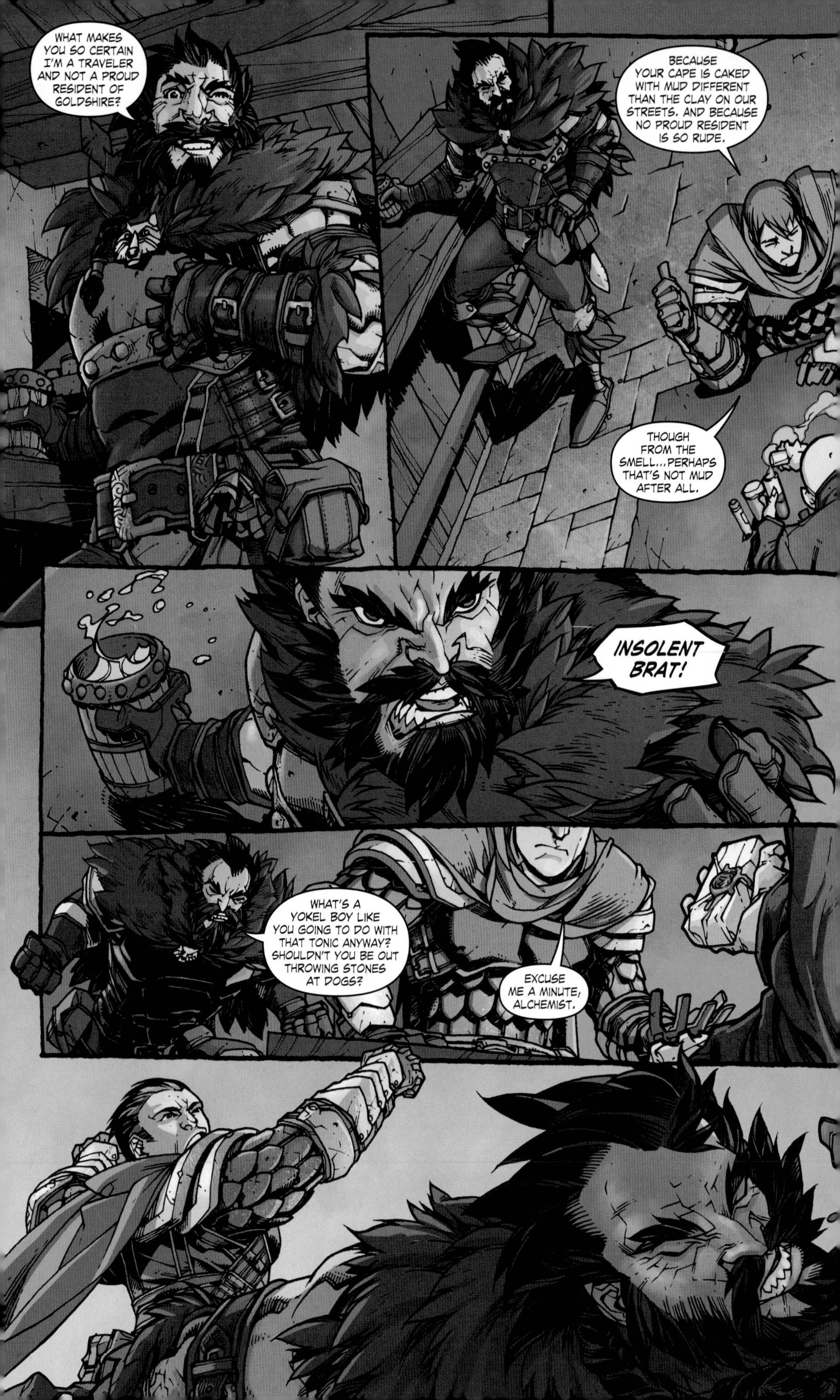
WHAT MAKES YOU SO CERTAIN I'M A TRAVELER AND NOT A PROUD RESIDENT OF GOLDSHIRE?
BECAUSE YOUR CAPE IS CAKED WITH MUD DIFFERENT THAN THE CLAY ON OUR STREETS. AND BECAUSE NO PROUD RESIDENT IS SO RUDE.
THOUGH FROM THE SMELL...PERHAPS THAT'S NOT MUD AFTER ALL.
INSOLENT BRAT!
WHAT'S A YOKEL BOY LIKE YOU GOING TO DO WITH THAT TONIC ANYWAY? SHOULDN'T YOU BE OUT THROWING STONES AT DOGS?
EXCUSE ME A MINUTE, ALCHEMIST.

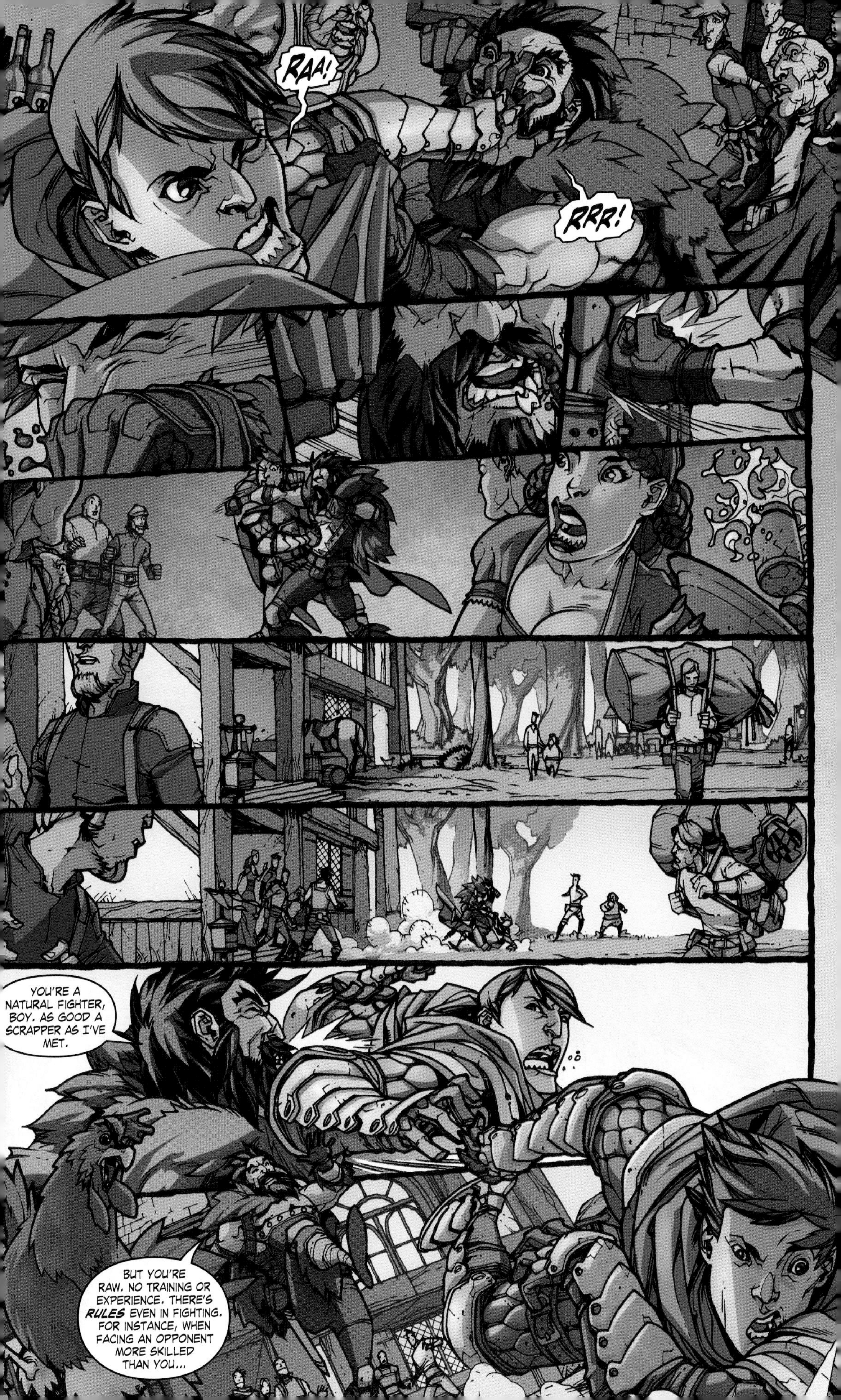
RAA!
RRR!
YOU'RE A NATURAL FIGHTER, BOY. AS GOOD A SCRAPPER AS I'VE MET.
BUT YOU'RE RAW. NO TRAINING OR EXPERIENCE. THERE'S *RULES* EVEN IN FIGHTING. FOR INSTANCE, WHEN FACING AN OPPONENT MORE SKILLED THAN YOU...

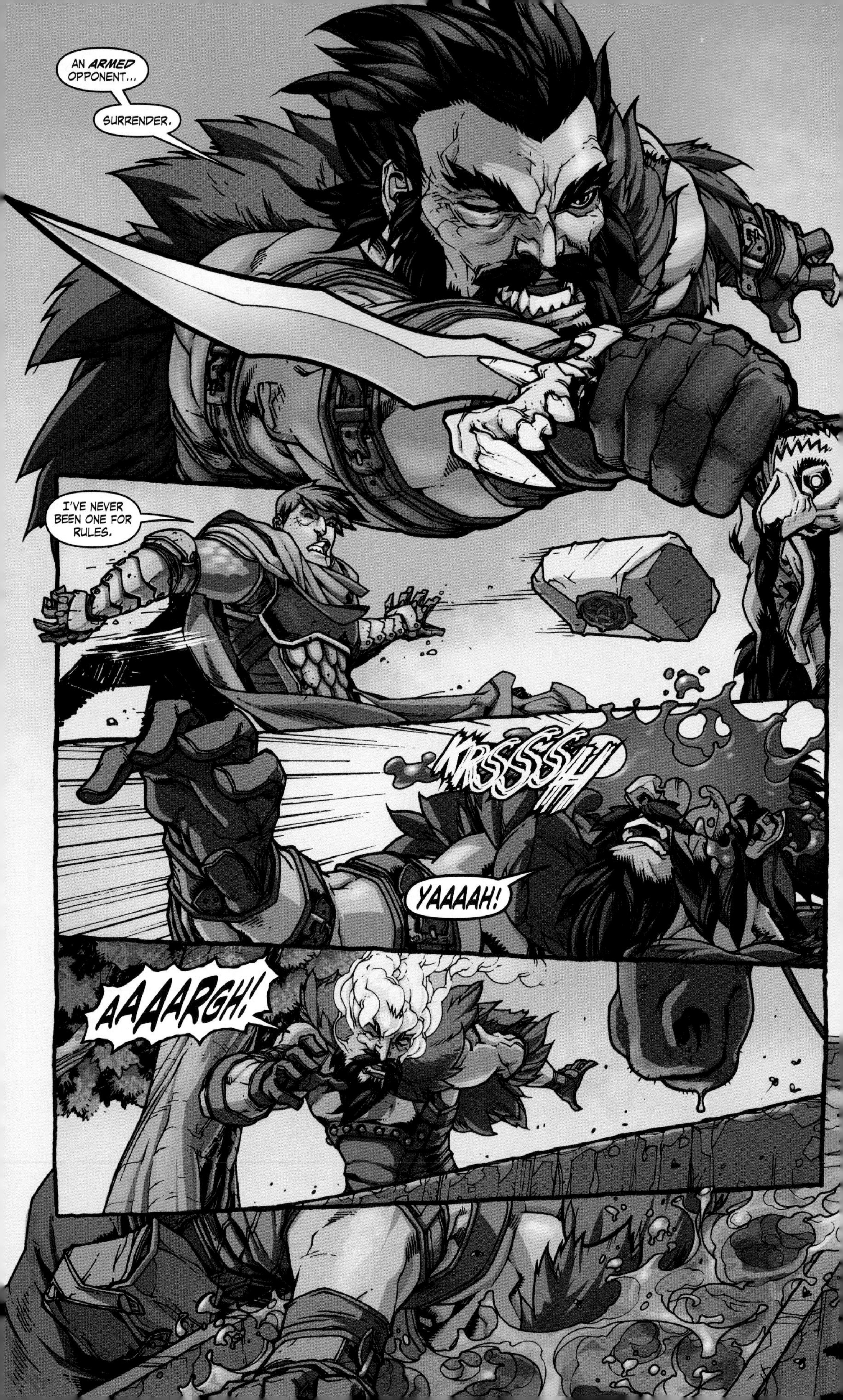
AN ARMED OPPONENT...
SURRENDER.
I'VE NEVER BEEN ONE FOR RULES.
KRSSSSH
YAAAAH!
AAAARGH!

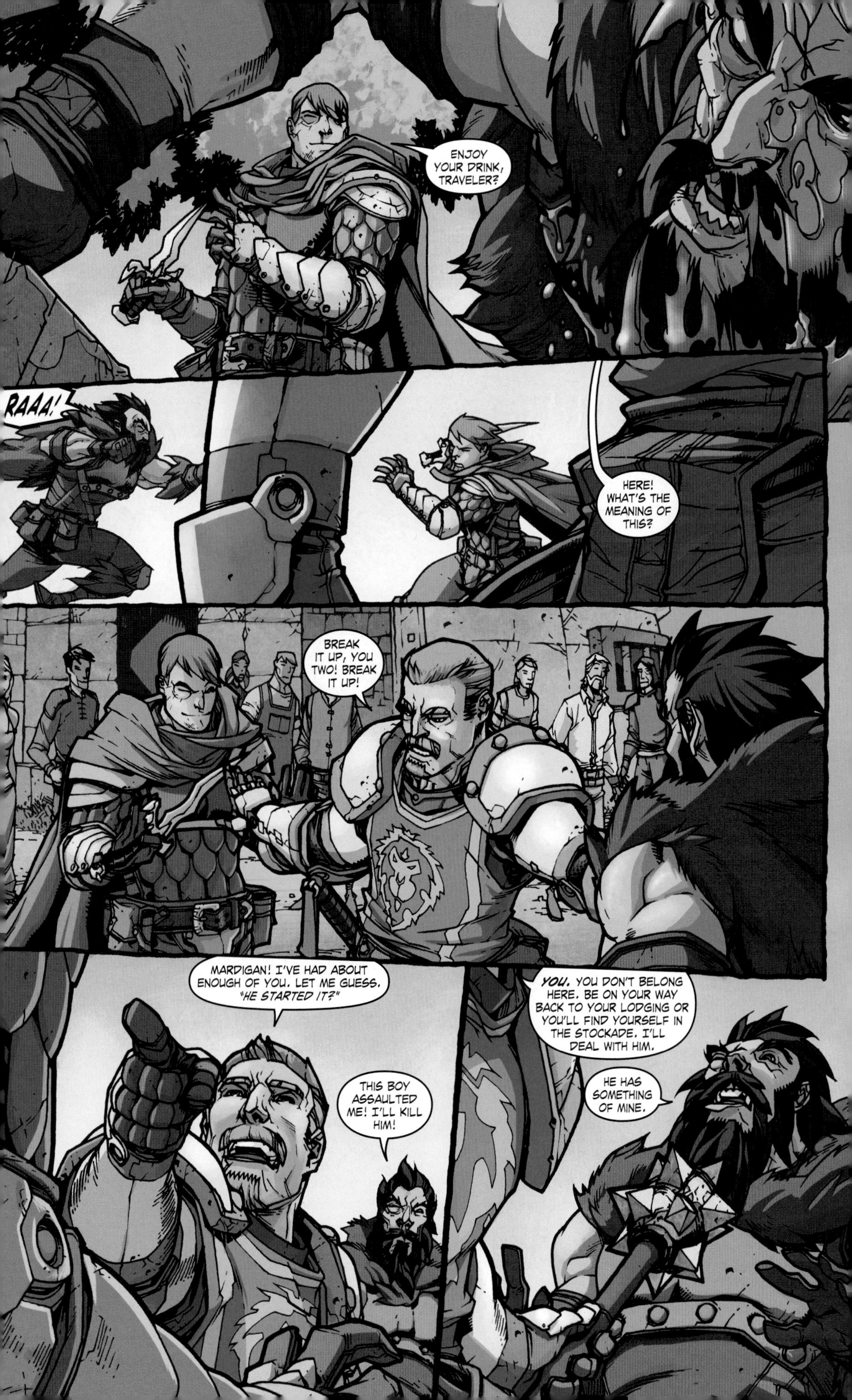
ENJOY YOUR DRINK, TRAVELER?
RAAA!
HERE! WHAT'S THE MEANING OF THIS?
BREAK IT UP, YOU TWO! BREAK IT UP!
MARDIGAN! I'VE HAD ABOUT ENOUGH OF YOU. LET ME GUESS. "HE STARTED IT?"
THIS BOY ASSAULTED ME! I'LL KILL HIM!
YOU. YOU DON'T BELONG HERE. BE ON YOUR WAY BACK TO YOUR LODGING OR YOU'LL FIND YOURSELF IN THE STOCKADE. I'LL DEAL WITH HIM.
HE HAS SOMETHING OF MINE.

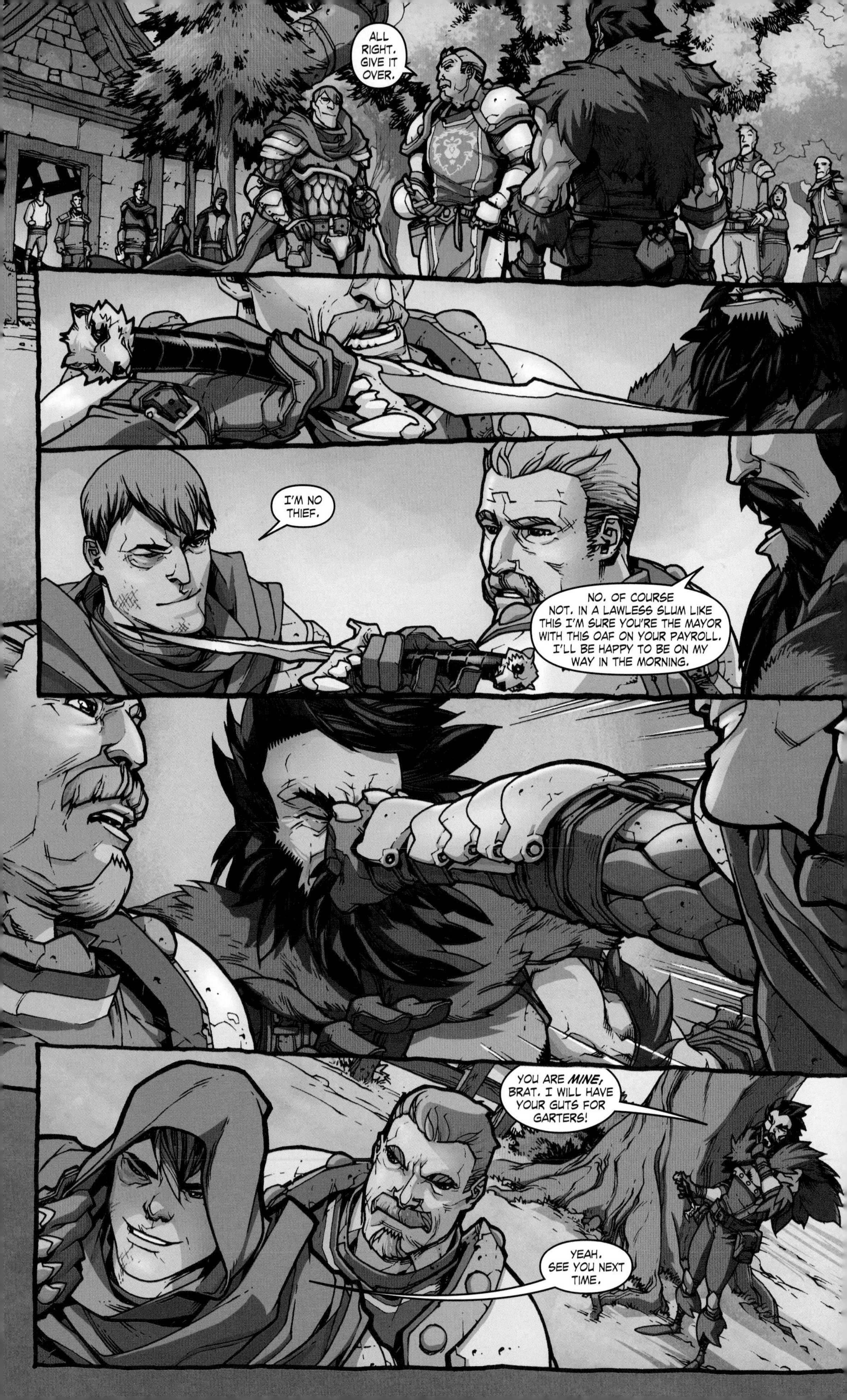

ALL RIGHT. GIVE IT OVER.
I'M NO THIEF.
NO. OF COURSE NOT. IN A LAWLESS SLUM LIKE THIS I'M SURE YOU'RE THE MAYOR WITH THIS OAF ON YOUR PAYROLL. I'LL BE HAPPY TO BE ON MY WAY IN THE MORNING.
YOU ARE *MINE,* BRAT. I WILL HAVE YOUR GUTS FOR GARTERS!
YEAH. SEE YOU NEXT TIME.

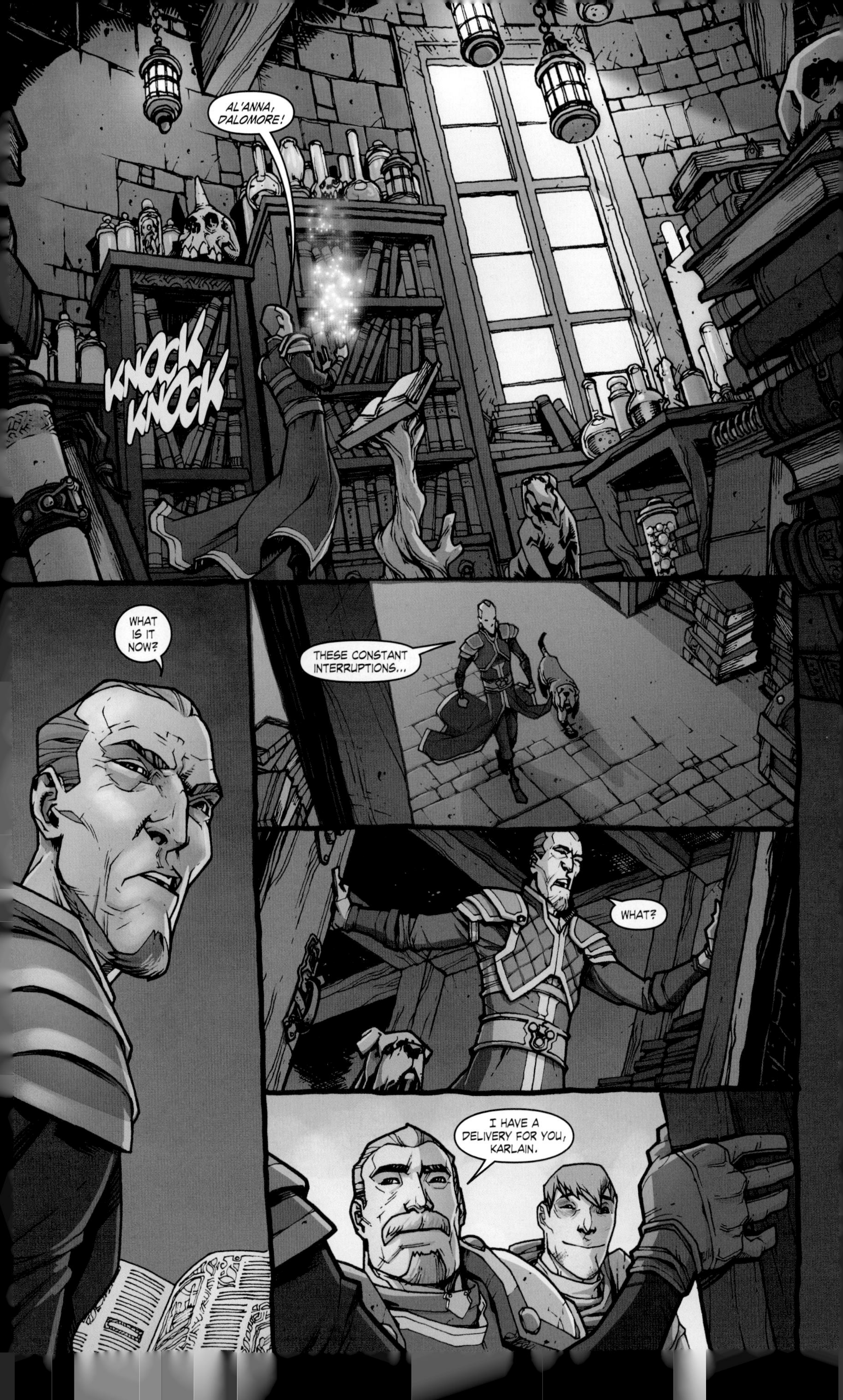
AL'ANNA, DALOMORE!
KNOCK KNOCK
WHAT IS IT NOW?
THESE CONSTANT INTERRUPTIONS...
WHAT?
I HAVE A DELIVERY FOR YOU, KARLAIN.

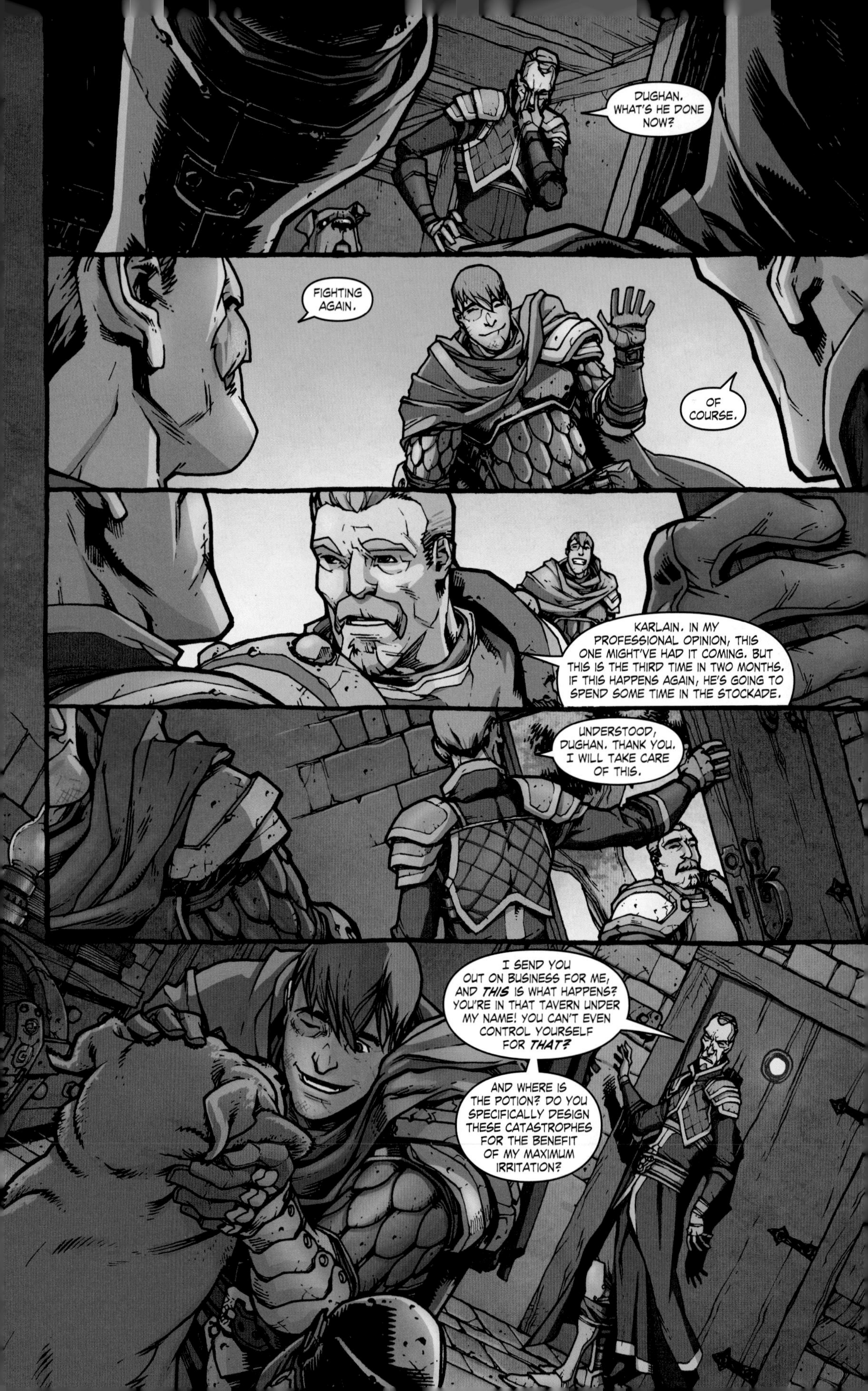
DUGHAN. WHAT'S HE DONE NOW?
FIGHTING AGAIN.
OF COURSE.
KARLAIN. IN MY PROFESSIONAL OPINION, THIS ONE MIGHT'VE HAD IT COMING. BUT THIS IS THE THIRD TIME IN TWO MONTHS. IF THIS HAPPENS AGAIN, HE'S GOING TO SPEND SOME TIME IN THE STOCKADE.
UNDERSTOOD, DUGHAN. THANK YOU. I WILL TAKE CARE OF THIS.
I SEND YOU OUT ON BUSINESS FOR ME, AND *THIS* IS WHAT HAPPENS? YOU'RE IN THAT TAVERN UNDER MY NAME! YOU CAN'T EVEN CONTROL YOURSELF FOR *THAT?*
AND WHERE IS THE POTION? DO YOU SPECIFICALLY DESIGN THESE CATASTROPHES FOR THE BENEFIT OF MY MAXIMUM IRRITATION?

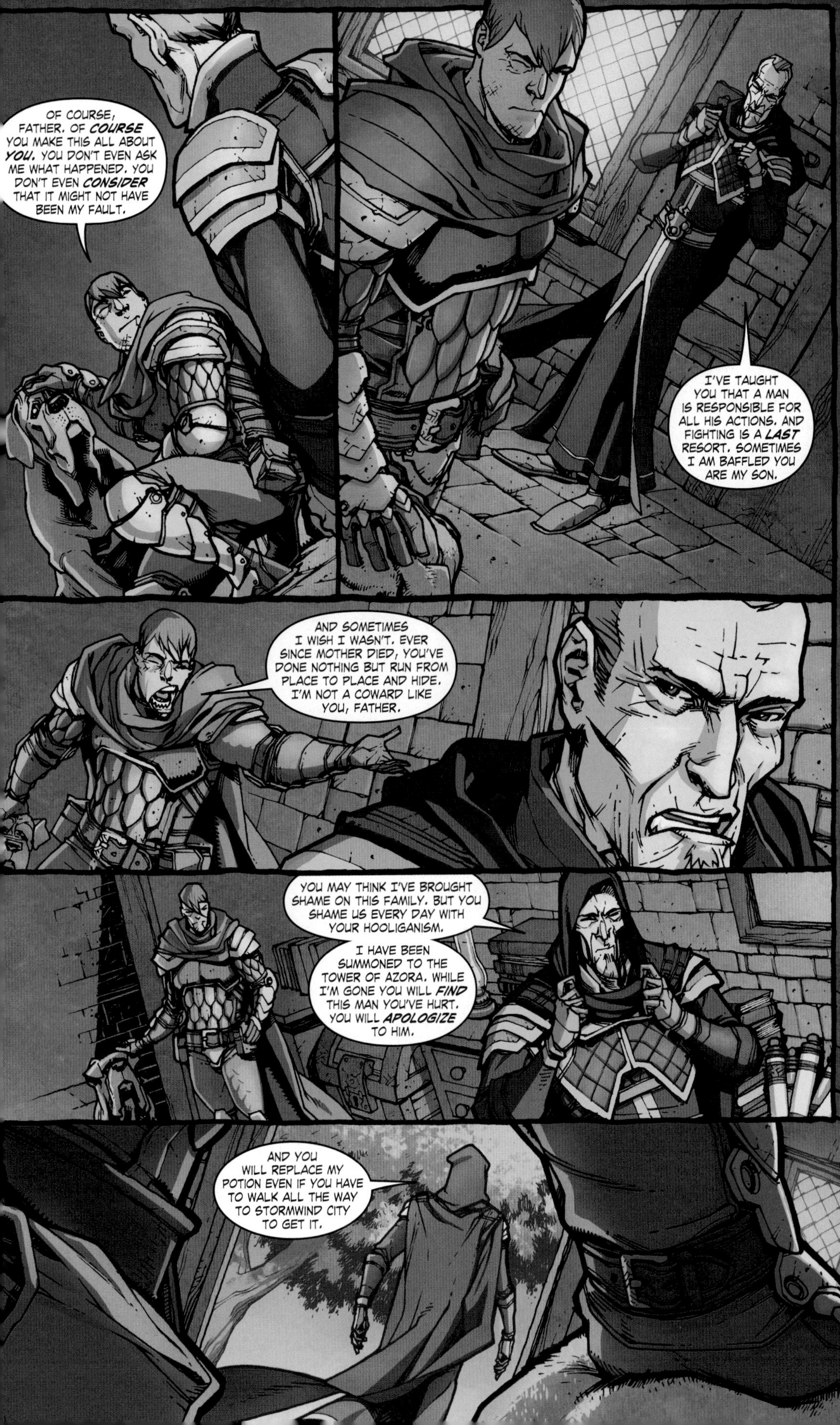
OF COURSE, FATHER. OF COURSE YOU MAKE THIS ALL ABOUT YOU. YOU DON'T EVEN ASK ME WHAT HAPPENED. YOU DON'T EVEN CONSIDER THAT IT MIGHT NOT HAVE BEEN MY FAULT.
I'VE TAUGHT YOU THAT A MAN IS RESPONSIBLE FOR ALL HIS ACTIONS. AND FIGHTING IS A LAST RESORT. SOMETIMES I AM BAFFLED YOU ARE MY SON.
AND SOMETIMES I WISH I WASN'T. EVER SINCE MOTHER DIED, YOU'VE DONE NOTHING BUT RUN FROM PLACE TO PLACE AND HIDE. I'M NOT A COWARD LIKE YOU, FATHER.
YOU MAY THINK I'VE BROUGHT SHAME ON THIS FAMILY. BUT YOU SHAME US EVERY DAY WITH YOUR HOOLIGANISM.
I HAVE BEEN SUMMONED TO THE TOWER OF AZORA. WHILE I'M GONE YOU WILL FIND THIS MAN YOU'VE HURT. YOU WILL APOLOGIZE TO HIM.
AND YOU WILL REPLACE MY POTION EVEN IF YOU HAVE TO WALK ALL THE WAY TO STORMWIND CITY TO GET IT.

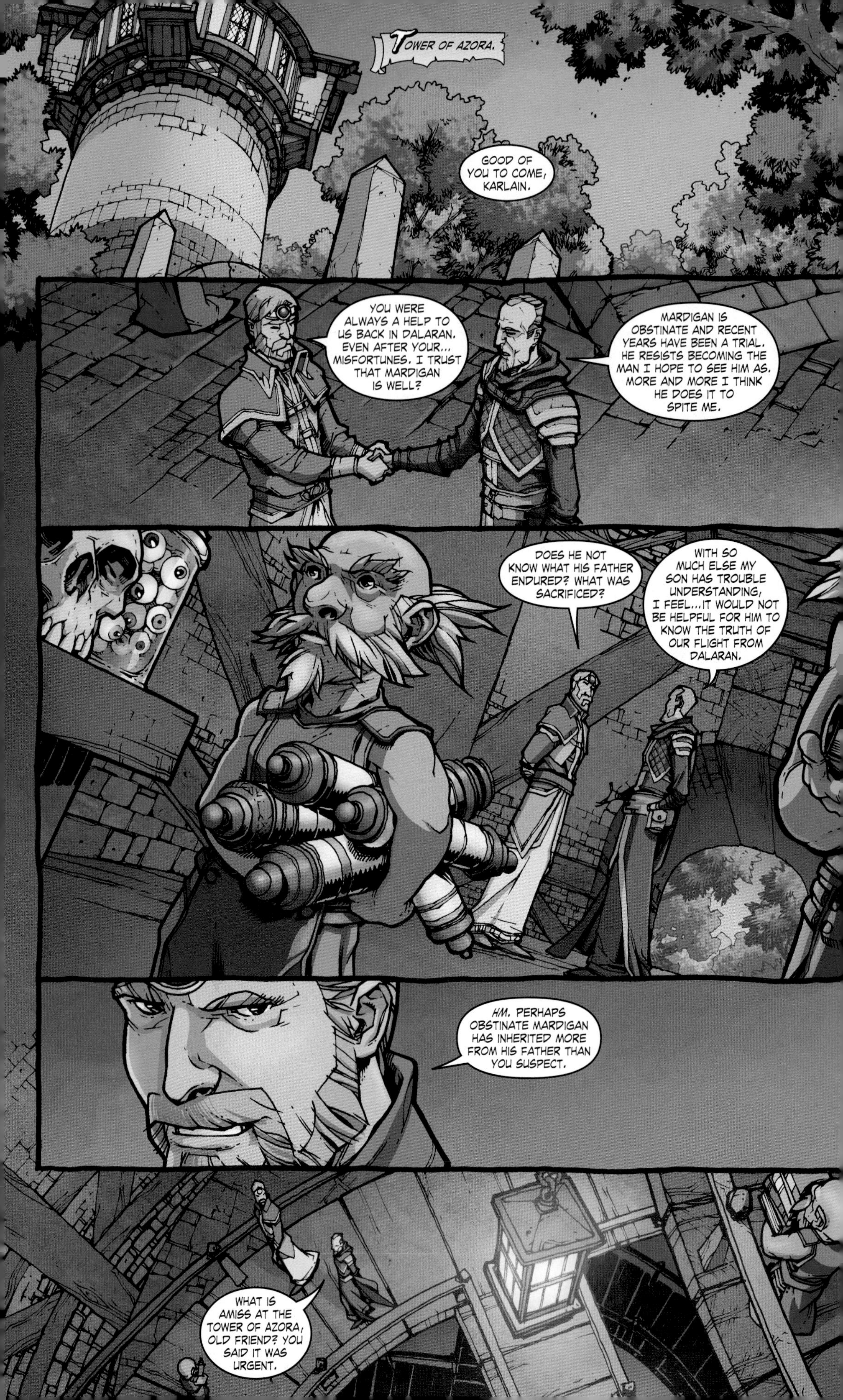

TOWER OF AZORA.
GOOD OF YOU TO COME, KARLAIN.
YOU WERE ALWAYS A HELP TO US BACK IN DALARAN. EVEN AFTER YOUR... MISFORTUNES. I TRUST THAT MARDIGAN IS WELL?
MARDIGAN IS OBSTINATE AND RECENT YEARS HAVE BEEN A TRIAL. HE RESISTS BECOMING THE MAN I HOPE TO SEE HIM AS. MORE AND MORE I THINK HE DOES IT TO SPITE ME.
DOES HE NOT KNOW WHAT HIS FATHER ENDURED? WHAT WAS SACRIFICED?
WITH SO MUCH ELSE MY SON HAS TROUBLE UNDERSTANDING, I FEEL...IT WOULD NOT BE HELPFUL FOR HIM TO KNOW THE TRUTH OF OUR FLIGHT FROM DALARAN.
HM. PERHAPS OBSTINATE MARDIGAN HAS INHERITED MORE FROM HIS FATHER THAN YOU SUSPECT.
WHAT IS AMISS AT THE TOWER OF AZORA, OLD FRIEND? YOU SAID IT WAS URGENT.

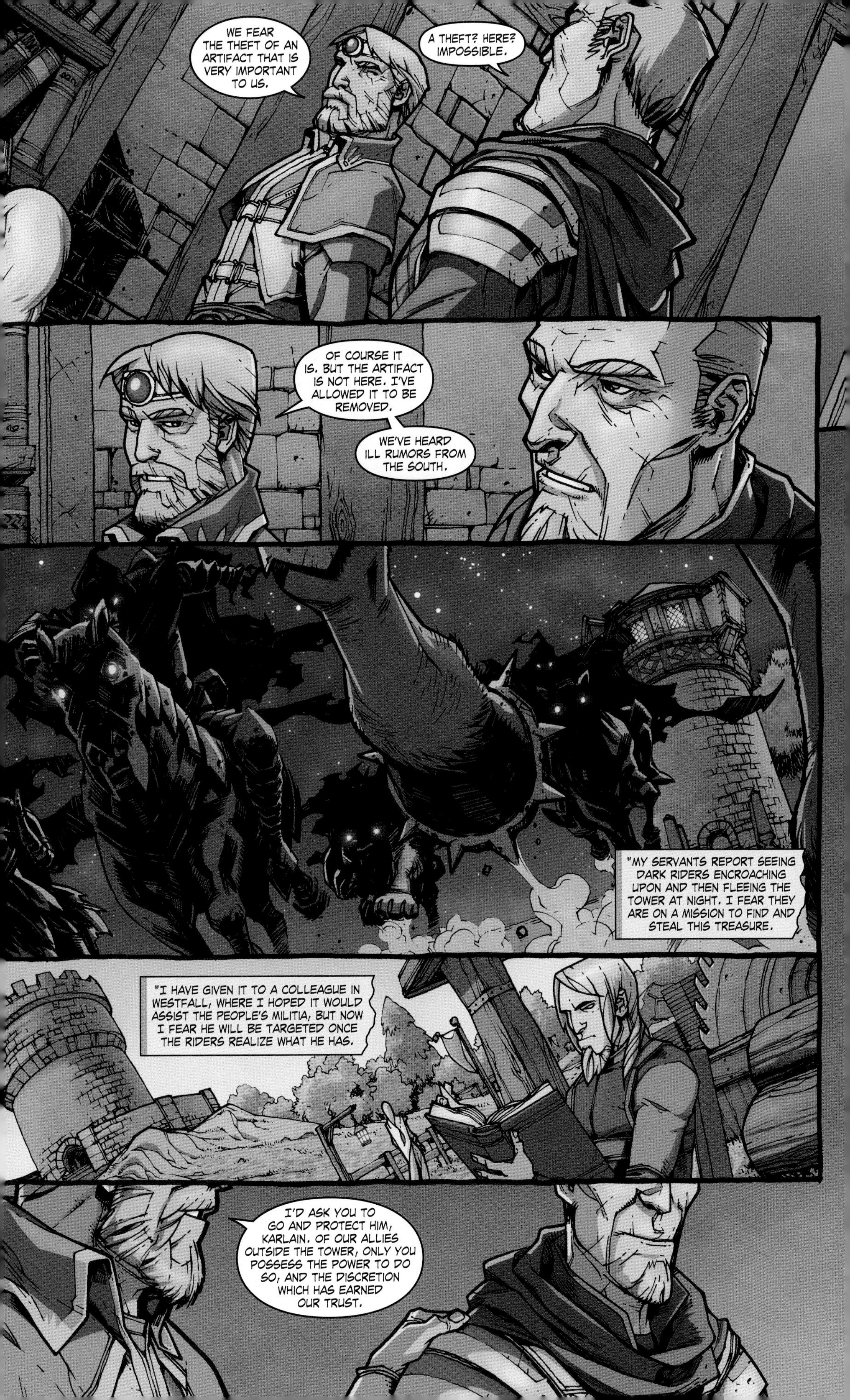
WE FEAR THE THEFT OF AN ARTIFACT THAT IS VERY IMPORTANT TO US.
A THEFT? HERE? IMPOSSIBLE.
OF COURSE IT IS. BUT THE ARTIFACT IS NOT HERE. I'VE ALLOWED IT TO BE REMOVED.
WE'VE HEARD ILL RUMORS FROM THE SOUTH.
"MY SERVANTS REPORT SEEING DARK RIDERS ENCROACHING UPON AND THEN FLEEING THE TOWER AT NIGHT. I FEAR THEY ARE ON A MISSION TO FIND AND STEAL THIS TREASURE.
"I HAVE GIVEN IT TO A COLLEAGUE IN WESTFALL, WHERE I HOPED IT WOULD ASSIST THE PEOPLE'S MILITIA, BUT NOW I FEAR HE WILL BE TARGETED ONCE THE RIDERS REALIZE WHAT HE HAS.
I'D ASK YOU TO GO AND PROTECT HIM, KARLAIN. OF OUR ALLIES OUTSIDE THE TOWER, ONLY YOU POSSESS THE POWER TO DO SO, AND THE DISCRETION WHICH HAS EARNED OUR TRUST.

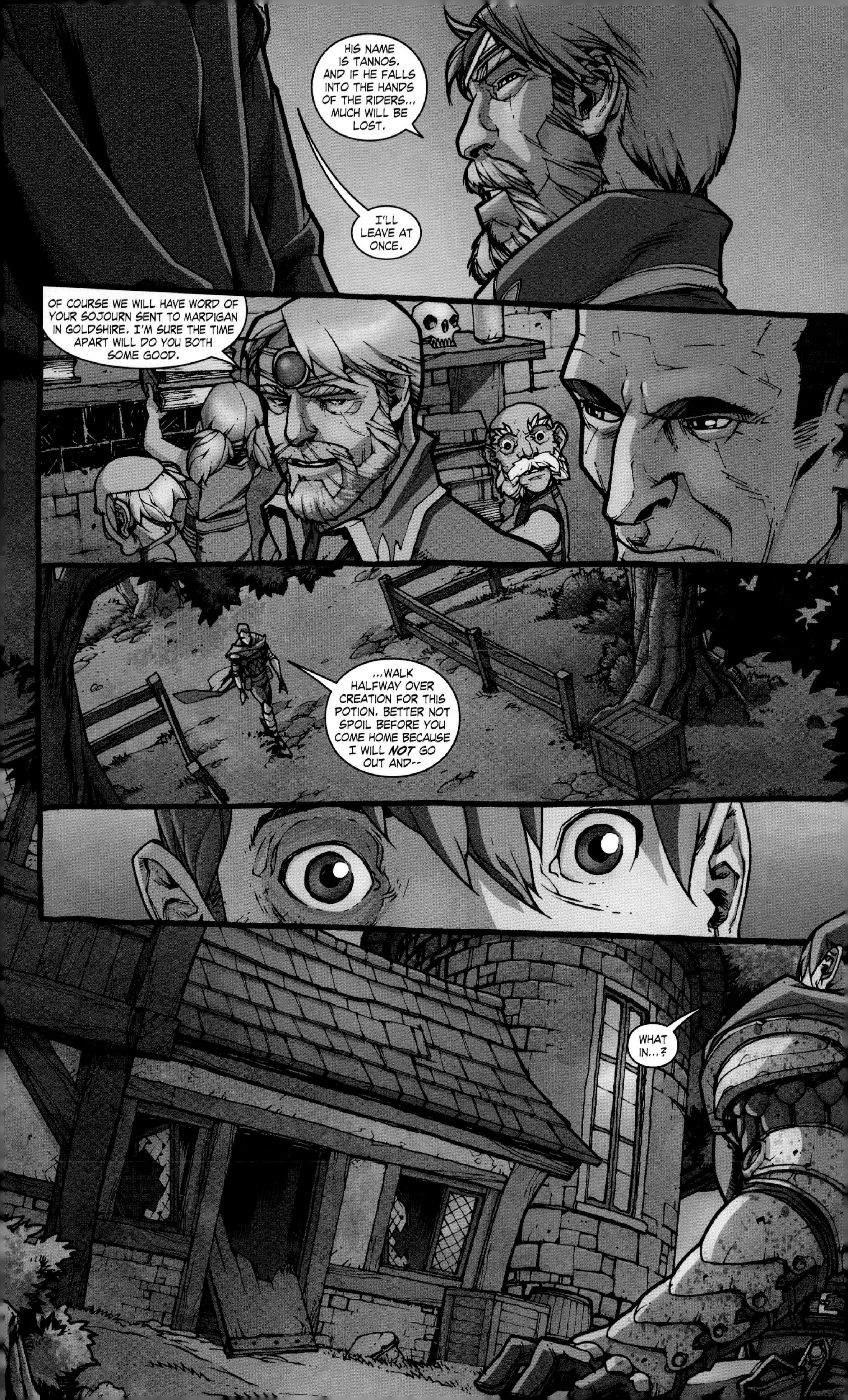
HIS NAME IS TANNOS. AND IF HE FALLS INTO THE HANDS OF THE RIDERS... MUCH WILL BE LOST.
I'LL LEAVE AT ONCE.
OF COURSE WE WILL HAVE WORD OF YOUR SOJOURN SENT TO MARDIGAN IN GOLDSHIRE. I'M SURE THE TIME APART WILL DO YOU BOTH SOME GOOD.
...WALK HALFWAY OVER CREATION FOR THIS POTION. BETTER NOT SPOIL BEFORE YOU COME HOME BECAUSE I WILL NOT GO OUT AND--
WHAT IN...?

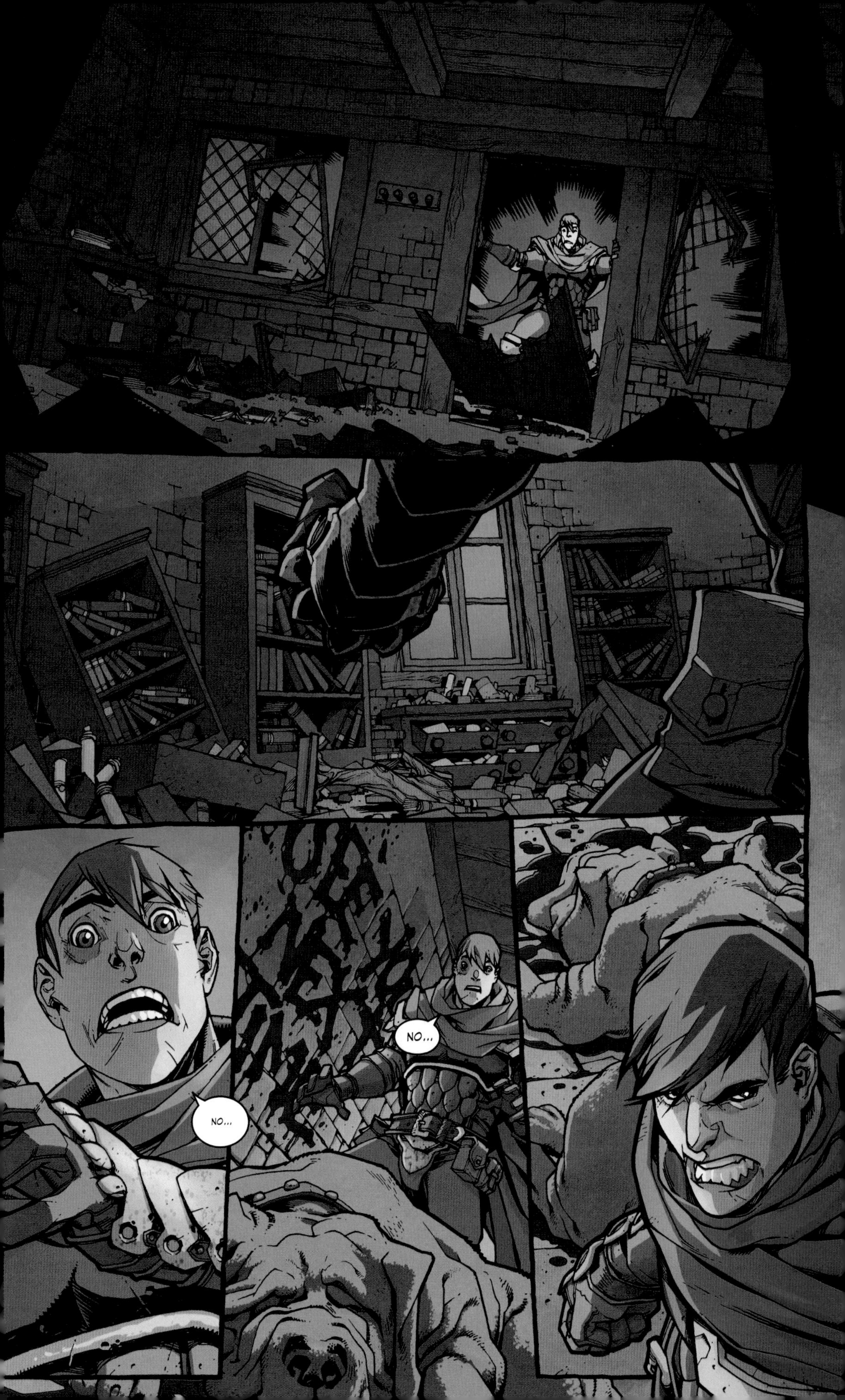
NO...
NO...

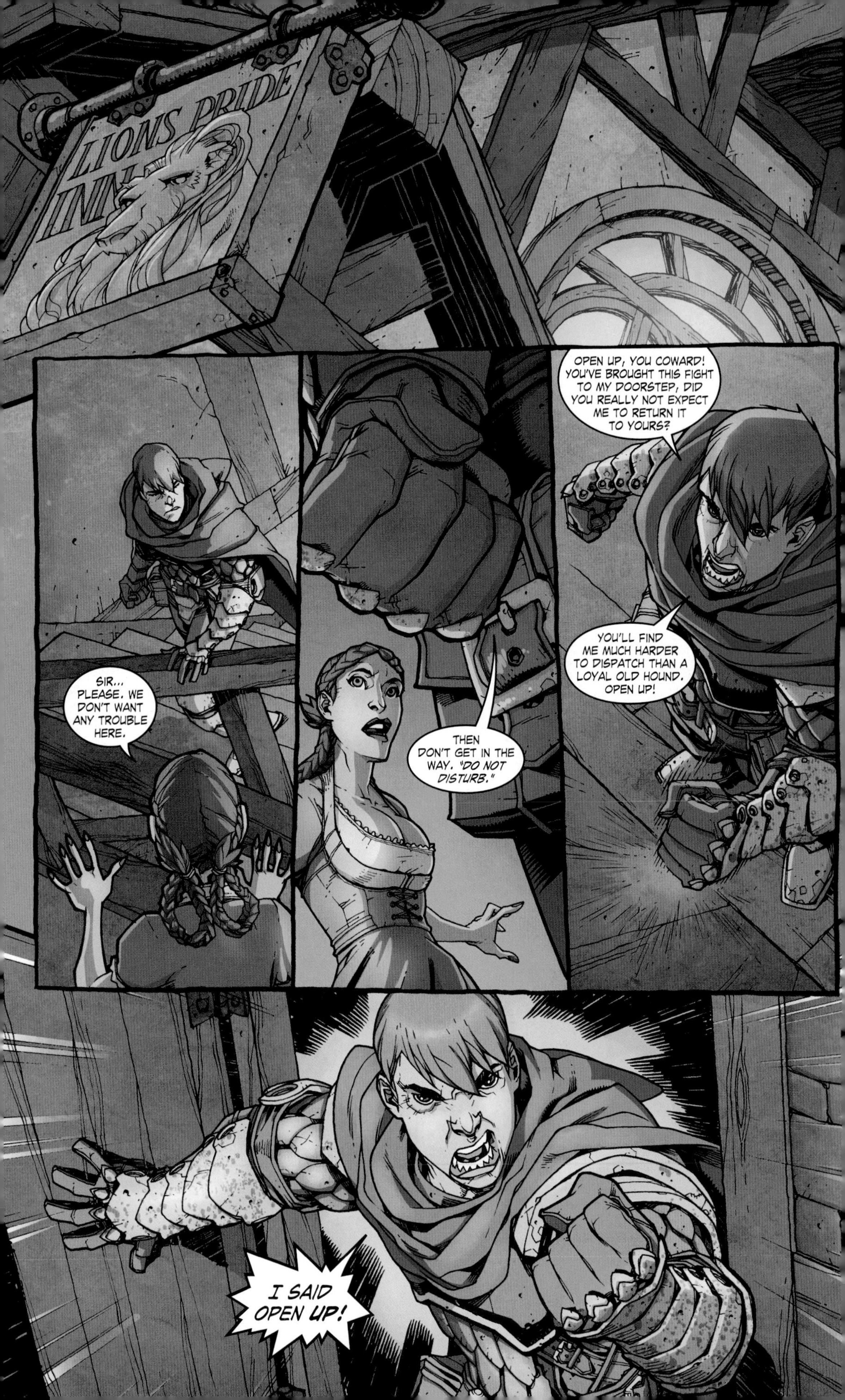
LIONS PRIDE INN
SIR... PLEASE. WE DON'T WANT ANY TROUBLE HERE.
THEN DON'T GET IN THE WAY. "DO NOT DISTURB."
OPEN UP, YOU COWARD! YOU'VE BROUGHT THIS FIGHT TO MY DOORSTEP, DID YOU REALLY NOT EXPECT ME TO RETURN IT TO YOURS?
YOU'LL FIND ME MUCH HARDER TO DISPATCH THAN A LOYAL OLD HOUND. OPEN UP!
I SAID OPEN UP!

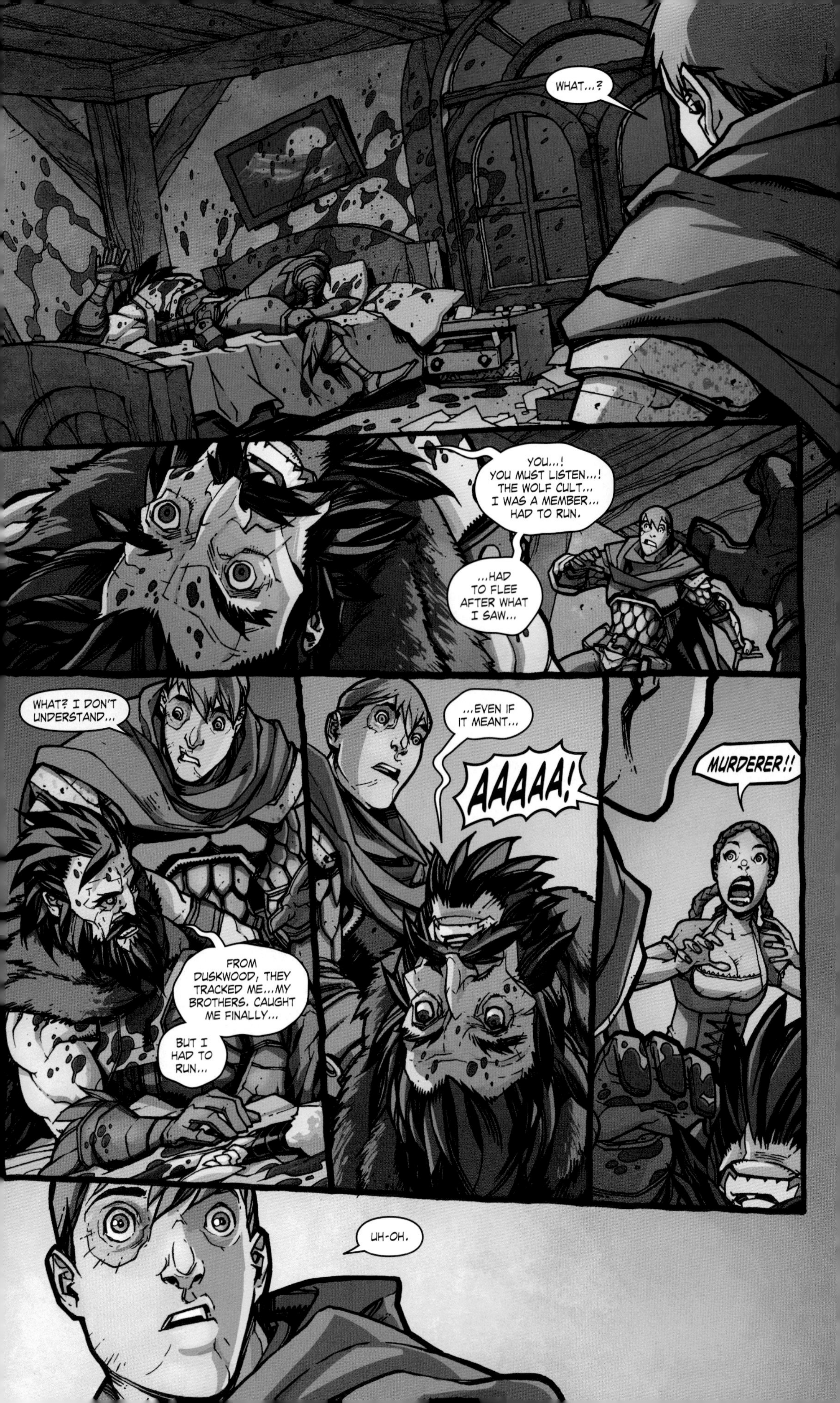
WHAT...?
YOU...! YOU MUST LISTEN...! THE WOLF CULT... I WAS A MEMBER... HAD TO RUN.
...HAD TO FLEE AFTER WHAT I SAW...
WHAT? I DON'T UNDERSTAND...
FROM DUSKWOOD, THEY TRACKED ME...MY BROTHERS. CAUGHT ME FINALLY...
BUT I HAD TO RUN...
...EVEN IF IT MEANT...
AAAAA!
MURDERER!!
UH-OH.

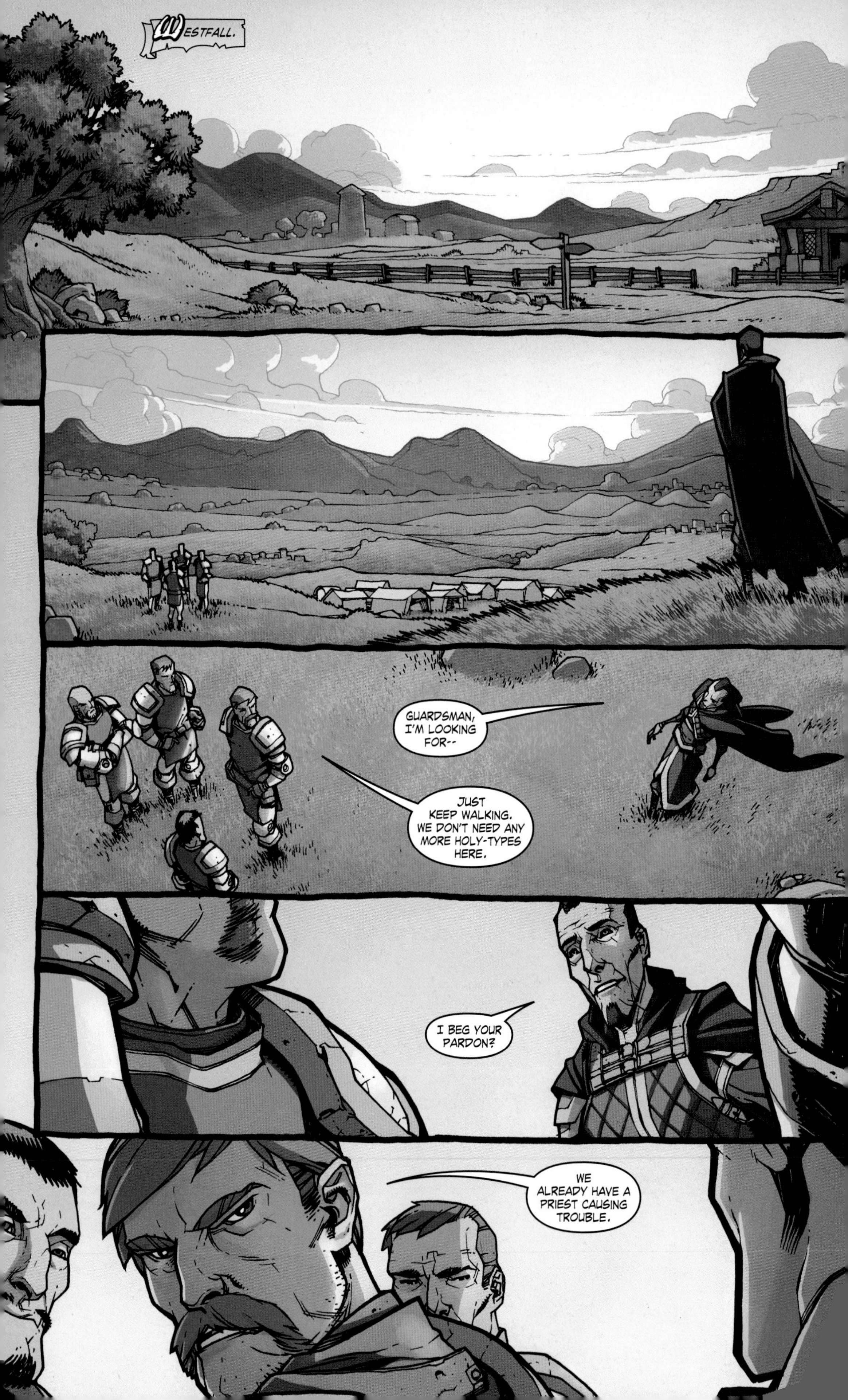
WESTFALL.
GUARDSMAN, I'M LOOKING FOR--
JUST KEEP WALKING. WE DON'T NEED ANY MORE HOLY-TYPES HERE.
I BEG YOUR PARDON?
WE ALREADY HAVE A PRIEST CAUSING TROUBLE.

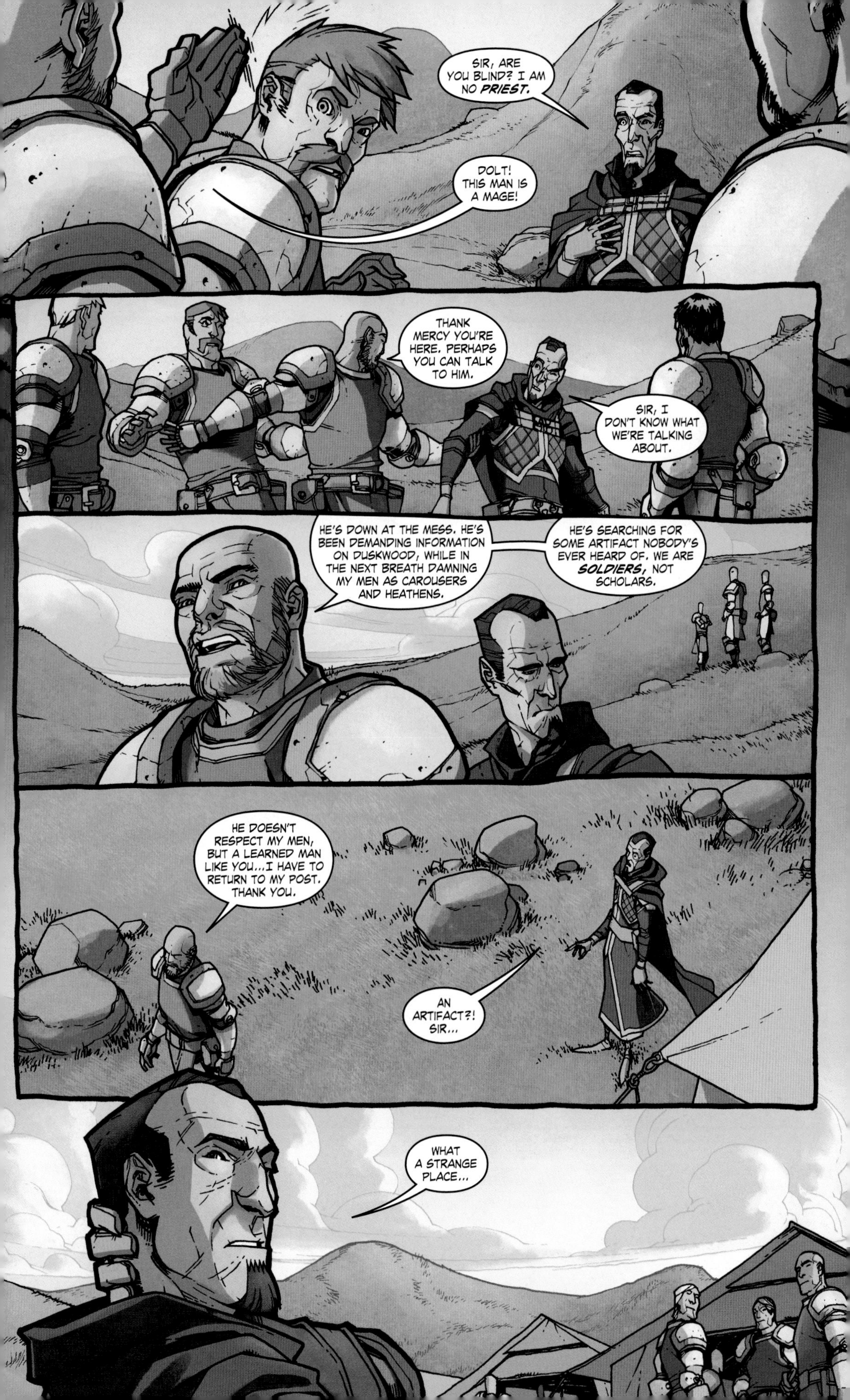
SIR, ARE YOU BLIND? I AM NO PRIEST.
DOLT! THIS MAN IS A MAGE!
THANK MERCY YOU'RE HERE. PERHAPS YOU CAN TALK TO HIM.
SIR, I DON'T KNOW WHAT WE'RE TALKING ABOUT.
HE'S DOWN AT THE MESS. HE'S BEEN DEMANDING INFORMATION ON DUSKWOOD, WHILE IN THE NEXT BREATH DAMNING MY MEN AS CAROUSERS AND HEATHENS.
HE'S SEARCHING FOR SOME ARTIFACT NOBODY'S EVER HEARD OF. WE ARE SOLDIERS, NOT SCHOLARS.
HE DOESN'T RESPECT MY MEN, BUT A LEARNED MAN LIKE YOU...I HAVE TO RETURN TO MY POST. THANK YOU.
AN ARTIFACT?! SIR...
WHAT A STRANGE PLACE...

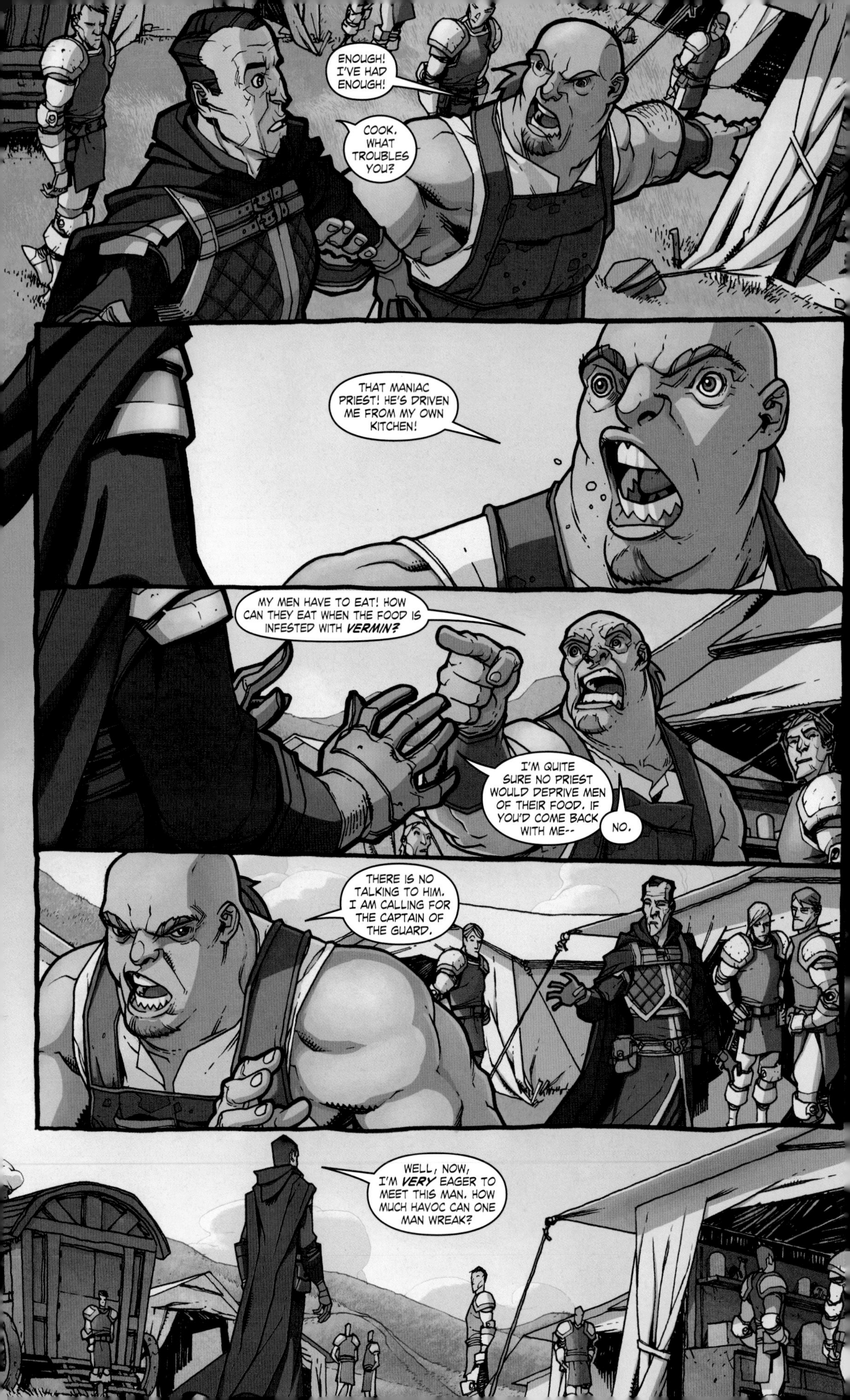
ENOUGH! I'VE HAD ENOUGH!
COOK. WHAT TROUBLES YOU?
THAT MANIAC PRIEST! HE'S DRIVEN ME FROM MY OWN KITCHEN!
MY MEN HAVE TO EAT! HOW CAN THEY EAT WHEN THE FOOD IS INFESTED WITH *VERMIN?*
I'M QUITE SURE NO PRIEST WOULD DEPRIVE MEN OF THEIR FOOD. IF YOU'D COME BACK WITH ME--
NO.
THERE IS NO TALKING TO HIM. I AM CALLING FOR THE CAPTAIN OF THE GUARD.
WELL, NOW, I'M ***VERY*** EAGER TO MEET THIS MAN. HOW MUCH HAVOC CAN ONE MAN WREAK?

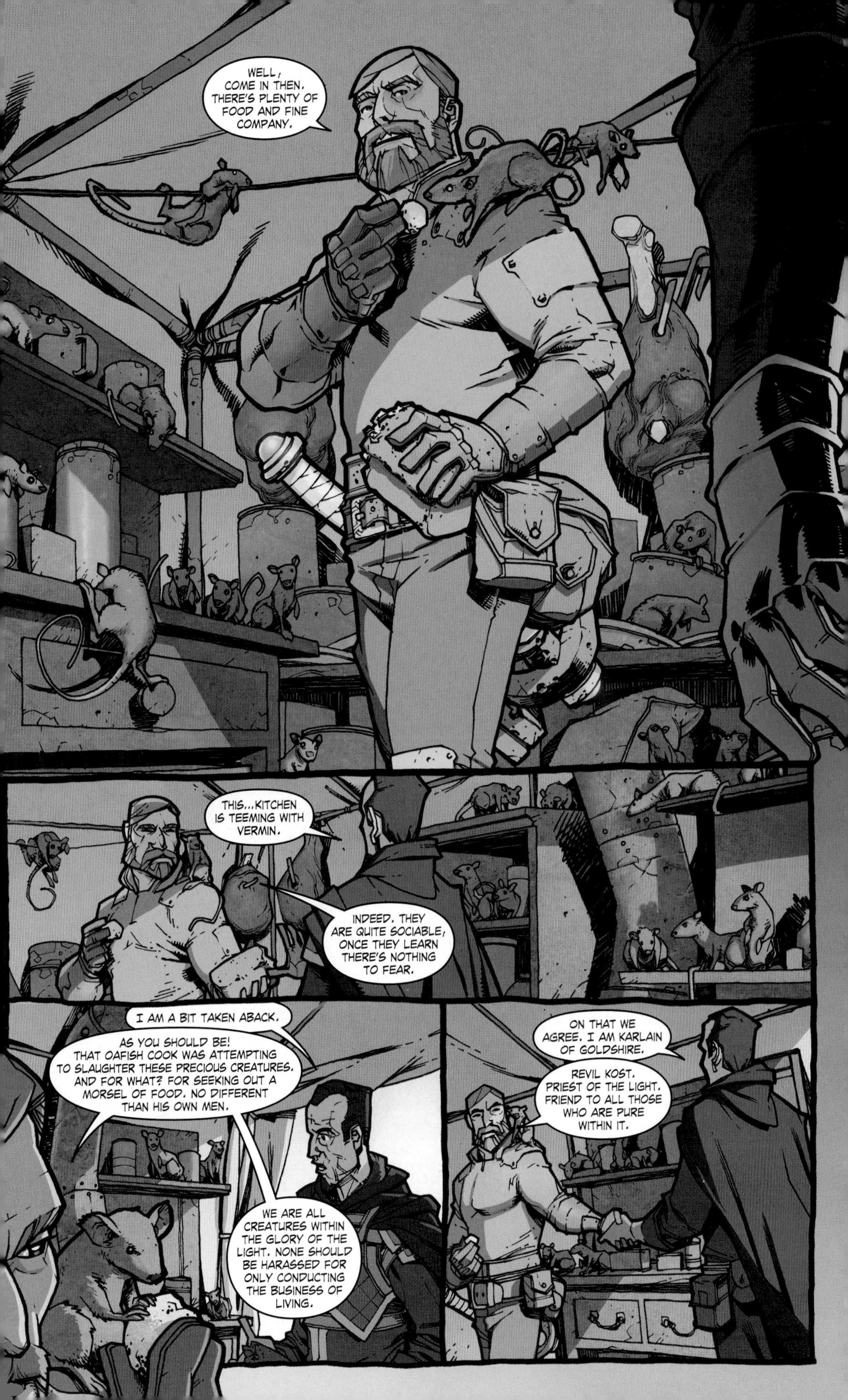
WELL, COME IN THEN. THERE'S PLENTY OF FOOD AND FINE COMPANY.
THIS...KITCHEN IS TEEMING WITH VERMIN.
INDEED. THEY ARE QUITE SOCIABLE, ONCE THEY LEARN THERE'S NOTHING TO FEAR.
I AM A BIT TAKEN ABACK.
AS YOU SHOULD BE! THAT OAFISH COOK WAS ATTEMPTING TO SLAUGHTER THESE PRECIOUS CREATURES. AND FOR WHAT? FOR SEEKING OUT A MORSEL OF FOOD. NO DIFFERENT THAN HIS OWN MEN.
WE ARE ALL CREATURES WITHIN THE GLORY OF THE LIGHT. NONE SHOULD BE HARASSED FOR ONLY CONDUCTING THE BUSINESS OF LIVING.
ON THAT WE AGREE. I AM KARLAIN OF GOLDSHIRE.
REVIL KOST. PRIEST OF THE LIGHT. FRIEND TO ALL THOSE WHO ARE PURE WITHIN IT.

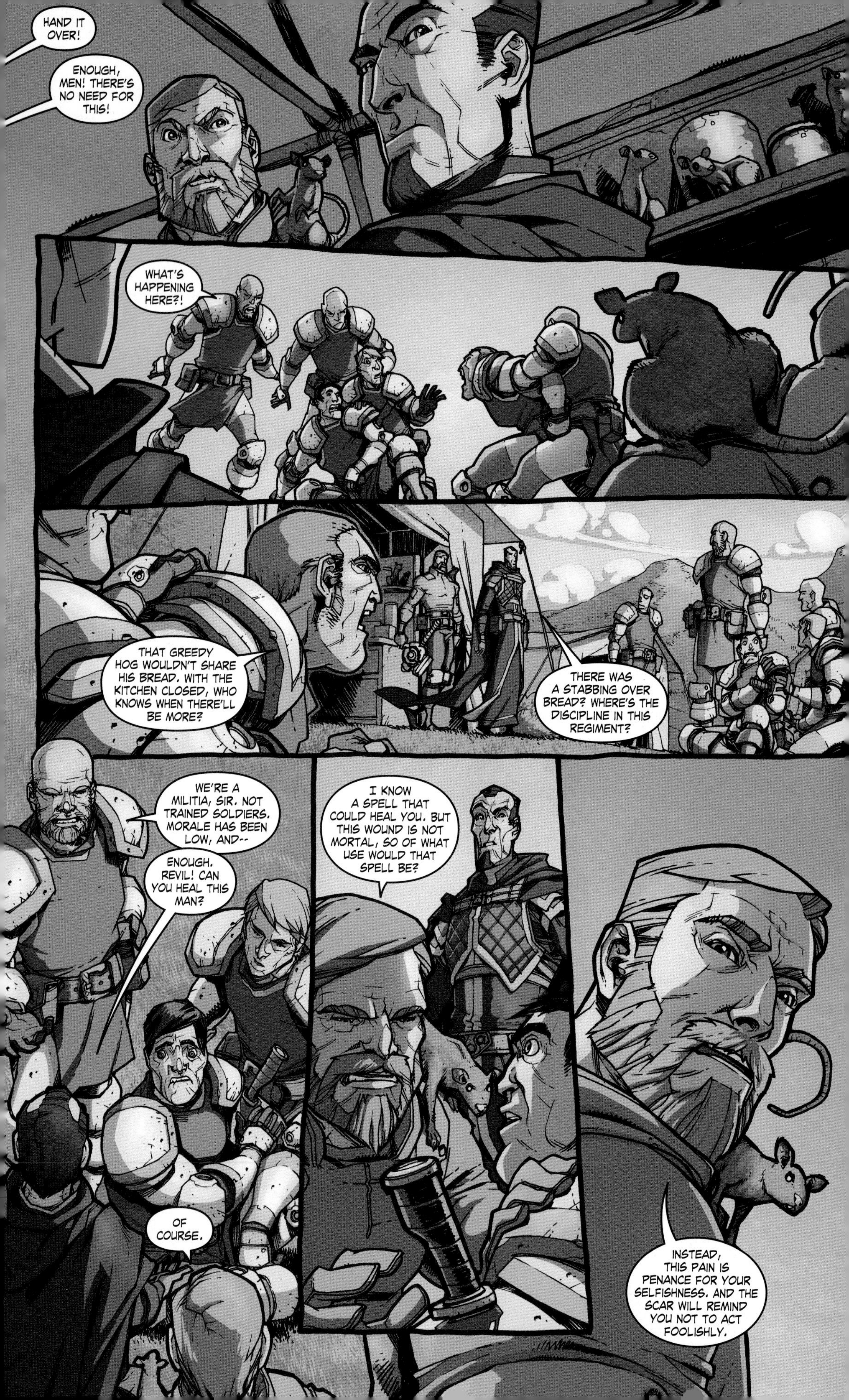
HAND IT OVER!
ENOUGH, MEN! THERE'S NO NEED FOR THIS!
WHAT'S HAPPENING HERE?!
THAT GREEDY HOG WOULDN'T SHARE HIS BREAD. WITH THE KITCHEN CLOSED, WHO KNOWS WHEN THERE'LL BE MORE?
THERE WAS A STABBING OVER BREAD? WHERE'S THE DISCIPLINE IN THIS REGIMENT?
WE'RE A MILITIA, SIR. NOT TRAINED SOLDIERS. MORALE HAS BEEN LOW, AND--
ENOUGH. REVIL! CAN YOU HEAL THIS MAN?
OF COURSE.
I KNOW A SPELL THAT COULD HEAL YOU. BUT THIS WOUND IS NOT MORTAL, SO OF WHAT USE WOULD THAT SPELL BE?
INSTEAD, THIS PAIN IS PENANCE FOR YOUR SELFISHNESS. AND THE SCAR WILL REMIND YOU NOT TO ACT FOOLISHLY.

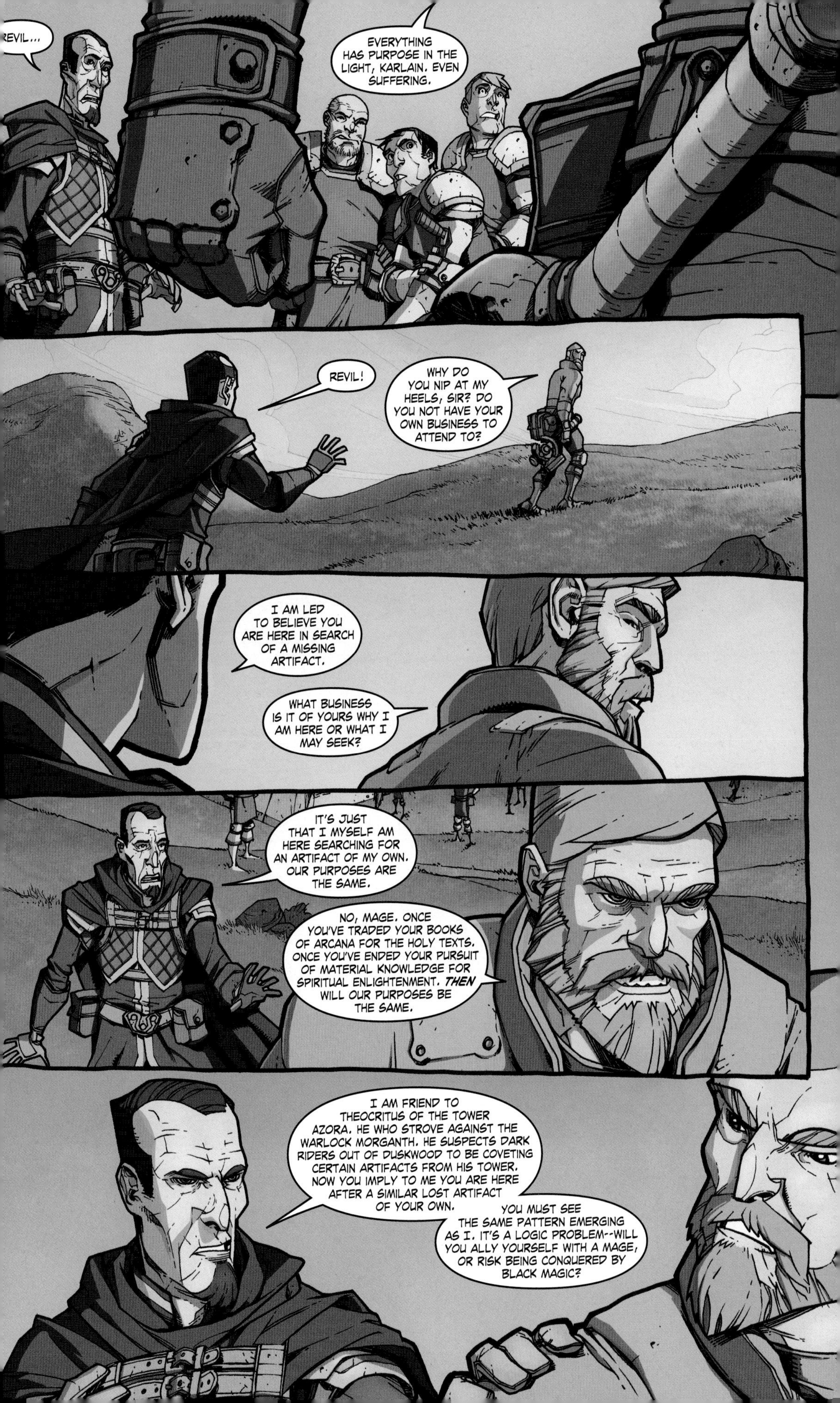

REVIL...
EVERYTHING HAS PURPOSE IN THE LIGHT, KARLAIN. EVEN SUFFERING.
REVIL!
WHY DO YOU NIP AT MY HEELS, SIR? DO YOU NOT HAVE YOUR OWN BUSINESS TO ATTEND TO?
I AM LED TO BELIEVE YOU ARE HERE IN SEARCH OF A MISSING ARTIFACT.
WHAT BUSINESS IS IT OF YOURS WHY I AM HERE OR WHAT I MAY SEEK?
IT'S JUST THAT I MYSELF AM HERE SEARCHING FOR AN ARTIFACT OF MY OWN. OUR PURPOSES ARE THE SAME.
NO, MAGE. ONCE YOU'VE TRADED YOUR BOOKS OF ARCANA FOR THE HOLY TEXTS. ONCE YOU'VE ENDED YOUR PURSUIT OF MATERIAL KNOWLEDGE FOR SPIRITUAL ENLIGHTENMENT. *THEN* WILL OUR PURPOSES BE THE SAME.
I AM FRIEND TO THEOCRITUS OF THE TOWER AZORA. HE WHO STROVE AGAINST THE WARLOCK MORGANTH. HE SUSPECTS DARK RIDERS OUT OF DUSKWOOD TO BE COVETING CERTAIN ARTIFACTS FROM HIS TOWER. NOW YOU IMPLY TO ME YOU ARE HERE AFTER A SIMILAR LOST ARTIFACT OF YOUR OWN.
YOU MUST SEE THE SAME PATTERN EMERGING AS I. IT'S A LOGIC PROBLEM--WILL YOU ALLY YOURSELF WITH A MAGE, OR RISK BEING CONQUERED BY BLACK MAGIC?

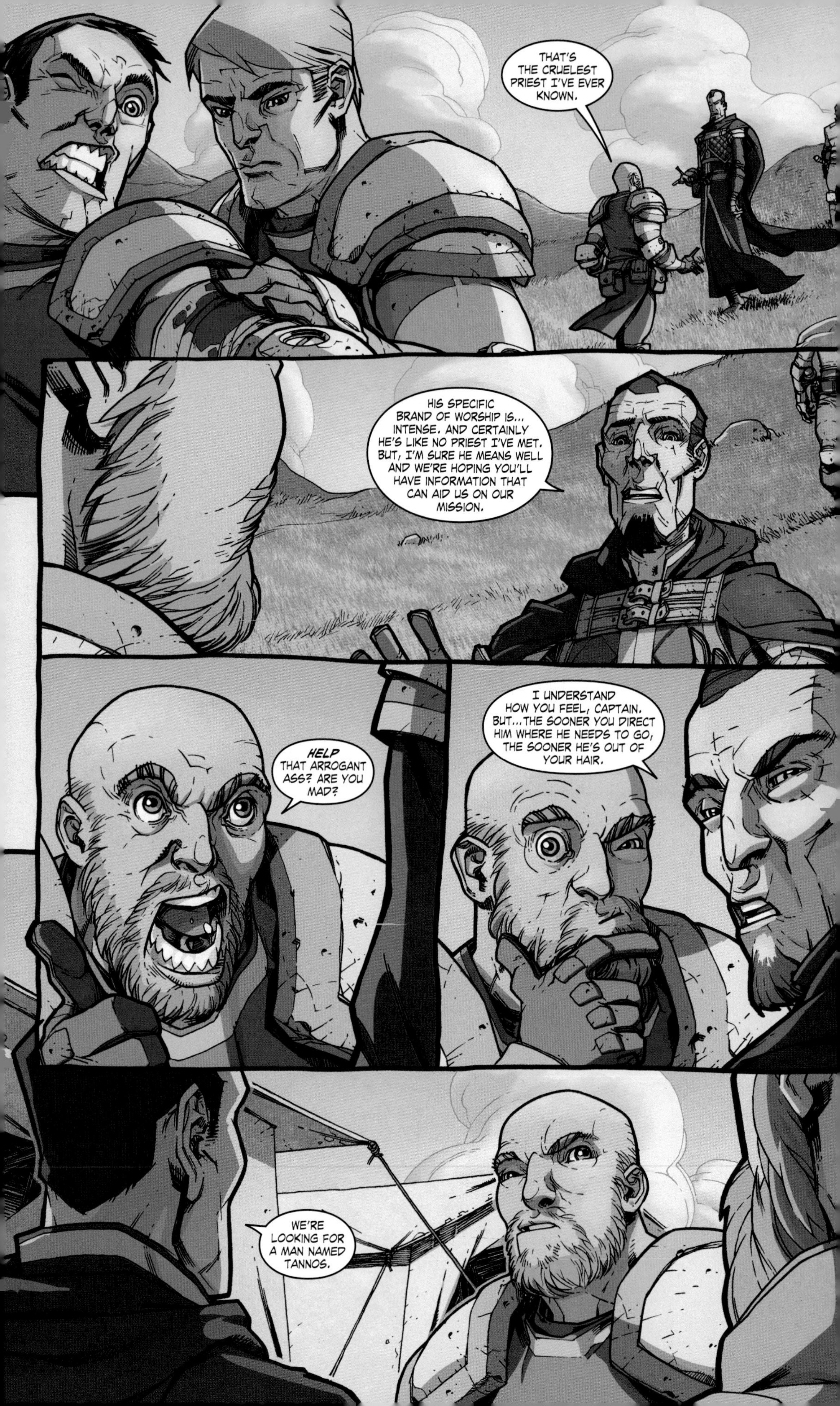
THAT'S THE CRUELEST PRIEST I'VE EVER KNOWN.
HIS SPECIFIC BRAND OF WORSHIP IS... INTENSE. AND CERTAINLY HE'S LIKE NO PRIEST I'VE MET. BUT, I'M SURE HE MEANS WELL AND WE'RE HOPING YOU'LL HAVE INFORMATION THAT CAN AID US ON OUR MISSION.
HELP THAT ARROGANT ASS? ARE YOU MAD?
I UNDERSTAND HOW YOU FEEL, CAPTAIN. BUT...THE SOONER YOU DIRECT HIM WHERE HE NEEDS TO GO, THE SOONER HE'S OUT OF YOUR HAIR.
WE'RE LOOKING FOR A MAN NAMED TANNOS.

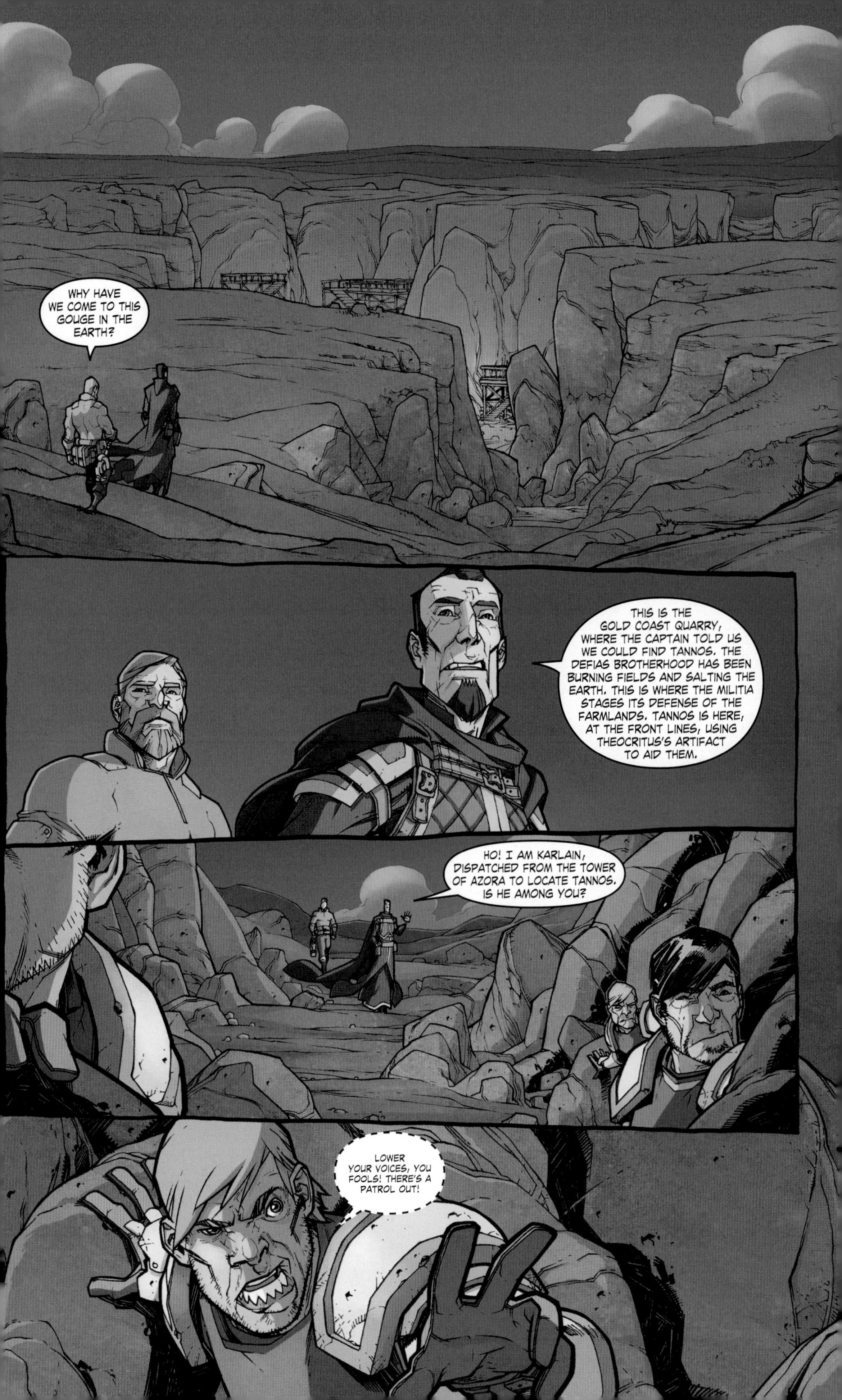
WHY HAVE WE COME TO THIS GOUGE IN THE EARTH?
THIS IS THE GOLD COAST QUARRY, WHERE THE CAPTAIN TOLD US WE COULD FIND TANNOS. THE DEFIAS BROTHERHOOD HAS BEEN BURNING FIELDS AND SALTING THE EARTH. THIS IS WHERE THE MILITIA STAGES ITS DEFENSE OF THE FARMLANDS. TANNOS IS HERE, AT THE FRONT LINES, USING THEOCRITUS'S ARTIFACT TO AID THEM.
HO! I AM KARLAIN, DISPATCHED FROM THE TOWER OF AZORA TO LOCATE TANNOS. IS HE AMONG YOU?
LOWER YOUR VOICES, YOU FOOLS! THERE'S A PATROL OUT!

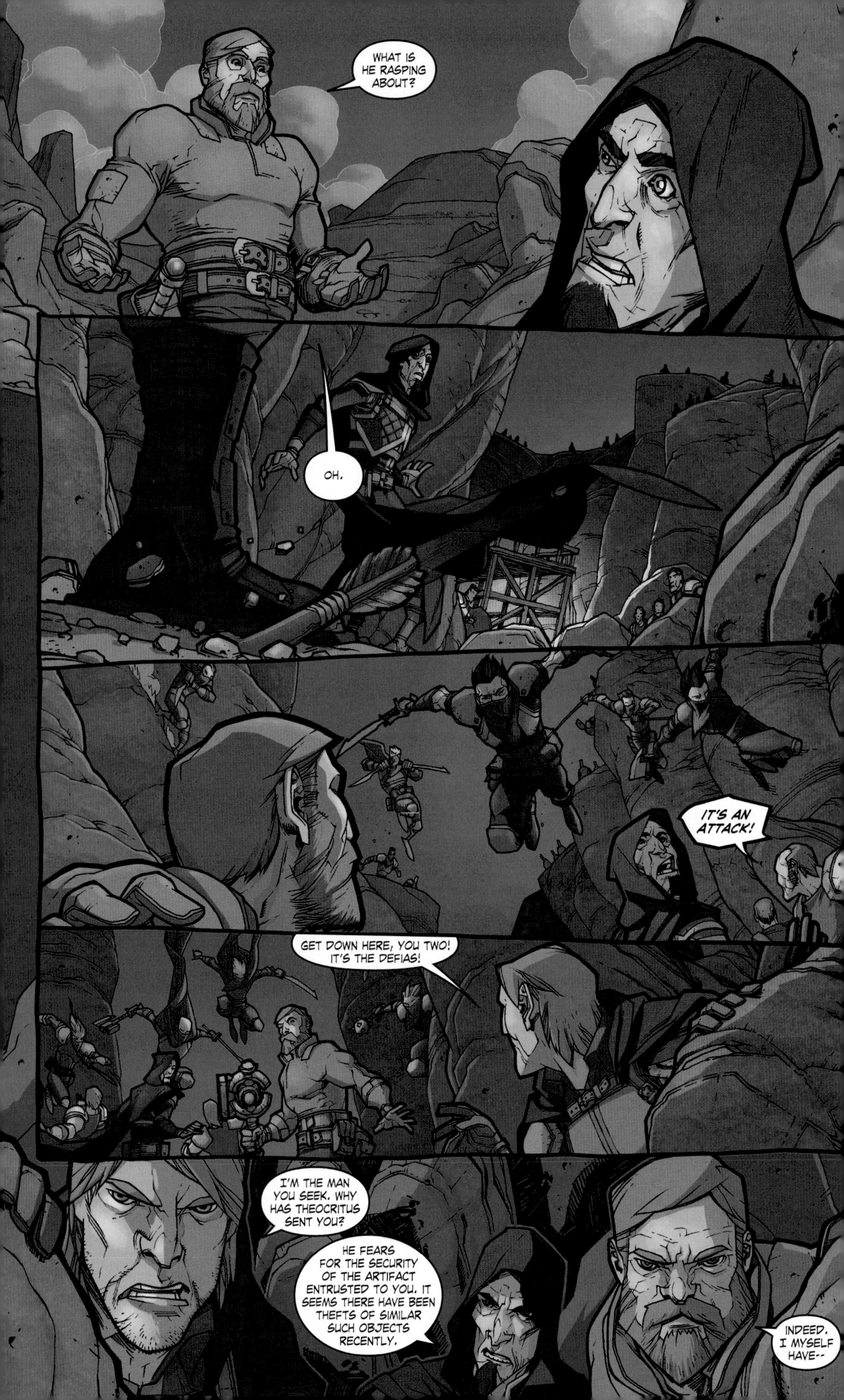
WHAT IS HE RASPING ABOUT?
OH.
IT'S AN ATTACK!
GET DOWN HERE, YOU TWO! IT'S THE DEFIAS!
I'M THE MAN YOU SEEK. WHY HAS THEOCRITUS SENT YOU?
HE FEARS FOR THE SECURITY OF THE ARTIFACT ENTRUSTED TO YOU. IT SEEMS THERE HAVE BEEN THEFTS OF SIMILAR SUCH OBJECTS RECENTLY.
INDEED. I MYSELF HAVE--

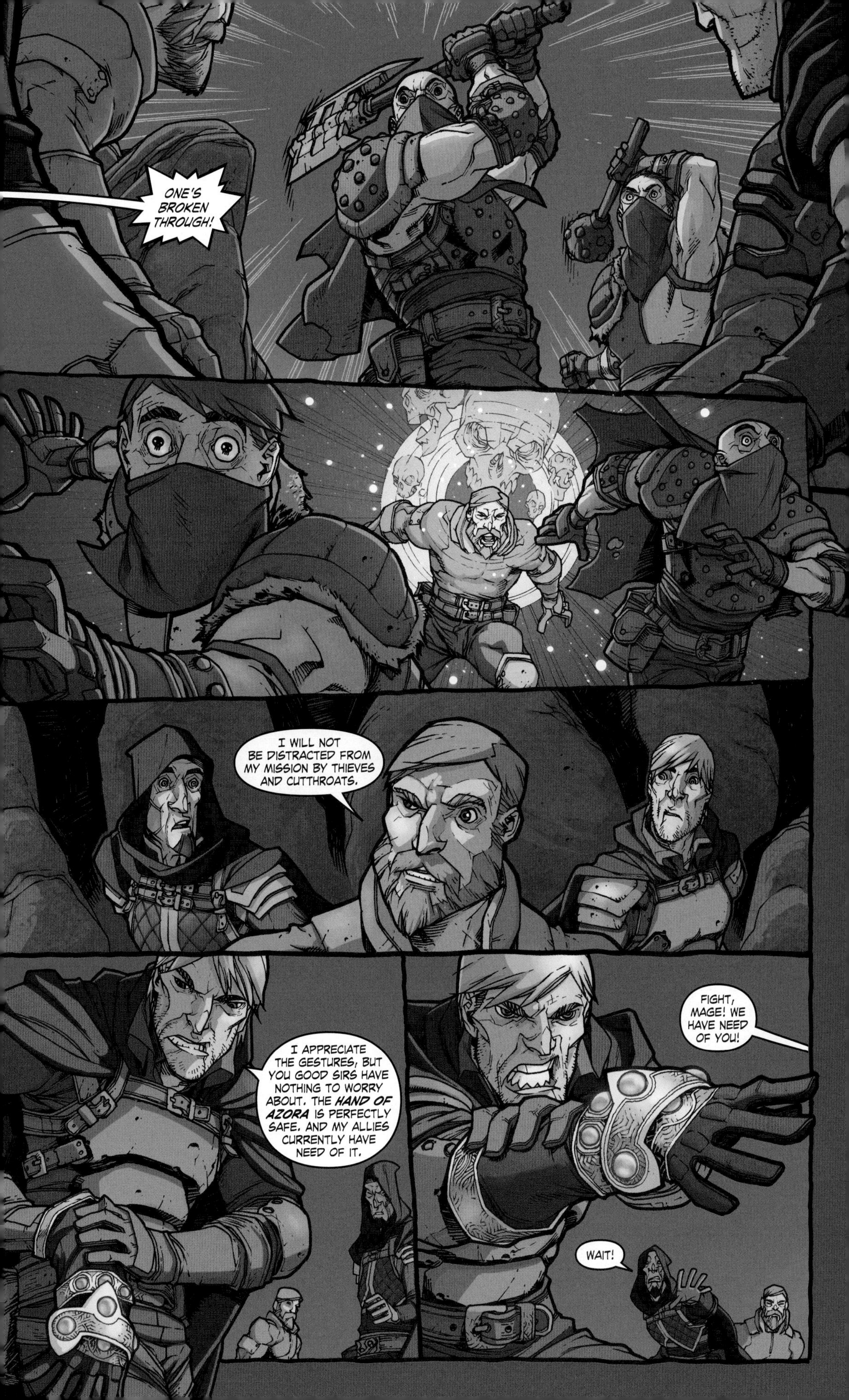
ONE'S BROKEN THROUGH!
I WILL NOT BE DISTRACTED FROM MY MISSION BY THIEVES AND CUTTHROATS.
I APPRECIATE THE GESTURES, BUT YOU GOOD SIRS HAVE NOTHING TO WORRY ABOUT. THE HAND OF AZORA IS PERFECTLY SAFE. AND MY ALLIES CURRENTLY HAVE NEED OF IT.
FIGHT, MAGE! WE HAVE NEED OF YOU!
WAIT!

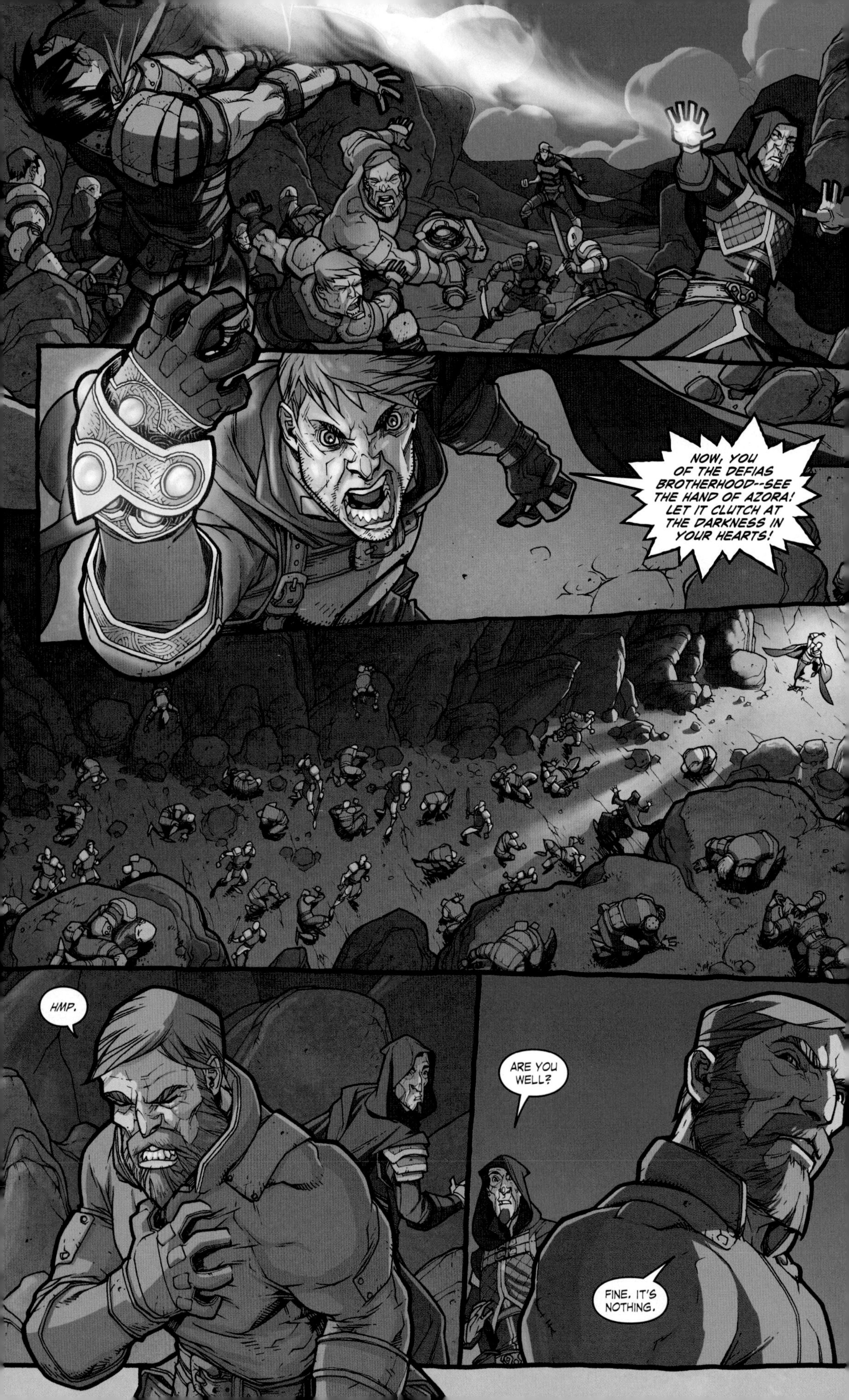
NOW, YOU OF THE DEFIAS BROTHERHOOD--SEE THE HAND OF AZORA! LET IT CLUTCH AT THE DARKNESS IN YOUR HEARTS!
HMP.
ARE YOU WELL?
FINE. IT'S NOTHING.

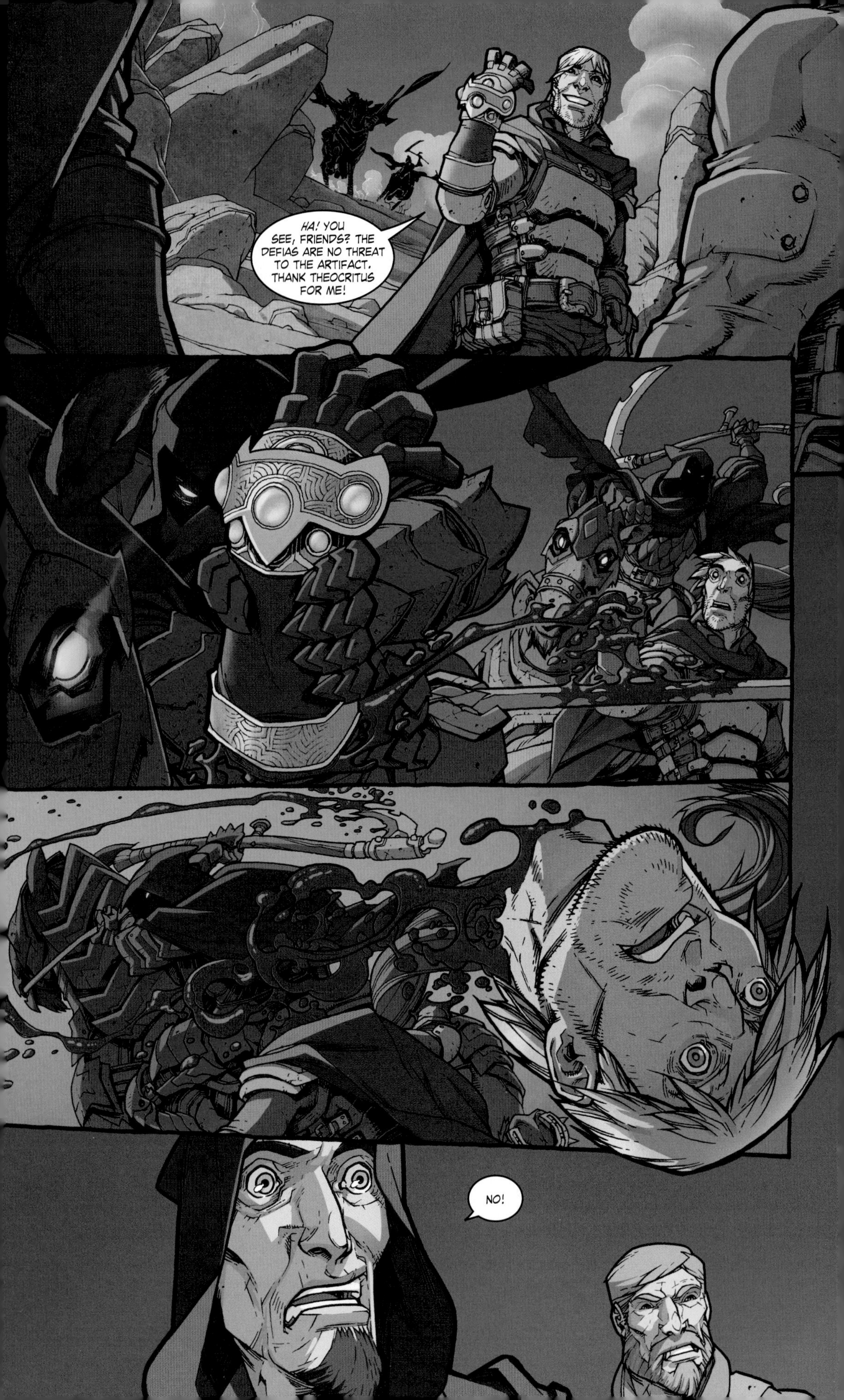
HA! YOU SEE, FRIENDS? THE DEFIAS ARE NO THREAT TO THE ARTIFACT. THANK THEOCRITUS FOR ME!
NO!

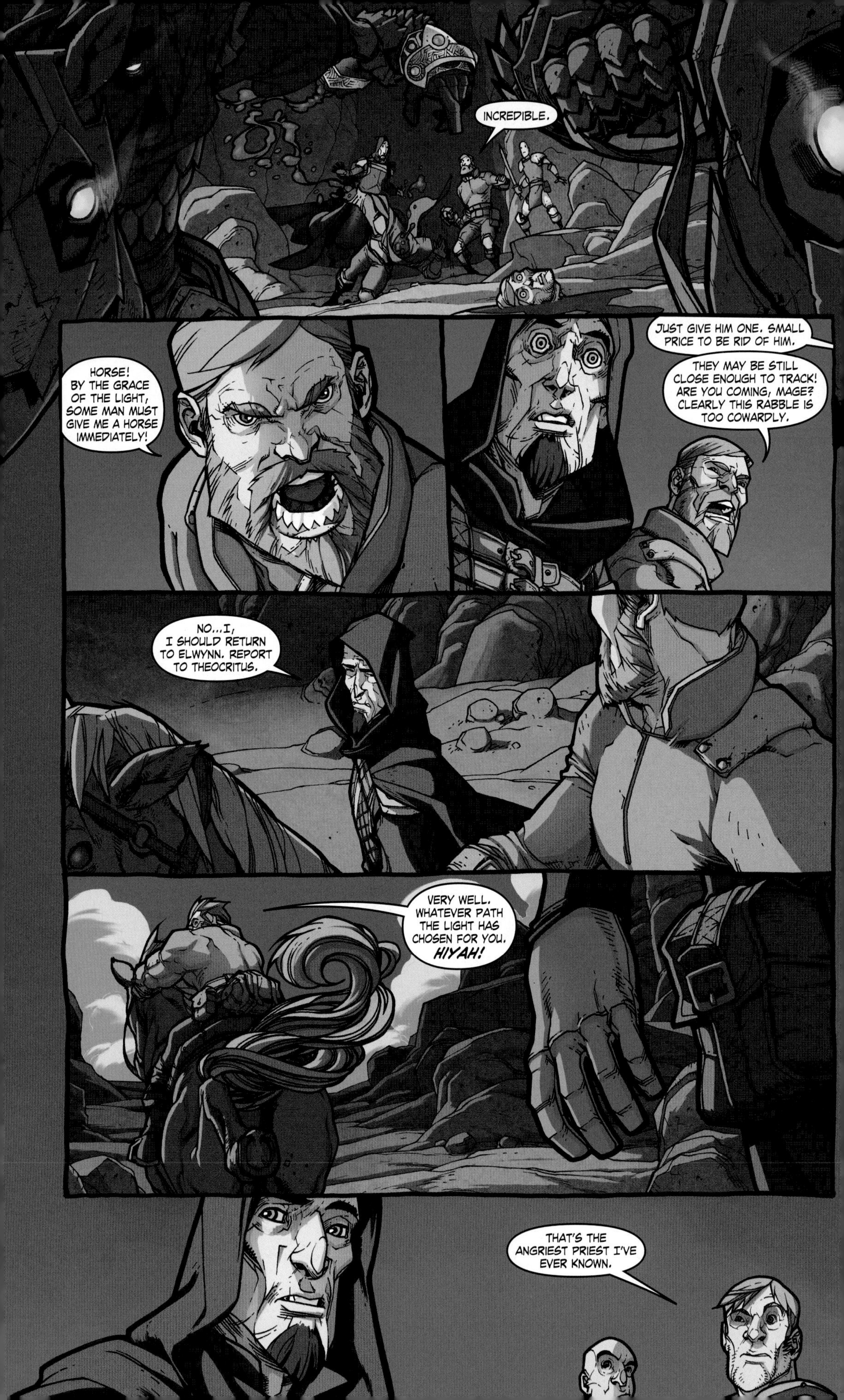
INCREDIBLE.
HORSE! BY THE GRACE OF THE LIGHT, SOME MAN MUST GIVE ME A HORSE IMMEDIATELY!
JUST GIVE HIM ONE. SMALL PRICE TO BE RID OF HIM.
THEY MAY BE STILL CLOSE ENOUGH TO TRACK! ARE YOU COMING, MAGE? CLEARLY THIS RABBLE IS TOO COWARDLY.
NO...I, I SHOULD RETURN TO ELWYNN. REPORT TO THEOCRITUS.
VERY WELL. WHATEVER PATH THE LIGHT HAS CHOSEN FOR YOU. HIYAH!
THAT'S THE ANGRIEST PRIEST I'VE EVER KNOWN.

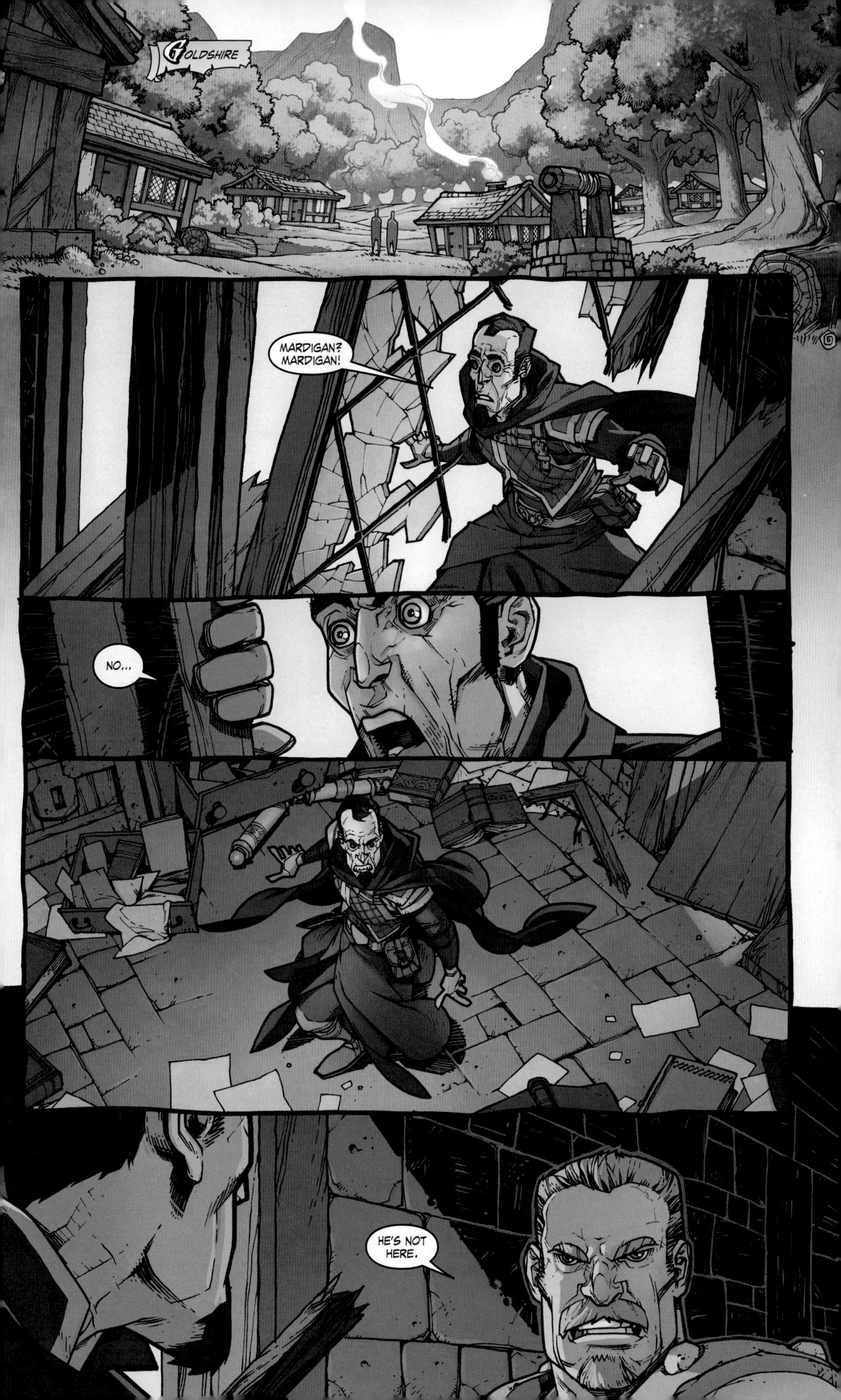
GOLDSHIRE
MARDIGAN? MARDIGAN!
NO...
HE'S NOT HERE.

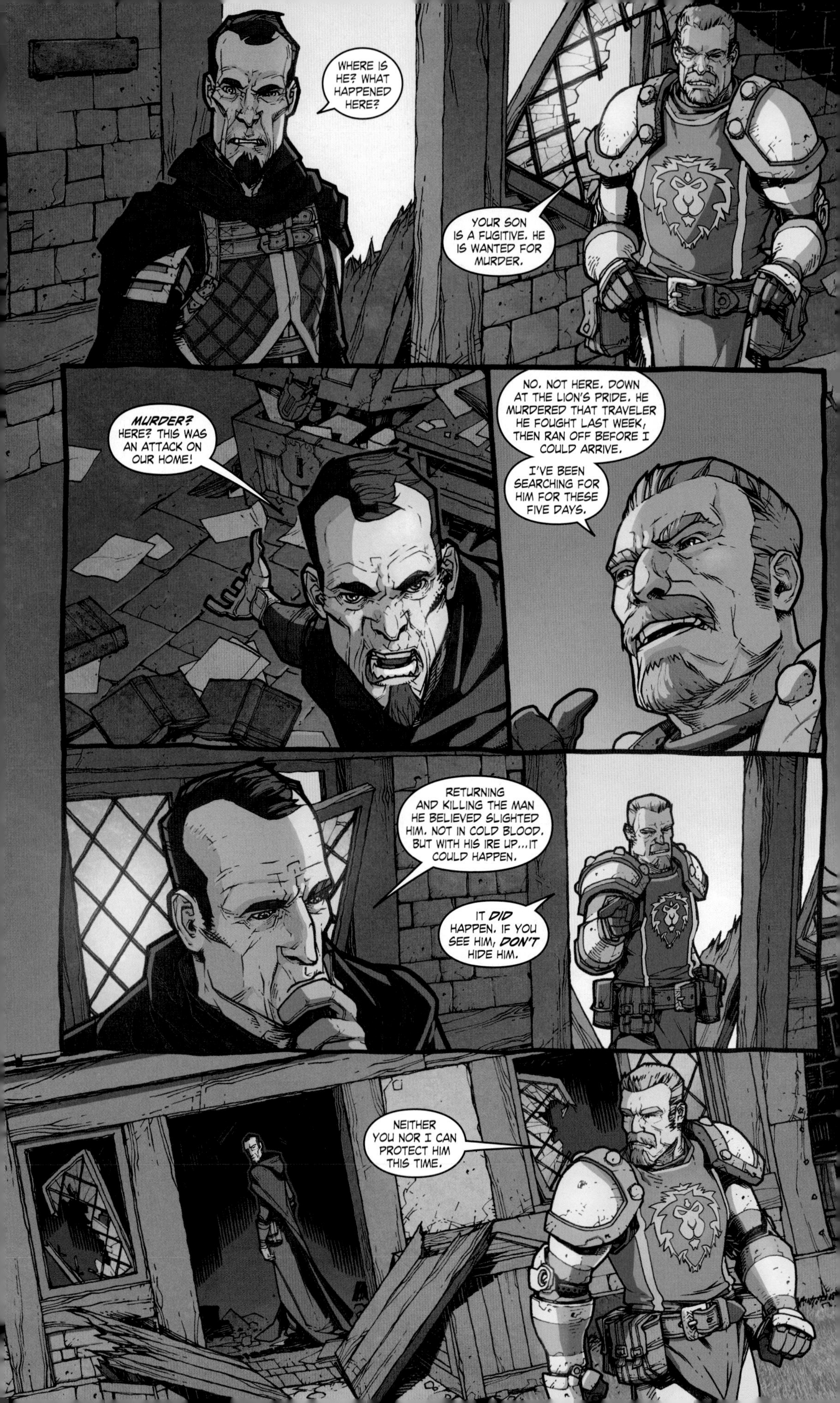
WHERE IS HE? WHAT HAPPENED HERE?
YOUR SON IS A FUGITIVE. HE IS WANTED FOR MURDER.
MURDER? HERE? THIS WAS AN ATTACK ON OUR HOME!
NO. NOT HERE. DOWN AT THE LION'S PRIDE. HE MURDERED THAT TRAVELER HE FOUGHT LAST WEEK, THEN RAN OFF BEFORE I COULD ARRIVE.
I'VE BEEN SEARCHING FOR HIM FOR THESE FIVE DAYS.
RETURNING AND KILLING THE MAN HE BELIEVED SLIGHTED HIM. NOT IN COLD BLOOD. BUT WITH HIS IRE UP...IT COULD HAPPEN.
IT DID HAPPEN. IF YOU SEE HIM, DON'T HIDE HIM.
NEITHER YOU NOR I CAN PROTECT HIM THIS TIME.

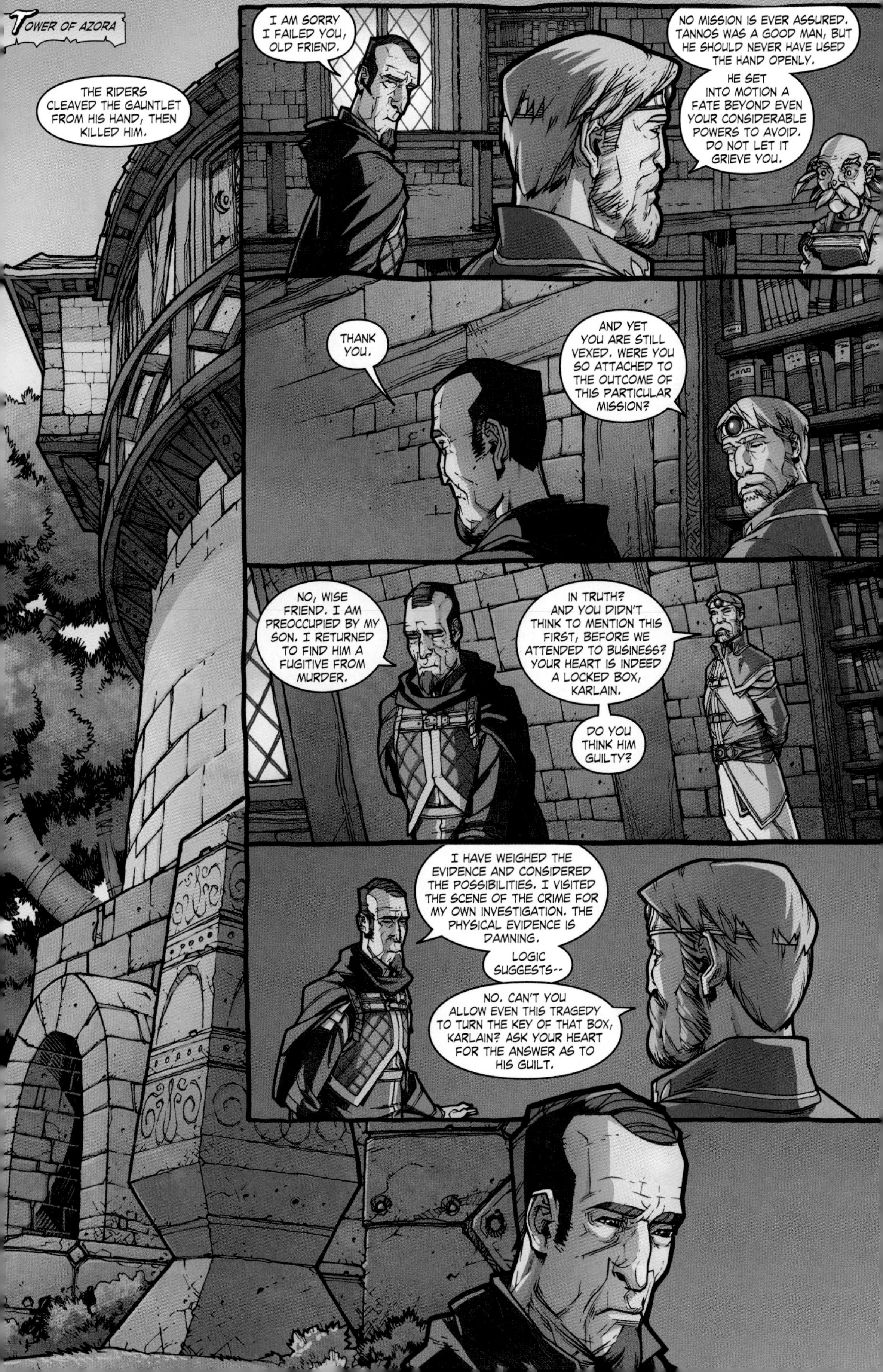
TOWER OF AZORA
THE RIDERS CLEAVED THE GAUNTLET FROM HIS HAND, THEN KILLED HIM.
I AM SORRY I FAILED YOU, OLD FRIEND.
NO MISSION IS EVER ASSURED. TANNOS WAS A GOOD MAN, BUT HE SHOULD NEVER HAVE USED THE HAND OPENLY.
HE SET INTO MOTION A FATE BEYOND EVEN YOUR CONSIDERABLE POWERS TO AVOID. DO NOT LET IT GRIEVE YOU.
THANK YOU.
AND YET YOU ARE STILL VEXED. WERE YOU SO ATTACHED TO THE OUTCOME OF THIS PARTICULAR MISSION?
NO, WISE FRIEND. I AM PREOCCUPIED BY MY SON. I RETURNED TO FIND HIM A FUGITIVE FROM MURDER.
IN TRUTH? AND YOU DIDN'T THINK TO MENTION THIS FIRST, BEFORE WE ATTENDED TO BUSINESS? YOUR HEART IS INDEED A LOCKED BOX, KARLAIN.
DO YOU THINK HIM GUILTY?
I HAVE WEIGHED THE EVIDENCE AND CONSIDERED THE POSSIBILITIES. I VISITED THE SCENE OF THE CRIME FOR MY OWN INVESTIGATION. THE PHYSICAL EVIDENCE IS DAMNING.
LOGIC SUGGESTS--
NO. CAN'T YOU ALLOW EVEN THIS TRAGEDY TO TURN THE KEY OF THAT BOX, KARLAIN? ASK YOUR HEART FOR THE ANSWER AS TO HIS GUILT.

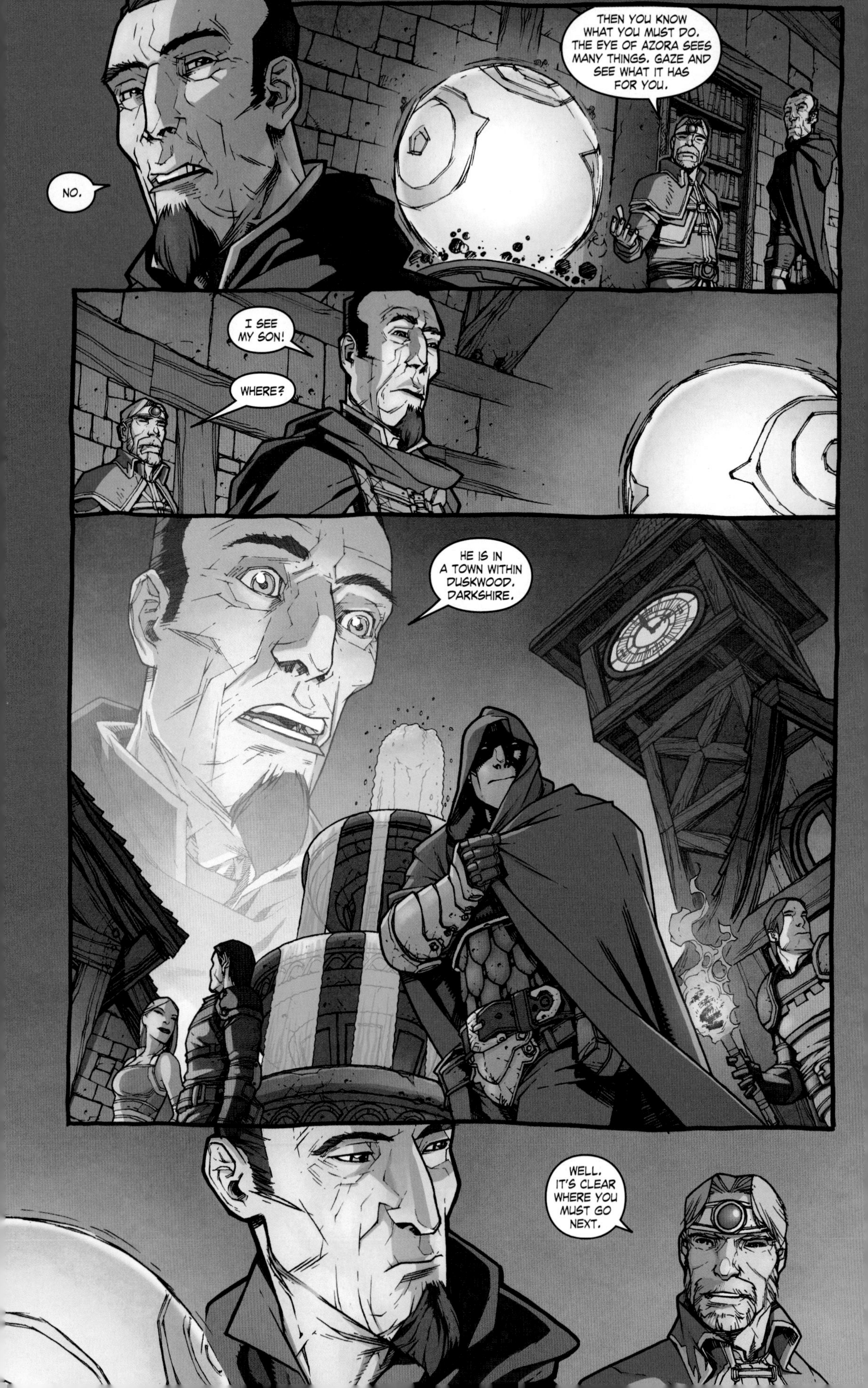
NO.
THEN YOU KNOW WHAT YOU MUST DO. THE EYE OF AZORA SEES MANY THINGS. GAZE AND SEE WHAT IT HAS FOR YOU.
I SEE MY SON!
WHERE?
HE IS IN A TOWN WITHIN DUSKWOOD. DARKSHIRE.
WELL. IT'S CLEAR WHERE YOU MUST GO NEXT.

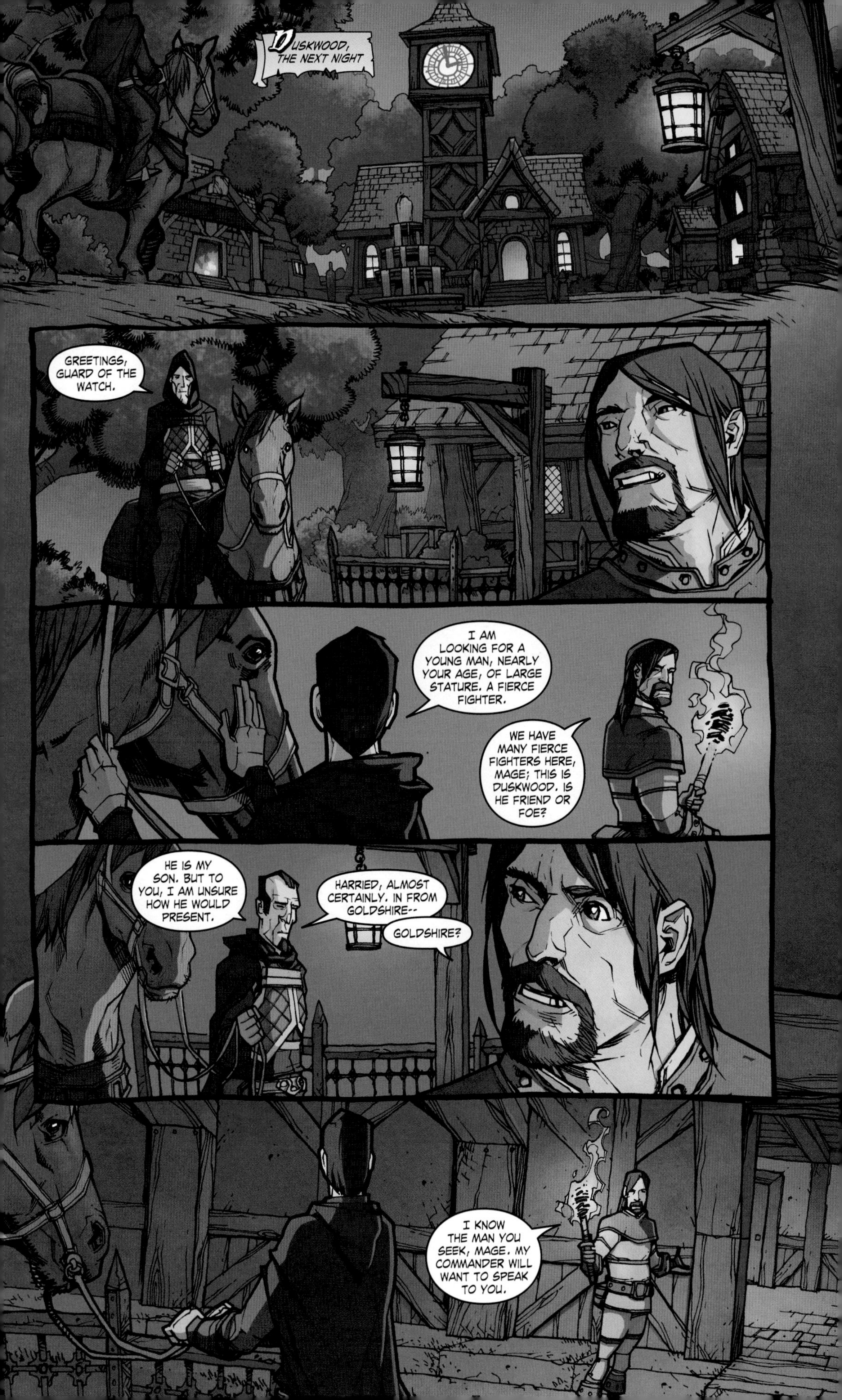
DUSKWOOD, THE NEXT NIGHT
GREETINGS, GUARD OF THE WATCH.
I AM LOOKING FOR A YOUNG MAN, NEARLY YOUR AGE, OF LARGE STATURE. A FIERCE FIGHTER.
WE HAVE MANY FIERCE FIGHTERS HERE, MAGE; THIS IS DUSKWOOD. IS HE FRIEND OR FOE?
HE IS MY SON. BUT TO YOU, I AM UNSURE HOW HE WOULD PRESENT.
HARRIED, ALMOST CERTAINLY. IN FROM GOLDSHIRE--
GOLDSHIRE?
I KNOW THE MAN YOU SEEK, MAGE. MY COMMANDER WILL WANT TO SPEAK TO YOU.

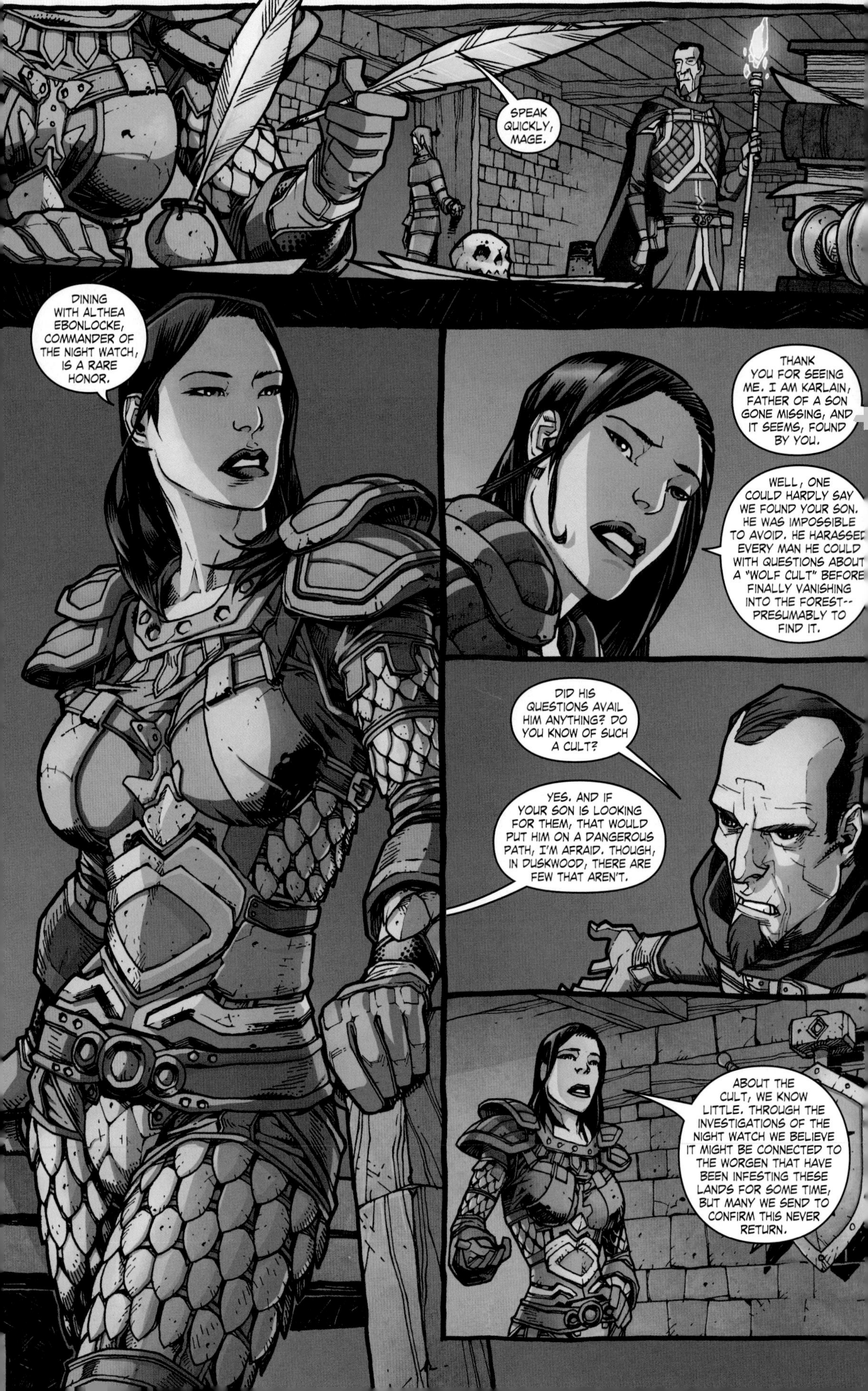
SPEAK QUICKLY, MAGE.
DINING WITH ALTHEA EBONLOCKE, COMMANDER OF THE NIGHT WATCH, IS A RARE HONOR.
THANK YOU FOR SEEING ME. I AM KARLAIN, FATHER OF A SON GONE MISSING, AND IT SEEMS, FOUND BY YOU.
WELL, ONE COULD HARDLY SAY WE FOUND YOUR SON. HE WAS IMPOSSIBLE TO AVOID. HE HARASSED EVERY MAN HE COULD WITH QUESTIONS ABOUT A "WOLF CULT" BEFORE FINALLY VANISHING INTO THE FOREST-- PRESUMABLY TO FIND IT.
DID HIS QUESTIONS AVAIL HIM ANYTHING? DO YOU KNOW OF SUCH A CULT?
YES. AND IF YOUR SON IS LOOKING FOR THEM, THAT WOULD PUT HIM ON A DANGEROUS PATH, I'M AFRAID. THOUGH, IN DUSKWOOD, THERE ARE FEW THAT AREN'T.
ABOUT THE CULT, WE KNOW LITTLE. THROUGH THE INVESTIGATIONS OF THE NIGHT WATCH WE BELIEVE IT MIGHT BE CONNECTED TO THE WORGEN THAT HAVE BEEN INFESTING THESE LANDS FOR SOME TIME, BUT MANY WE SEND TO CONFIRM THIS NEVER RETURN.

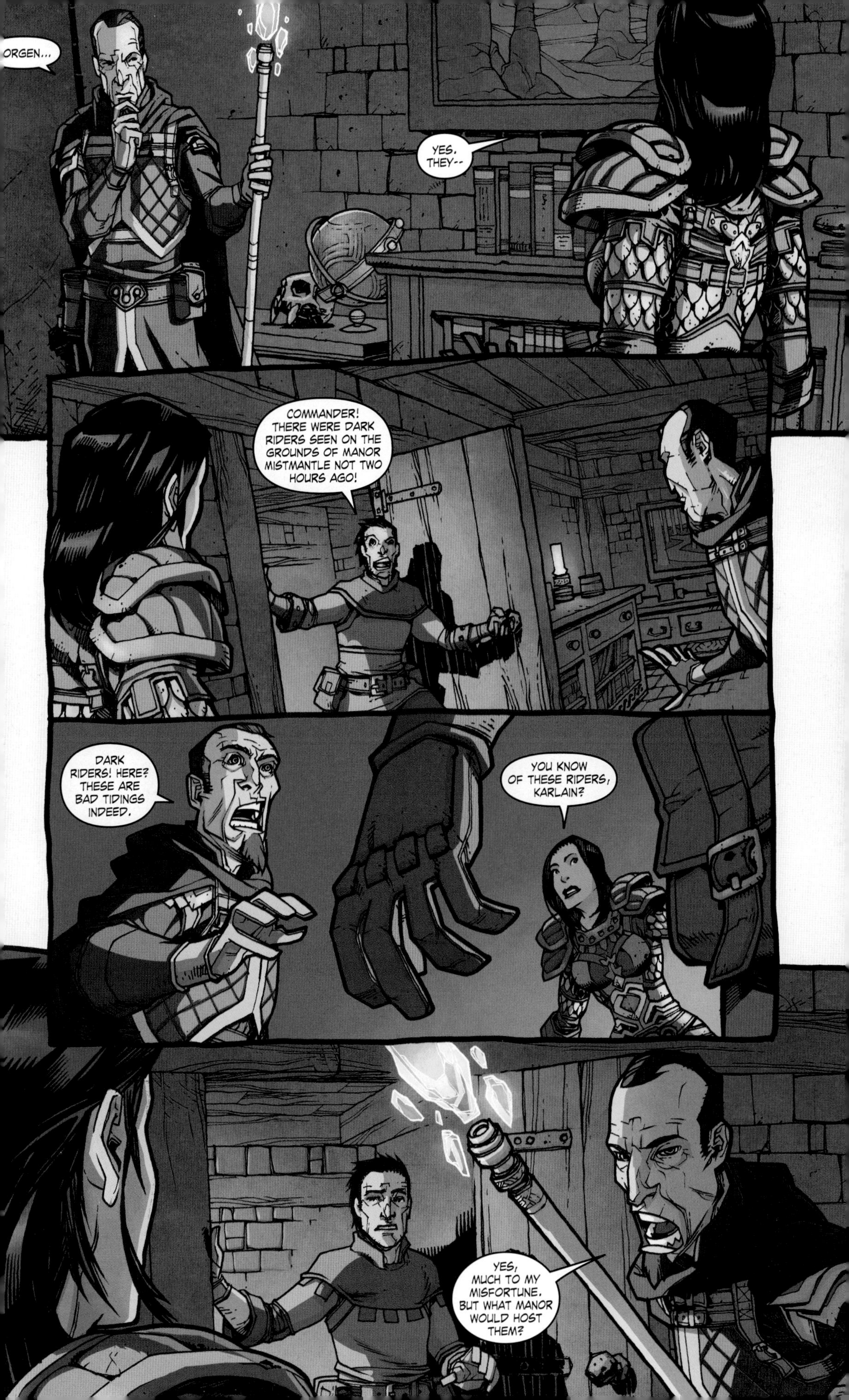
ORGEN...
YES. THEY--
COMMANDER! THERE WERE DARK RIDERS SEEN ON THE GROUNDS OF MANOR MISTMANTLE NOT TWO HOURS AGO!
DARK RIDERS! HERE? THESE ARE BAD TIDINGS INDEED.
YOU KNOW OF THESE RIDERS, KARLAIN?
YES, MUCH TO MY MISFORTUNE. BUT WHAT MANOR WOULD HOST THEM?

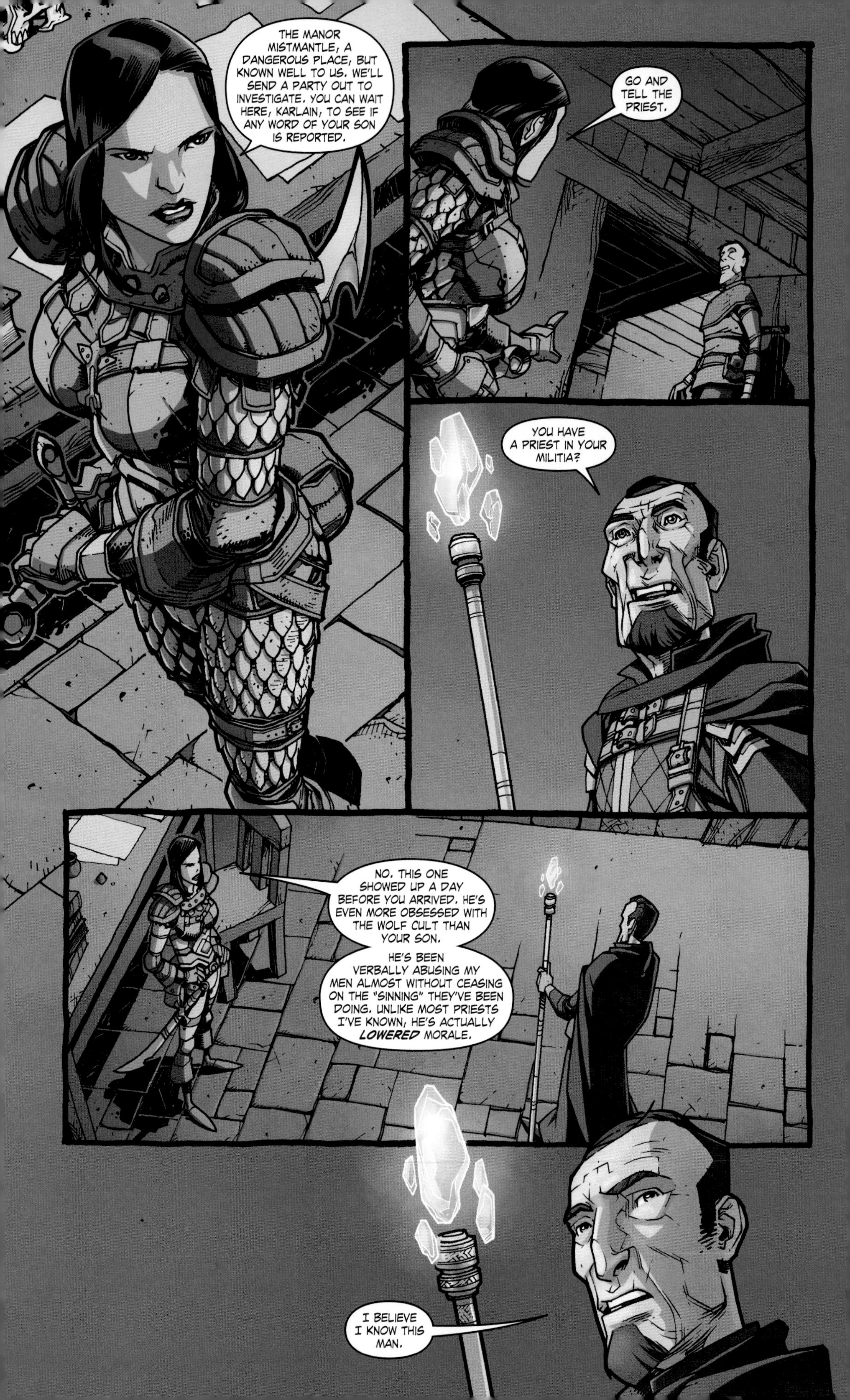
THE MANOR MISTMANTLE, A DANGEROUS PLACE, BUT KNOWN WELL TO US. WE'LL SEND A PARTY OUT TO INVESTIGATE. YOU CAN WAIT HERE, KARLAIN, TO SEE IF ANY WORD OF YOUR SON IS REPORTED.
GO AND TELL THE PRIEST.
YOU HAVE A PRIEST IN YOUR MILITIA?
NO. THIS ONE SHOWED UP A DAY BEFORE YOU ARRIVED. HE'S EVEN MORE OBSESSED WITH THE WOLF CULT THAN YOUR SON.
HE'S BEEN VERBALLY ABUSING MY MEN ALMOST WITHOUT CEASING ON THE "SINNING" THEY'VE BEEN DOING. UNLIKE MOST PRIESTS I'VE KNOWN, HE'S ACTUALLY *LOWERED* MORALE.
I BELIEVE I KNOW THIS MAN.

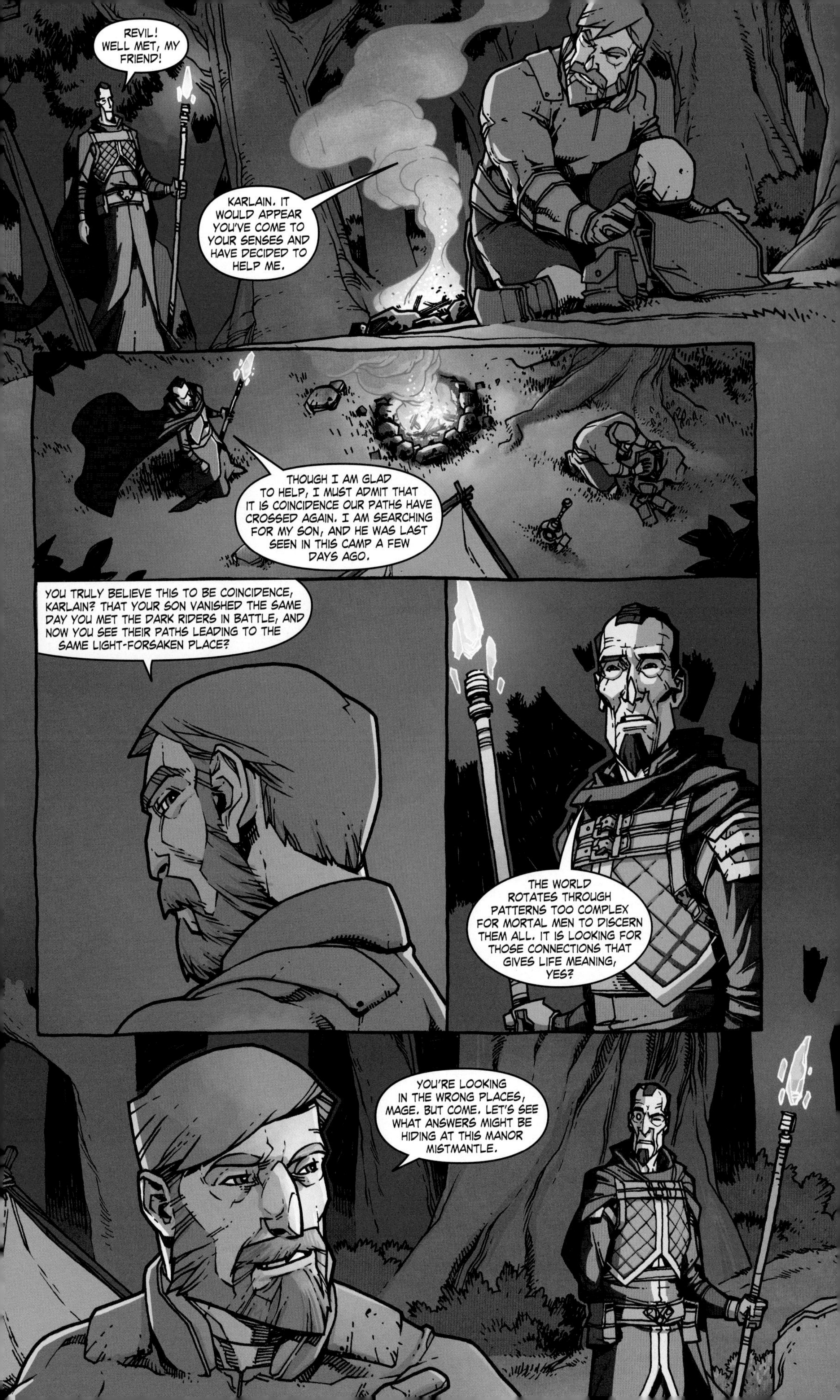
REVIL! WELL MET, MY FRIEND!
KARLAIN. IT WOULD APPEAR YOU'VE COME TO YOUR SENSES AND HAVE DECIDED TO HELP ME.
THOUGH I AM GLAD TO HELP, I MUST ADMIT THAT IT IS COINCIDENCE OUR PATHS HAVE CROSSED AGAIN. I AM SEARCHING FOR MY SON, AND HE WAS LAST SEEN IN THIS CAMP A FEW DAYS AGO.
YOU TRULY BELIEVE THIS TO BE COINCIDENCE, KARLAIN? THAT YOUR SON VANISHED THE SAME DAY YOU MET THE DARK RIDERS IN BATTLE, AND NOW YOU SEE THEIR PATHS LEADING TO THE SAME LIGHT-FORSAKEN PLACE?
THE WORLD ROTATES THROUGH PATTERNS TOO COMPLEX FOR MORTAL MEN TO DISCERN THEM ALL. IT IS LOOKING FOR THOSE CONNECTIONS THAT GIVES LIFE MEANING, YES?
YOU'RE LOOKING IN THE WRONG PLACES, MAGE. BUT COME. LET'S SEE WHAT ANSWERS MIGHT BE HIDING AT THIS MANOR MISTMANTLE.

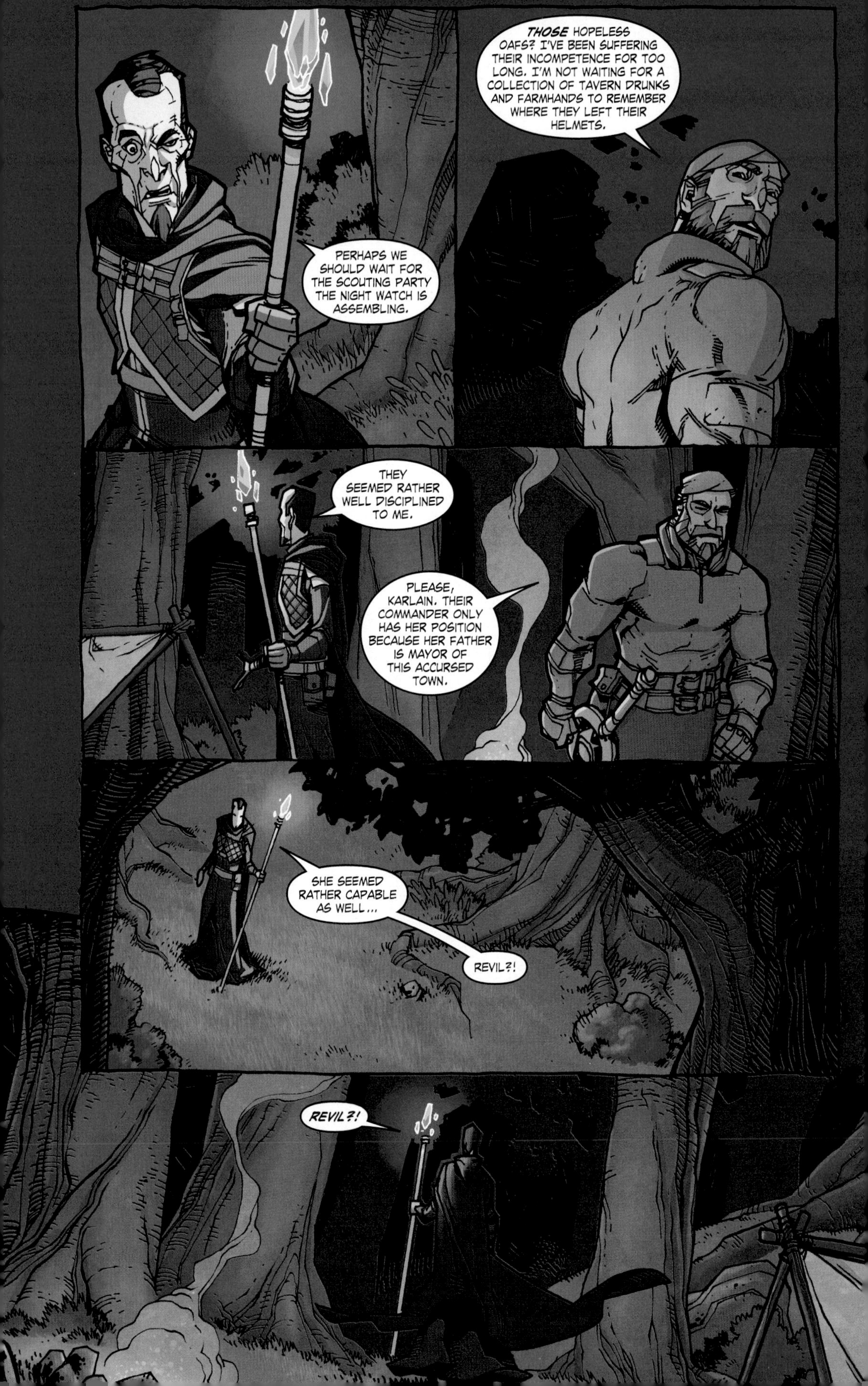
PERHAPS WE SHOULD WAIT FOR THE SCOUTING PARTY THE NIGHT WATCH IS ASSEMBLING.
THOSE HOPELESS OAFS? I'VE BEEN SUFFERING THEIR INCOMPETENCE FOR TOO LONG. I'M NOT WAITING FOR A COLLECTION OF TAVERN DRUNKS AND FARMHANDS TO REMEMBER WHERE THEY LEFT THEIR HELMETS.
THEY SEEMED RATHER WELL DISCIPLINED TO ME.
PLEASE, KARLAIN. THEIR COMMANDER ONLY HAS HER POSITION BECAUSE HER FATHER IS MAYOR OF THIS ACCURSED TOWN.
SHE SEEMED RATHER CAPABLE AS WELL...
REVIL?!
REVIL?!

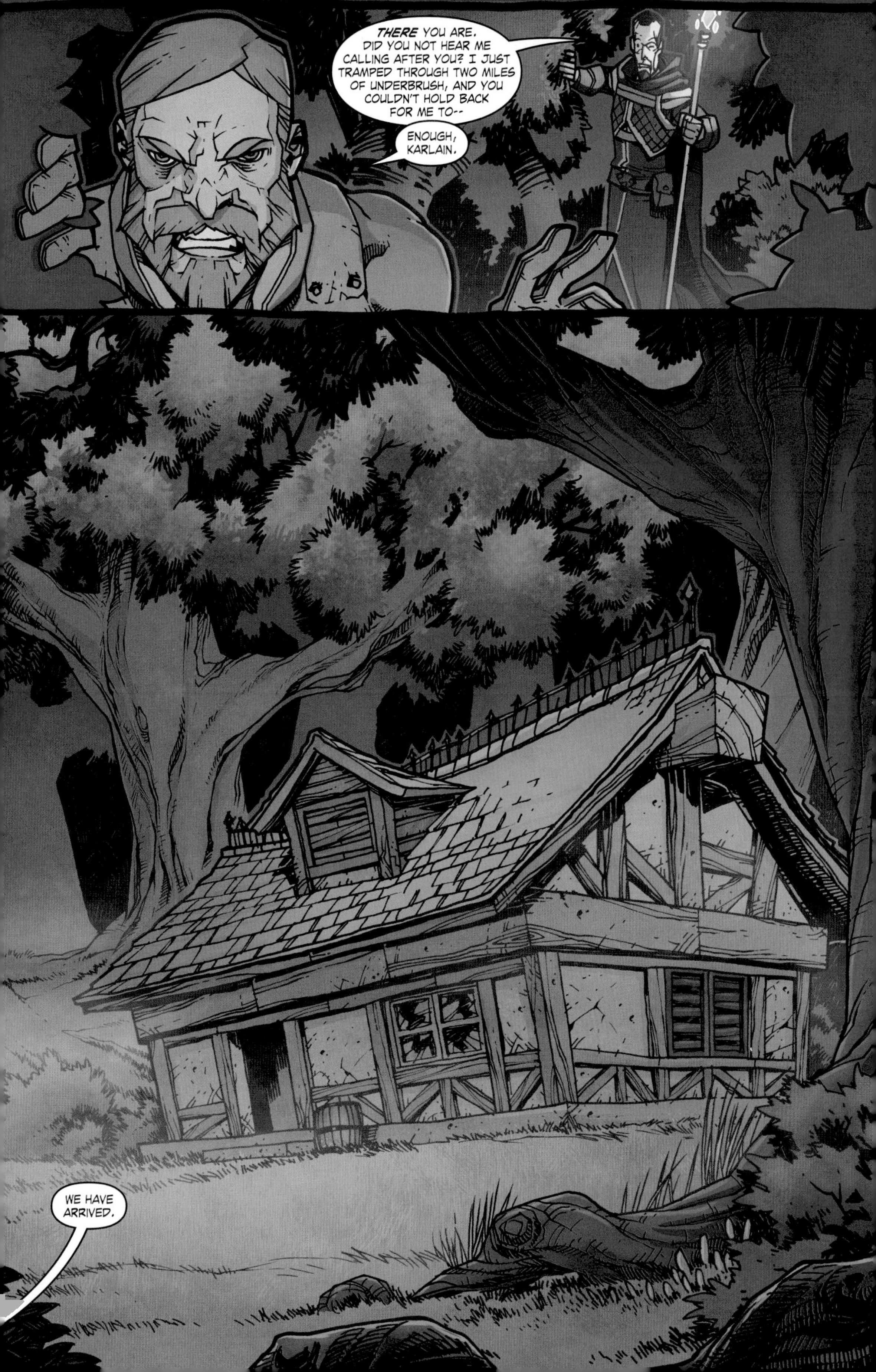
THERE YOU ARE. DID YOU NOT HEAR ME CALLING AFTER YOU? I JUST TRAMPED THROUGH TWO MILES OF UNDERBRUSH, AND YOU COULDN'T HOLD BACK FOR ME TO--
ENOUGH, KARLAIN.
WE HAVE ARRIVED.

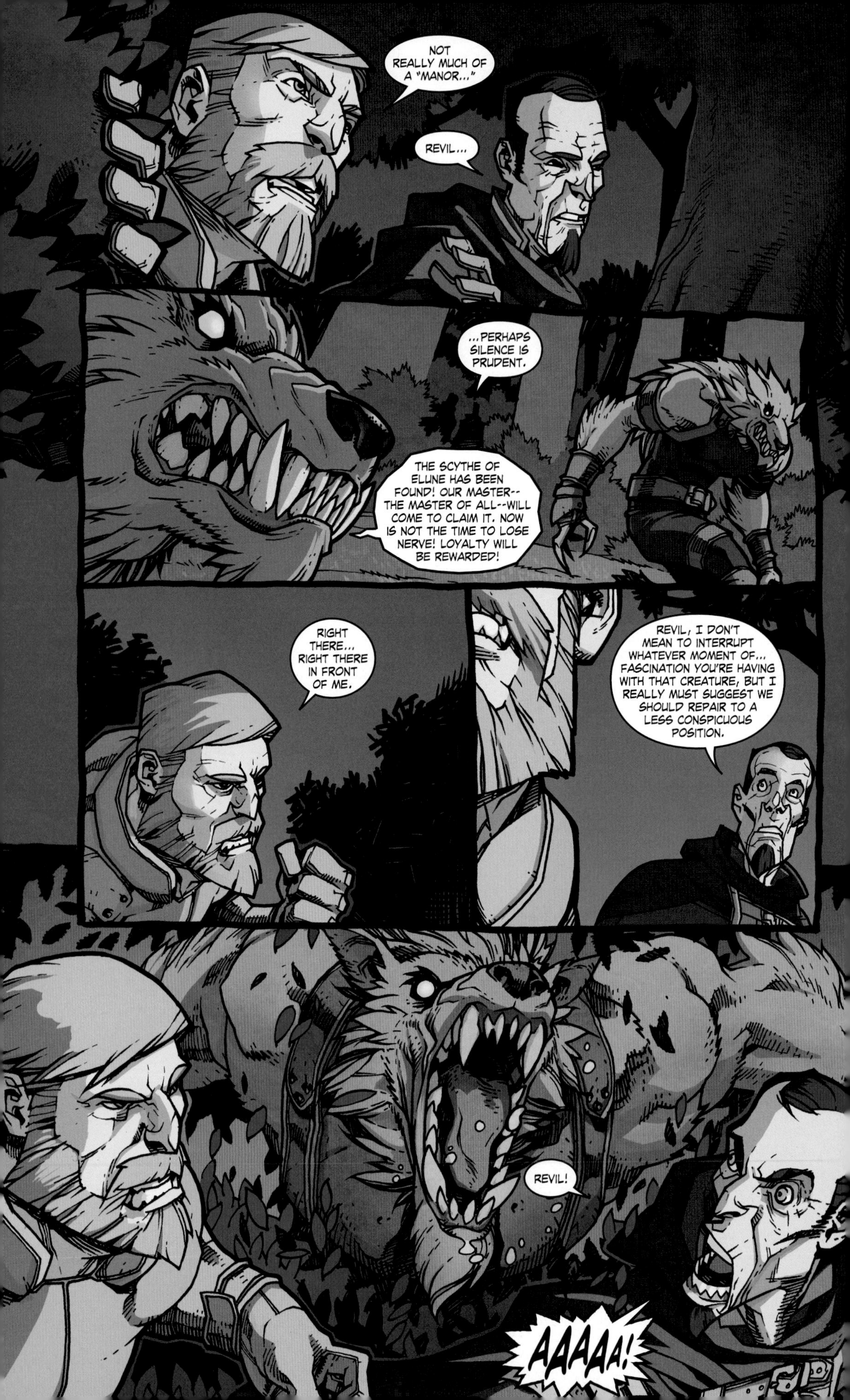
NOT REALLY MUCH OF A "MANOR..."
REVIL...
...PERHAPS SILENCE IS PRUDENT.
THE SCYTHE OF ELUNE HAS BEEN FOUND! OUR MASTER-- THE MASTER OF ALL--WILL COME TO CLAIM IT. NOW IS NOT THE TIME TO LOSE NERVE! LOYALTY WILL BE REWARDED!
RIGHT THERE... RIGHT THERE IN FRONT OF ME.
REVIL, I DON'T MEAN TO INTERRUPT WHATEVER MOMENT OF... FASCINATION YOU'RE HAVING WITH THAT CREATURE, BUT I REALLY MUST SUGGEST WE SHOULD REPAIR TO A LESS CONSPICUOUS POSITION.
REVIL!
AAAAA!

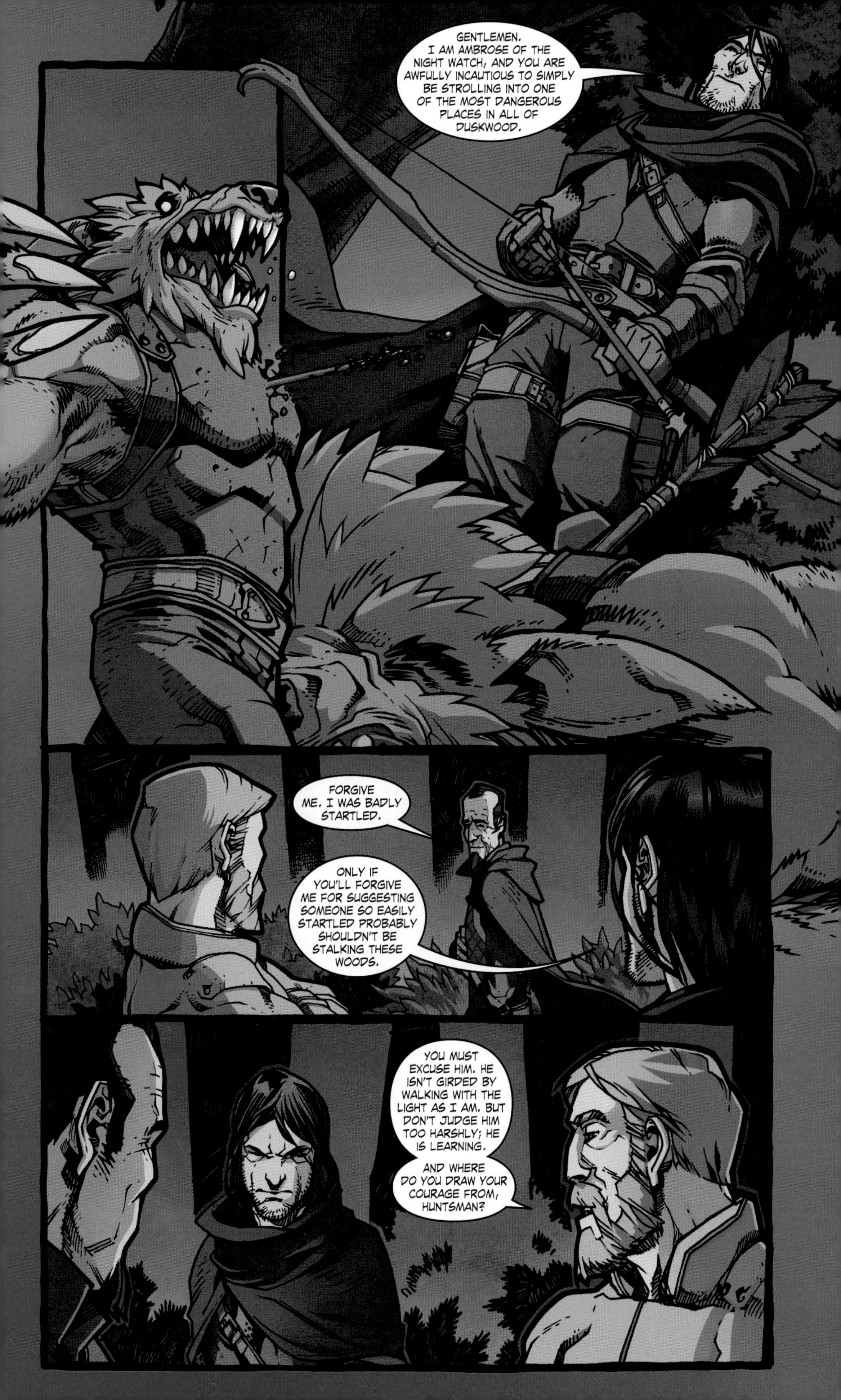
GENTLEMEN. I AM AMBROSE OF THE NIGHT WATCH, AND YOU ARE AWFULLY INCAUTIOUS TO SIMPLY BE STROLLING INTO ONE OF THE MOST DANGEROUS PLACES IN ALL OF DUSKWOOD.
FORGIVE ME. I WAS BADLY STARTLED.
ONLY IF YOU'LL FORGIVE ME FOR SUGGESTING SOMEONE SO EASILY STARTLED PROBABLY SHOULDN'T BE STALKING THESE WOODS.
YOU MUST EXCUSE HIM. HE ISN'T GIRDED BY WALKING WITH THE LIGHT AS I AM. BUT DON'T JUDGE HIM TOO HARSHLY; HE IS LEARNING.
AND WHERE DO YOU DRAW YOUR COURAGE FROM, HUNTSMAN?

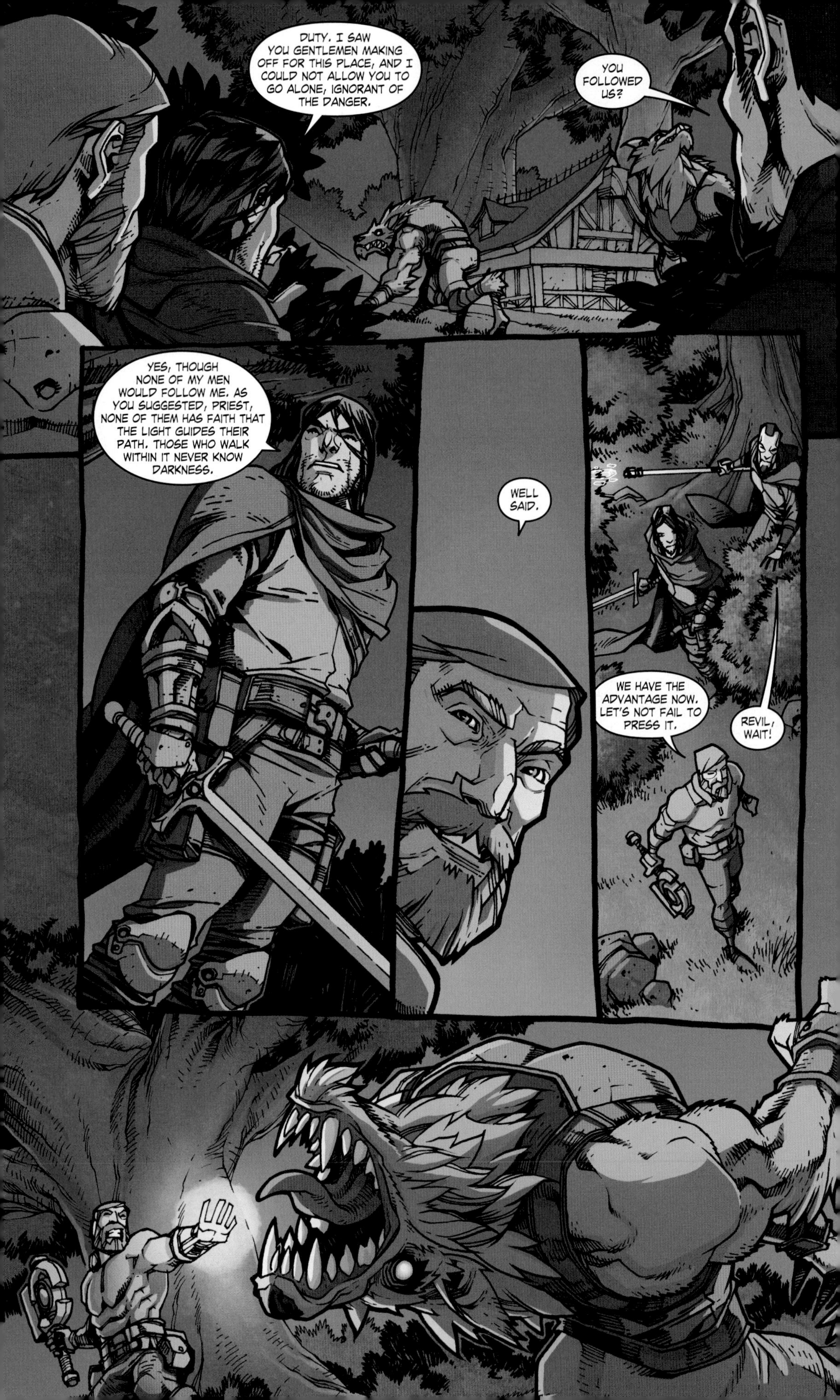
DUTY. I SAW YOU GENTLEMEN MAKING OFF FOR THIS PLACE, AND I COULD NOT ALLOW YOU TO GO ALONE, IGNORANT OF THE DANGER.
YOU FOLLOWED US?
YES, THOUGH NONE OF MY MEN WOULD FOLLOW ME. AS YOU SUGGESTED, PRIEST, NONE OF THEM HAS FAITH THAT THE LIGHT GUIDES THEIR PATH. THOSE WHO WALK WITHIN IT NEVER KNOW DARKNESS.
WELL SAID.
WE HAVE THE ADVANTAGE NOW. LET'S NOT FAIL TO PRESS IT.
REVIL, WAIT!

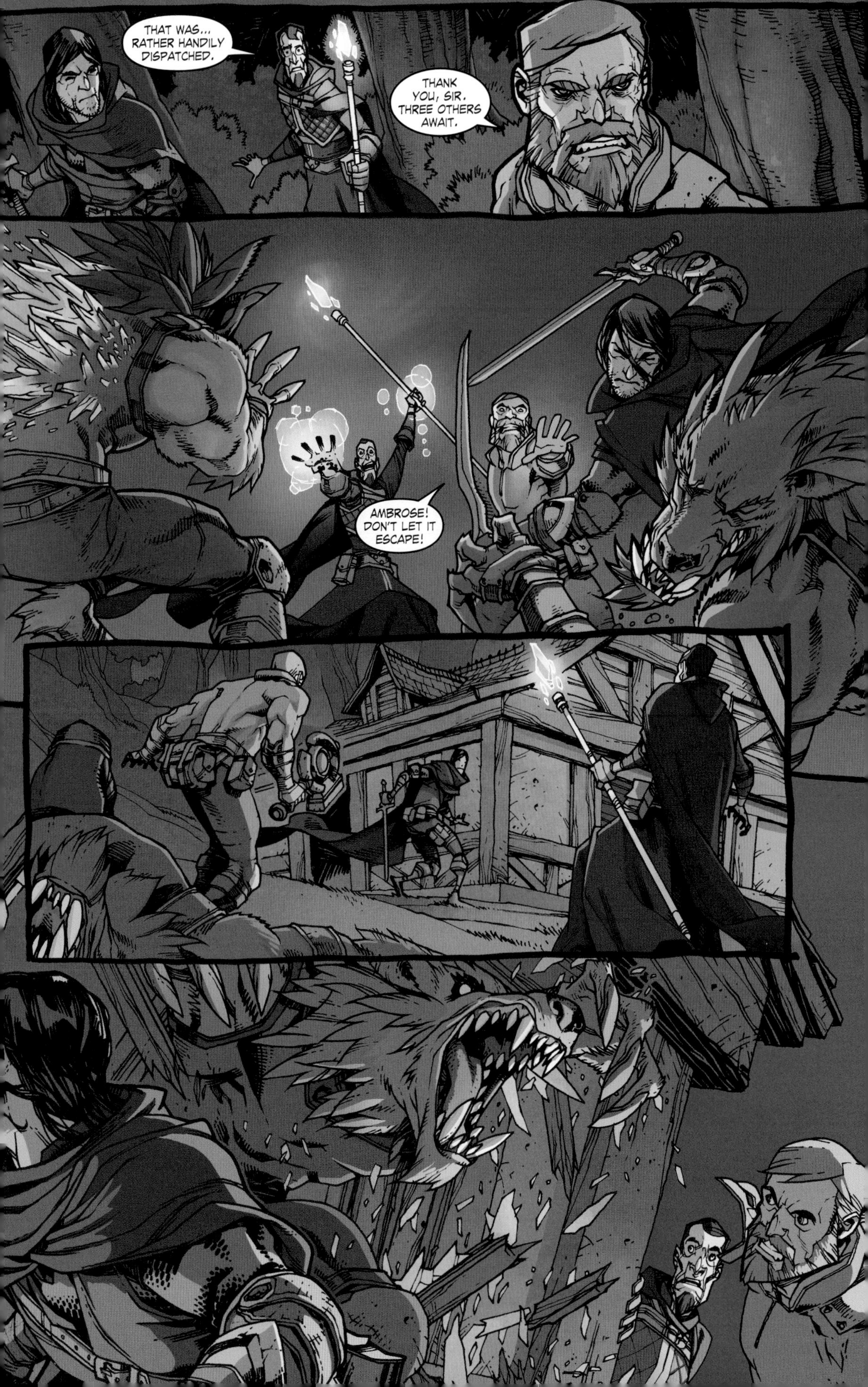
THAT WAS... RATHER HANDILY DISPATCHED.
THANK YOU, SIR. THREE OTHERS AWAIT.
AMBROSE! DON'T LET IT ESCAPE!

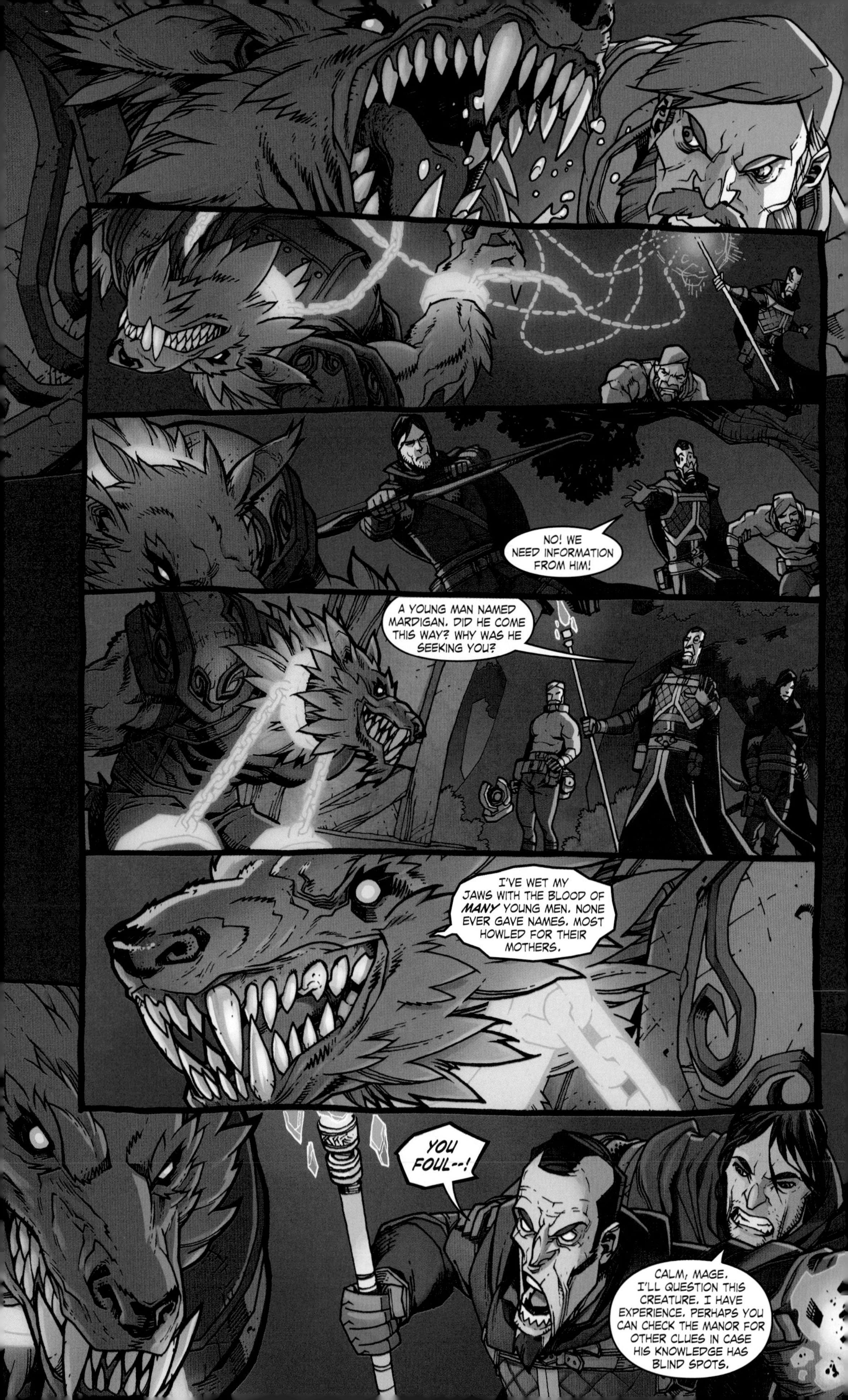
NO! WE NEED INFORMATION FROM HIM!
A YOUNG MAN NAMED MARDIGAN. DID HE COME THIS WAY? WHY WAS HE SEEKING YOU?
I'VE WET MY JAWS WITH THE BLOOD OF *MANY* YOUNG MEN. NONE EVER GAVE NAMES. MOST HOWLED FOR THEIR MOTHERS.
YOU FOUL--!
CALM, MAGE. I'LL QUESTION THIS CREATURE. I HAVE EXPERIENCE. PERHAPS YOU CAN CHECK THE MANOR FOR OTHER CLUES IN CASE HIS KNOWLEDGE HAS BLIND SPOTS.

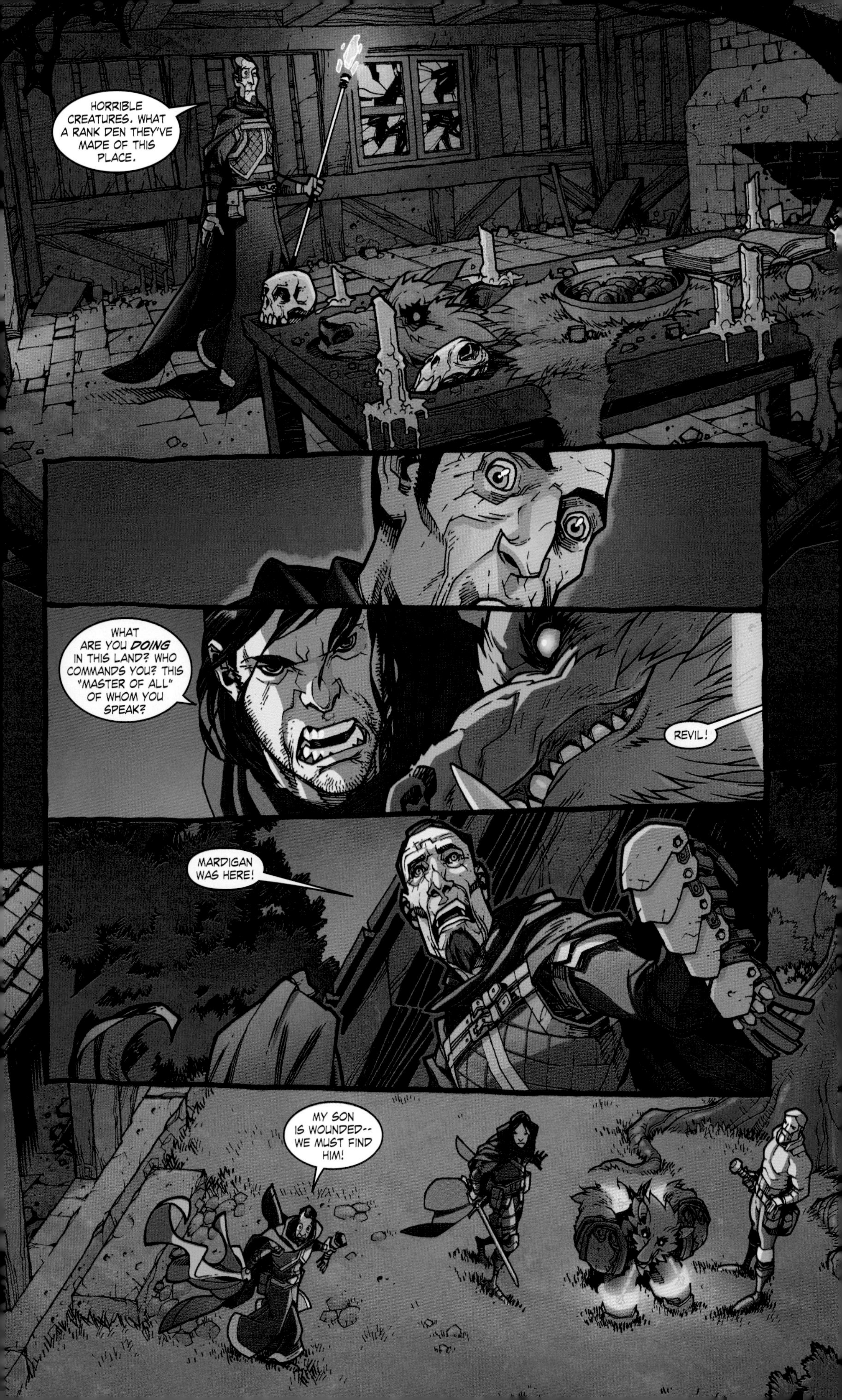

HORRIBLE CREATURES. WHAT A RANK DEN THEY'VE MADE OF THIS PLACE.
WHAT ARE YOU *DOING* IN THIS LAND? WHO COMMANDS YOU? THIS "MASTER OF ALL" OF WHOM YOU SPEAK?
REVIL!
MARDIGAN WAS HERE!
MY SON IS WOUNDED-- WE MUST FIND HIM!

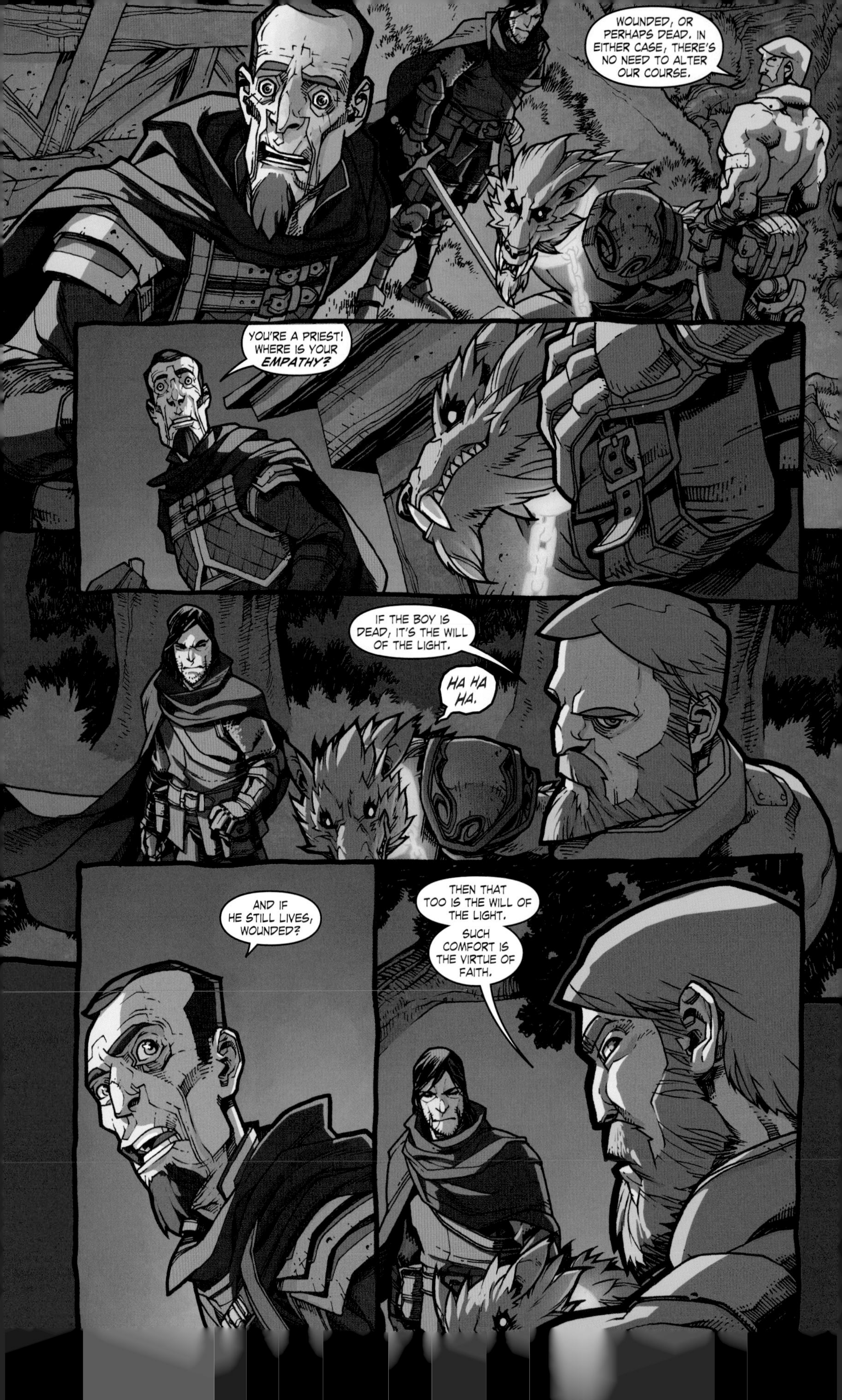
WOUNDED, OR PERHAPS DEAD. IN EITHER CASE, THERE'S NO NEED TO ALTER OUR COURSE.
YOU'RE A PRIEST! WHERE IS YOUR *EMPATHY?*
IF THE BOY IS DEAD, IT'S THE WILL OF THE LIGHT.
HA HA HA.
AND IF HE STILL LIVES, WOUNDED?
THEN THAT TOO IS THE WILL OF THE LIGHT.
SUCH COMFORT IS THE VIRTUE OF FAITH.

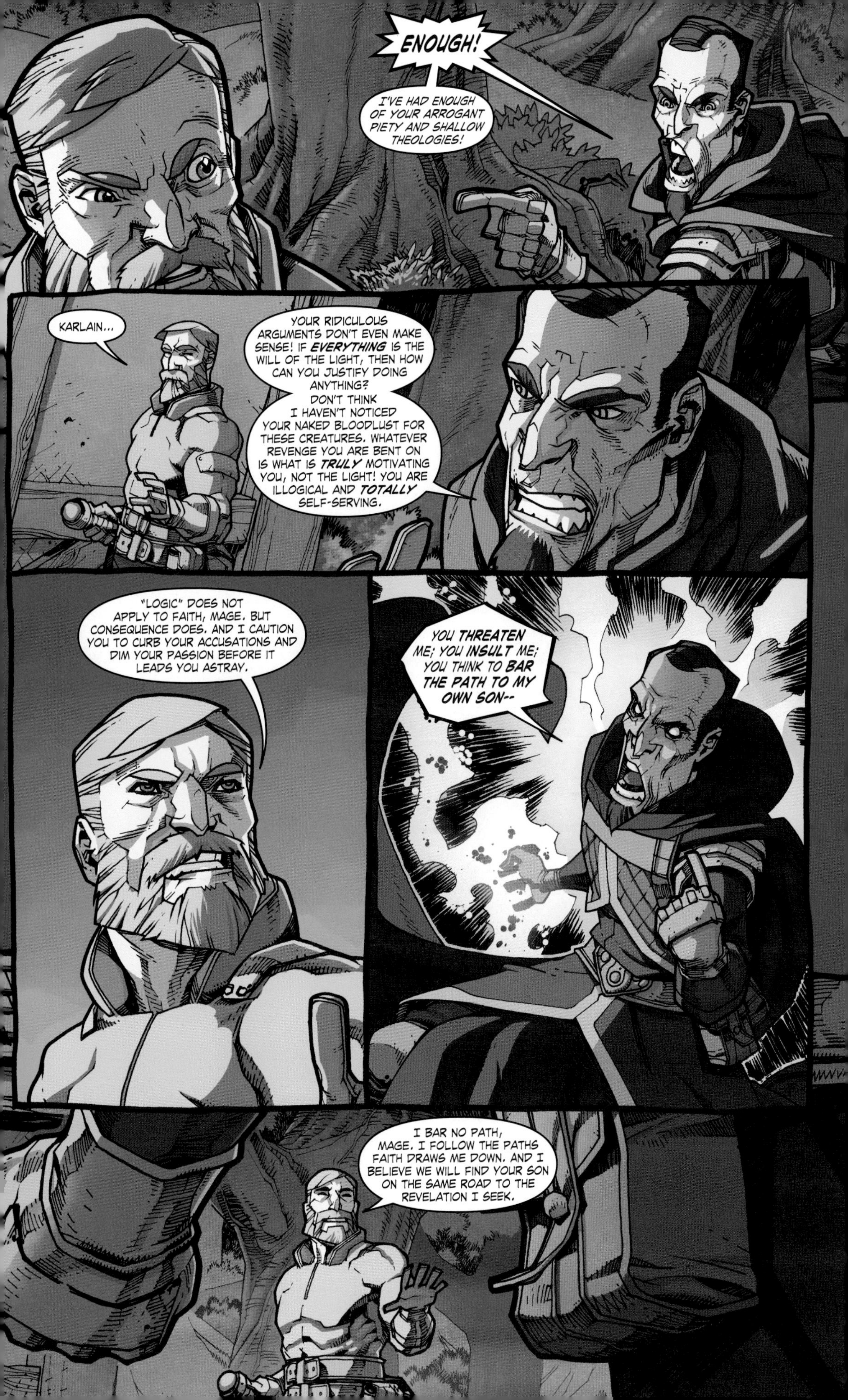
ENOUGH!
I'VE HAD ENOUGH OF YOUR ARROGANT PIETY AND SHALLOW THEOLOGIES!
KARLAIN...
YOUR RIDICULOUS ARGUMENTS DON'T EVEN MAKE SENSE! IF EVERYTHING IS THE WILL OF THE LIGHT, THEN HOW CAN YOU JUSTIFY DOING ANYTHING?
DON'T THINK I HAVEN'T NOTICED YOUR NAKED BLOODLUST FOR THESE CREATURES. WHATEVER REVENGE YOU ARE BENT ON IS WHAT IS TRULY MOTIVATING YOU, NOT THE LIGHT! YOU ARE ILLOGICAL AND TOTALLY SELF-SERVING.
"LOGIC" DOES NOT APPLY TO FAITH, MAGE. BUT CONSEQUENCE DOES. AND I CAUTION YOU TO CURB YOUR ACCUSATIONS AND DIM YOUR PASSION BEFORE IT LEADS YOU ASTRAY.
YOU THREATEN ME; YOU INSULT ME; YOU THINK TO BAR THE PATH TO MY OWN SON--
I BAR NO PATH, MAGE. I FOLLOW THE PATHS FAITH DRAWS ME DOWN. AND I BELIEVE WE WILL FIND YOUR SON ON THE SAME ROAD TO THE REVELATION I SEEK.

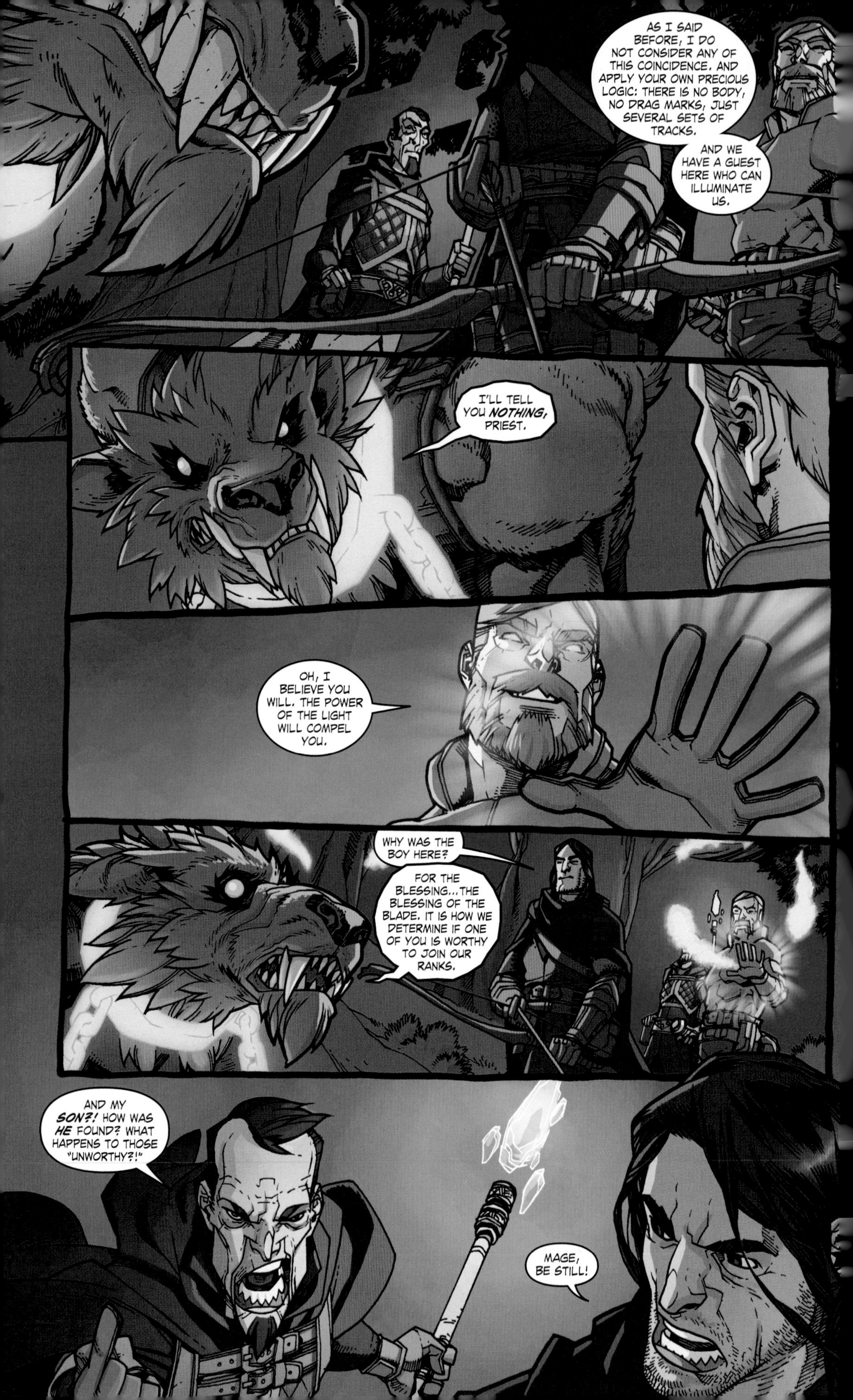
AS I SAID BEFORE, I DO NOT CONSIDER ANY OF THIS COINCIDENCE. AND APPLY YOUR OWN PRECIOUS LOGIC: THERE IS NO BODY, NO DRAG MARKS, JUST SEVERAL SETS OF TRACKS.
AND WE HAVE A GUEST HERE WHO CAN ILLUMINATE US.
I'LL TELL YOU *NOTHING,* PRIEST.
OH, I BELIEVE YOU WILL. THE POWER OF THE LIGHT WILL COMPEL YOU.
WHY WAS THE BOY HERE?
FOR THE BLESSING... THE BLESSING OF THE BLADE. IT IS HOW WE DETERMINE IF ONE OF YOU IS WORTHY TO JOIN OUR RANKS.
AND MY *SON?!* HOW WAS *HE* FOUND? WHAT HAPPENS TO THOSE "UNWORTHY?!"
MAGE, BE STILL!

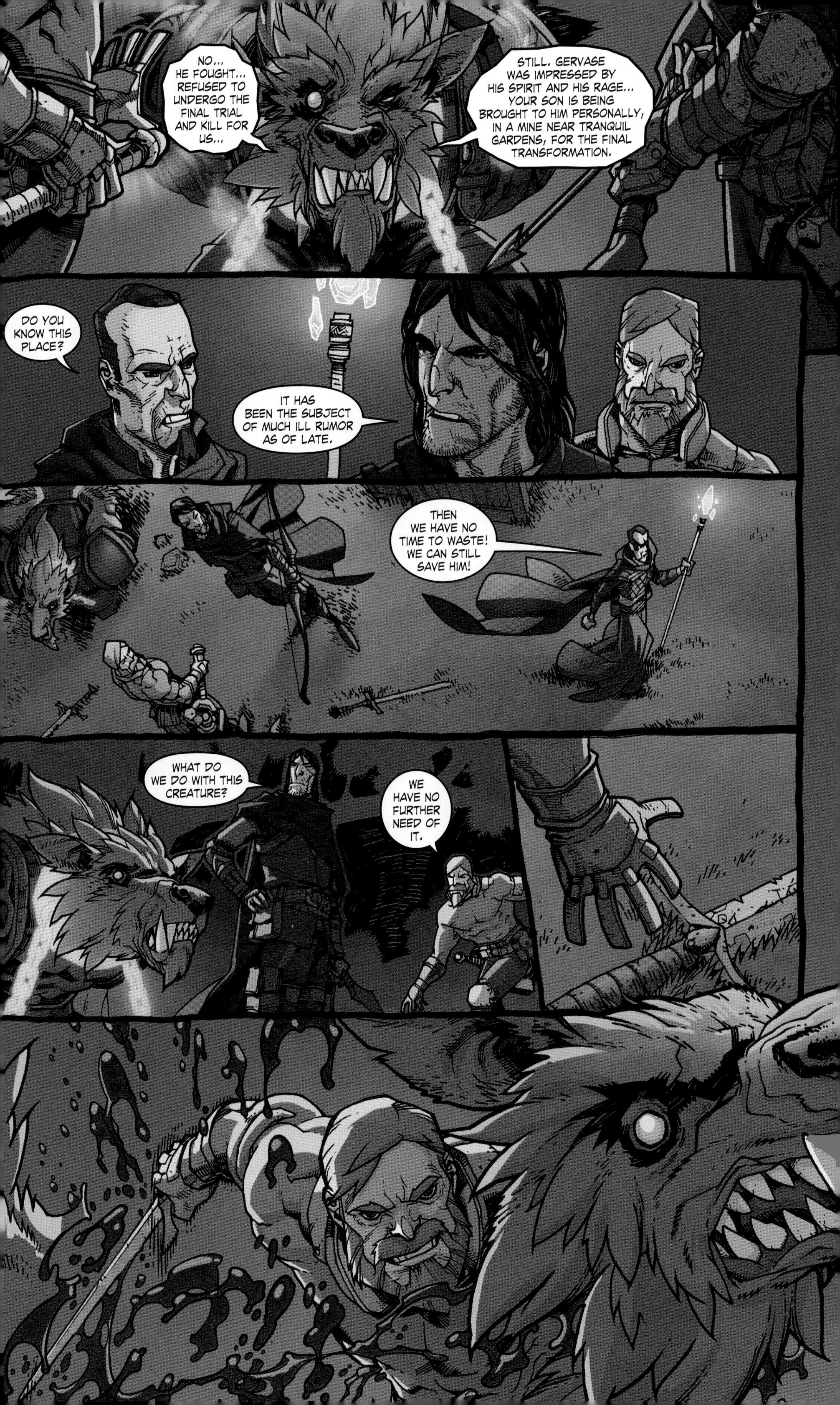
NO... HE FOUGHT... REFUSED TO UNDERGO THE FINAL TRIAL AND KILL FOR US...
STILL. GERVASE WAS IMPRESSED BY HIS SPIRIT AND HIS RAGE... YOUR SON IS BEING BROUGHT TO HIM PERSONALLY, IN A MINE NEAR TRANQUIL GARDENS, FOR THE FINAL TRANSFORMATION.
DO YOU KNOW THIS PLACE?
IT HAS BEEN THE SUBJECT OF MUCH ILL RUMOR AS OF LATE.
THEN WE HAVE NO TIME TO WASTE! WE CAN STILL SAVE HIM!
WHAT DO WE DO WITH THIS CREATURE?
WE HAVE NO FURTHER NEED OF IT.

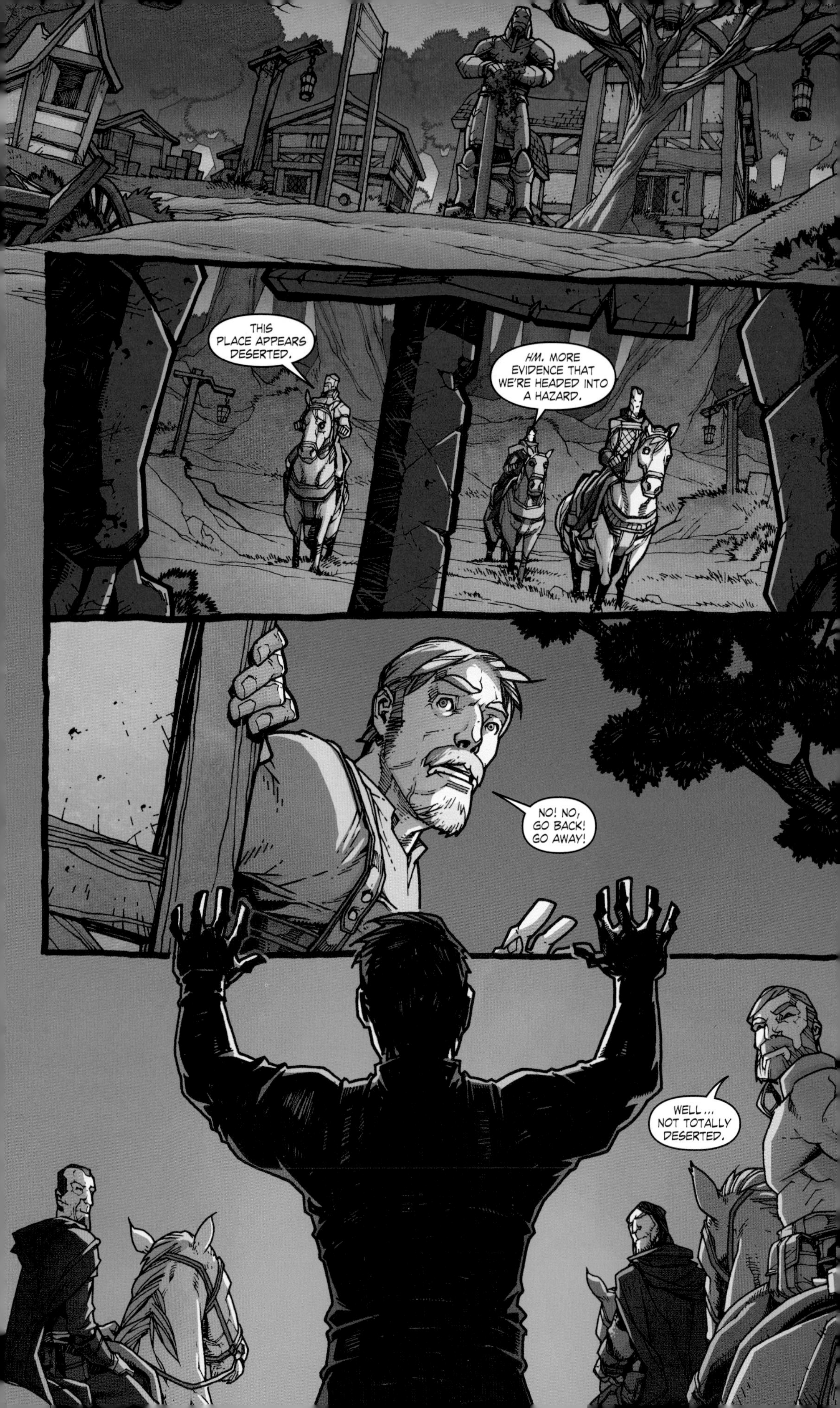
THIS PLACE APPEARS DESERTED.
HM. MORE EVIDENCE THAT WE'RE HEADED INTO A HAZARD.
NO! NO, GO BACK! GO AWAY!
WELL... NOT TOTALLY DESERTED.

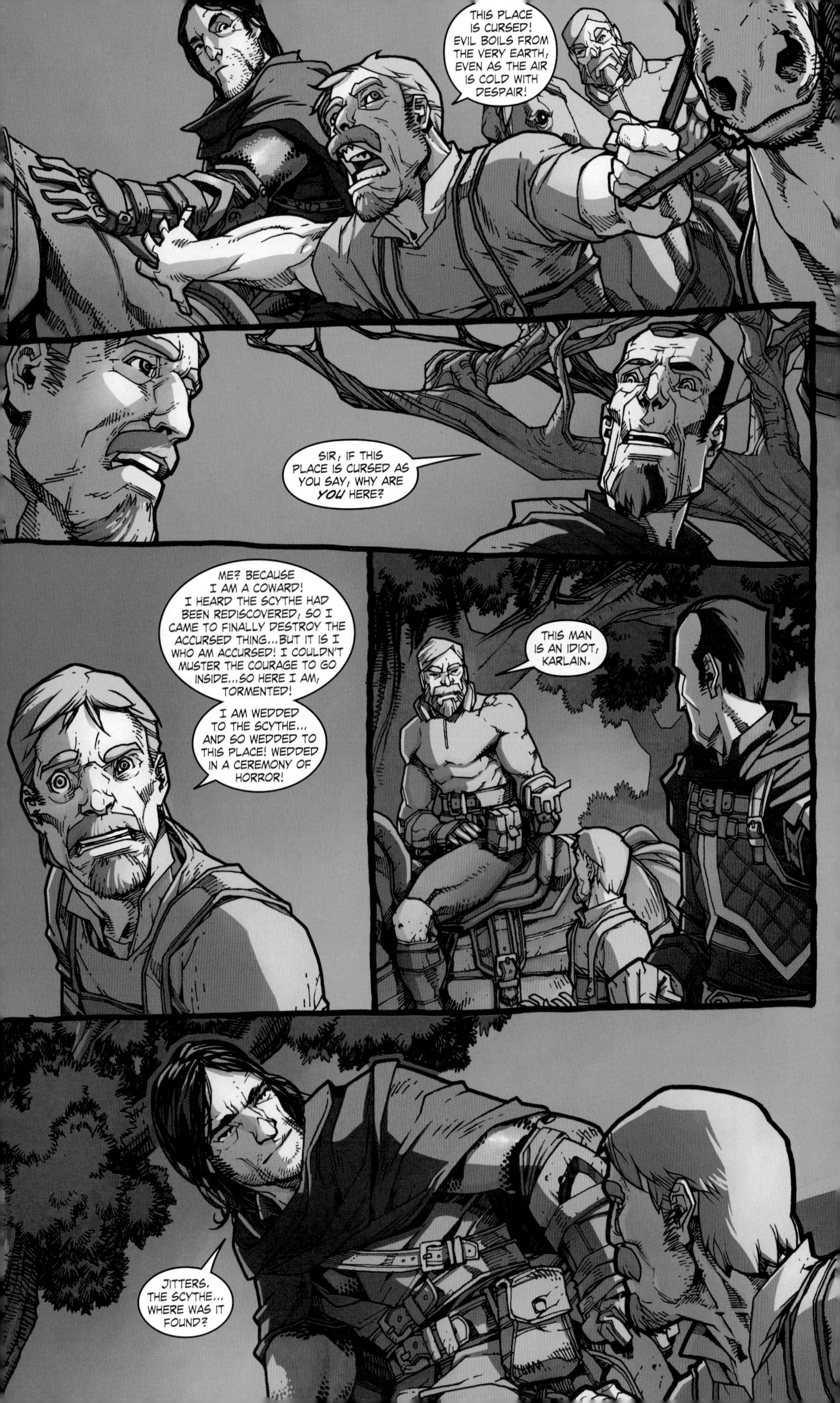
THIS PLACE IS CURSED! EVIL BOILS FROM THE VERY EARTH, EVEN AS THE AIR IS COLD WITH DESPAIR!
SIR, IF THIS PLACE IS CURSED AS YOU SAY, WHY ARE *YOU* HERE?
ME? BECAUSE I AM A COWARD! I HEARD THE SCYTHE HAD BEEN REDISCOVERED, SO I CAME TO FINALLY DESTROY THE ACCURSED THING...BUT IT IS I WHO AM ACCURSED! I COULDN'T MUSTER THE COURAGE TO GO INSIDE...SO HERE I AM, TORMENTED!
I AM WEDDED TO THE SCYTHE... AND SO WEDDED TO THIS PLACE! WEDDED IN A CEREMONY OF HORROR!
THIS MAN IS AN IDIOT, KARLAIN.
JITTERS. THE SCYTHE... WHERE WAS IT FOUND?

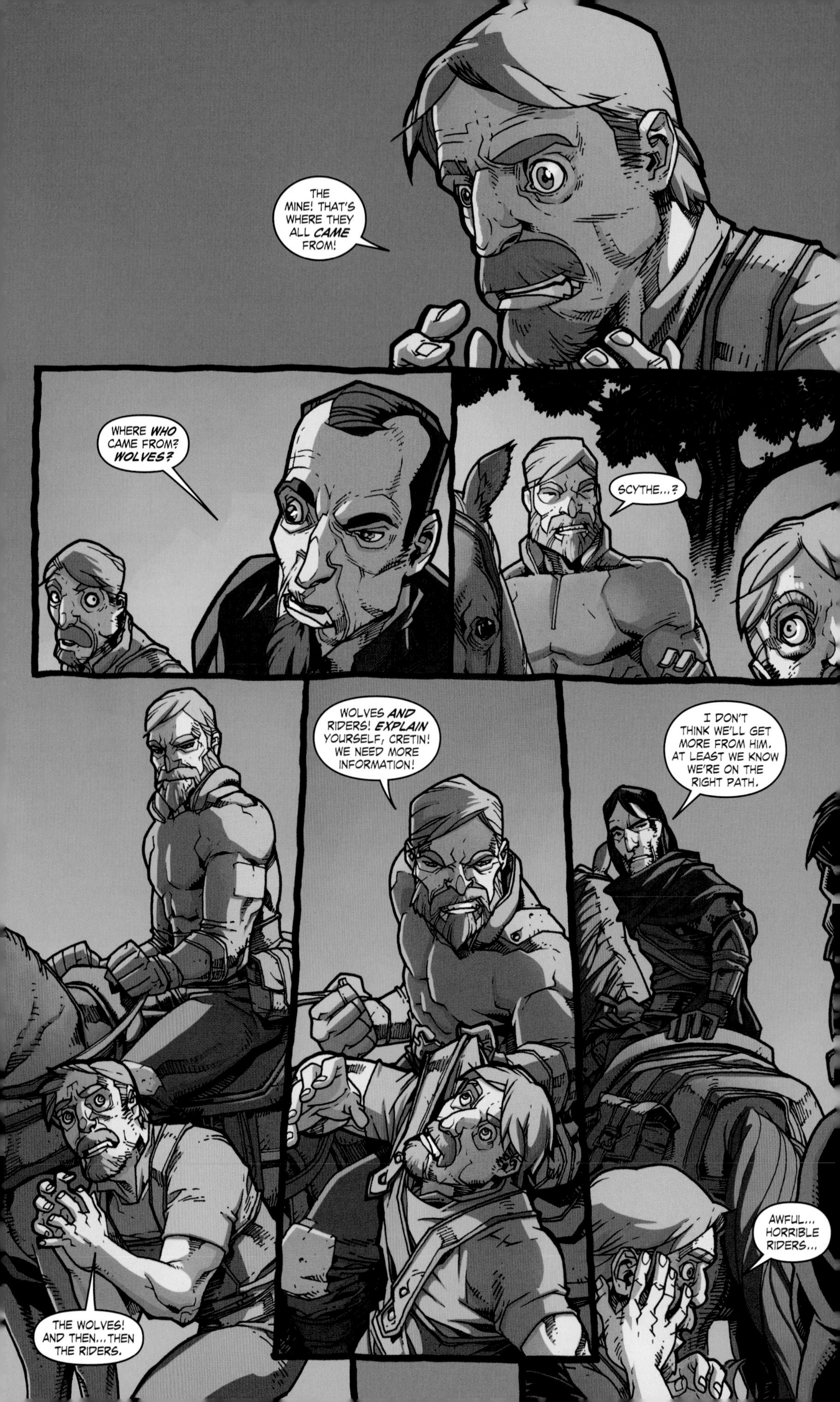
THE MINE! THAT'S WHERE THEY ALL *CAME* FROM!
WHERE *WHO* CAME FROM? *WOLVES?*
SCYTHE...?
THE WOLVES! AND THEN...THEN THE RIDERS.
WOLVES *AND* RIDERS! *EXPLAIN* YOURSELF, CRETIN! WE NEED MORE INFORMATION!
I DON'T THINK WE'LL GET MORE FROM HIM. AT LEAST WE KNOW WE'RE ON THE RIGHT PATH.
AWFUL... HORRIBLE RIDERS...

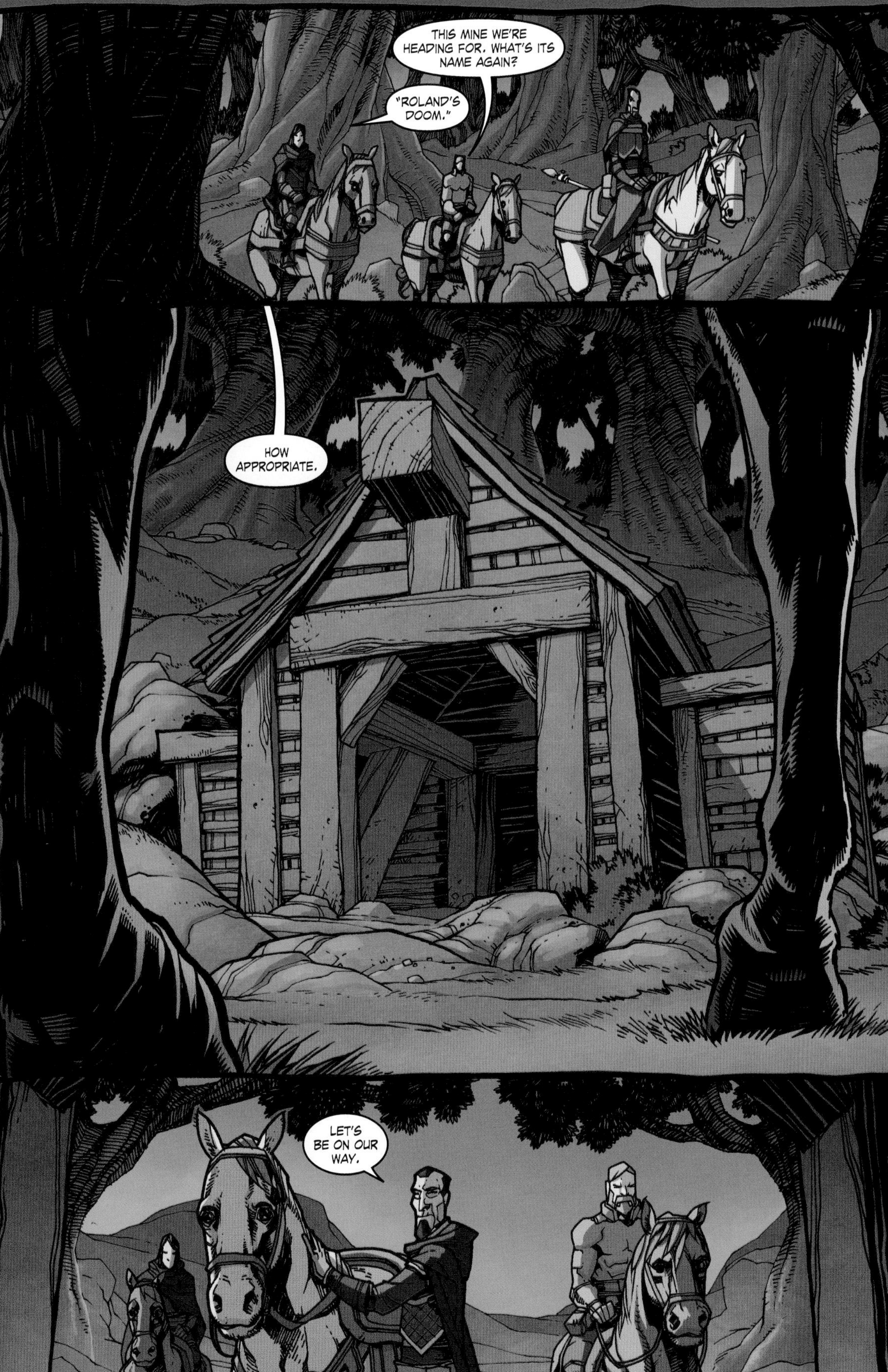
THIS MINE WE'RE HEADING FOR. WHAT'S ITS NAME AGAIN?
"ROLAND'S DOOM."
HOW APPROPRIATE.
LET'S BE ON OUR WAY.

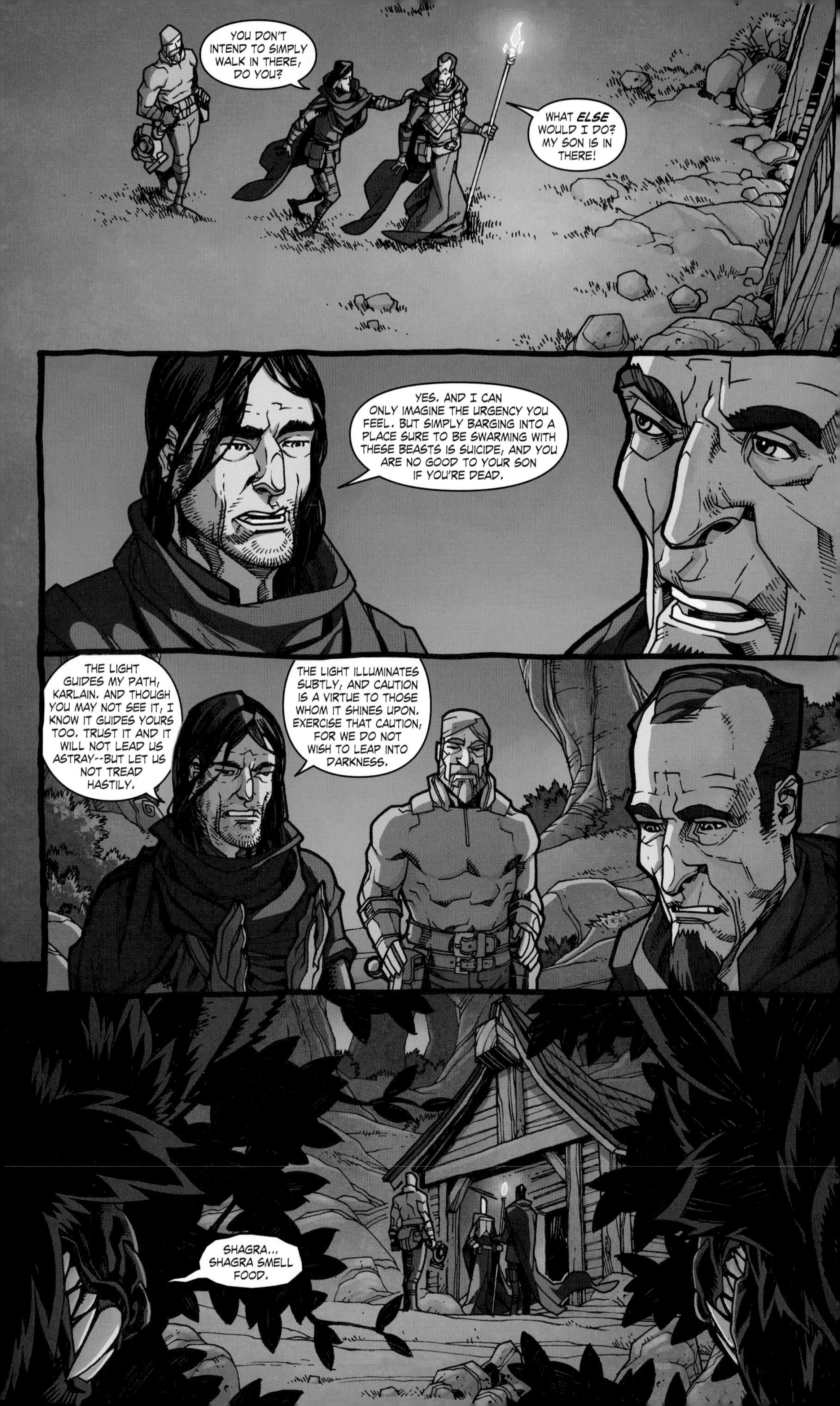
YOU DON'T INTEND TO SIMPLY WALK IN THERE, DO YOU?
WHAT ELSE WOULD I DO? MY SON IS IN THERE!
YES. AND I CAN ONLY IMAGINE THE URGENCY YOU FEEL. BUT SIMPLY BARGING INTO A PLACE SURE TO BE SWARMING WITH THESE BEASTS IS SUICIDE, AND YOU ARE NO GOOD TO YOUR SON IF YOU'RE DEAD.
THE LIGHT GUIDES MY PATH, KARLAIN. AND THOUGH YOU MAY NOT SEE IT, I KNOW IT GUIDES YOURS TOO. TRUST IT AND IT WILL NOT LEAD US ASTRAY--BUT LET US NOT TREAD HASTILY.
THE LIGHT ILLUMINATES SUBTLY, AND CAUTION IS A VIRTUE TO THOSE WHOM IT SHINES UPON. EXERCISE THAT CAUTION, FOR WE DO NOT WISH TO LEAP INTO DARKNESS.
SHAGRA... SHAGRA SMELL FOOD.

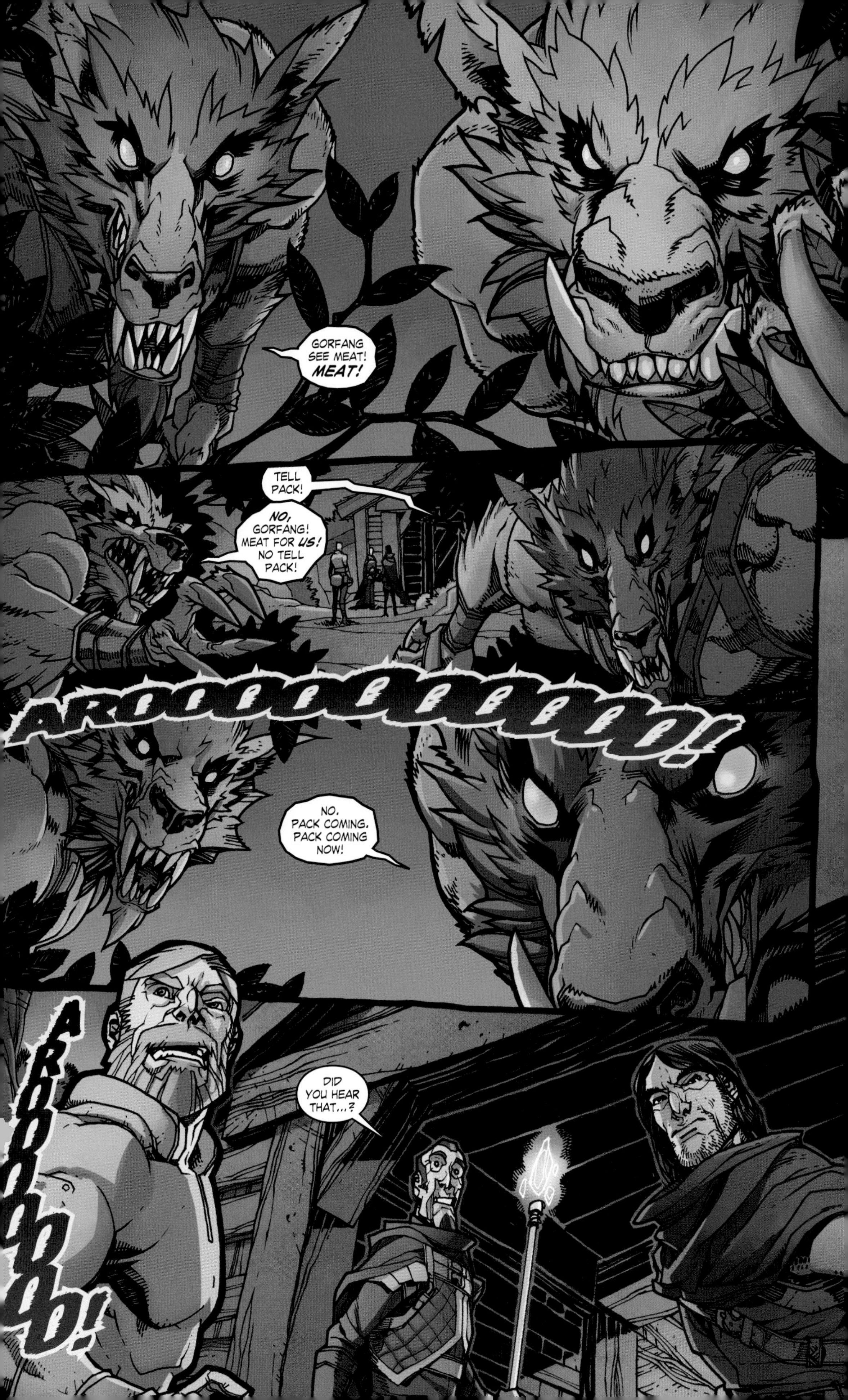
GORFANG SEE MEAT! MEAT!
TELL PACK!
NO, GORFANG! MEAT FOR US! NO TELL PACK!
AROOOOOOOOOO!
NO. PACK COMING. PACK COMING NOW!
AROOOOOO!
DID YOU HEAR THAT...?

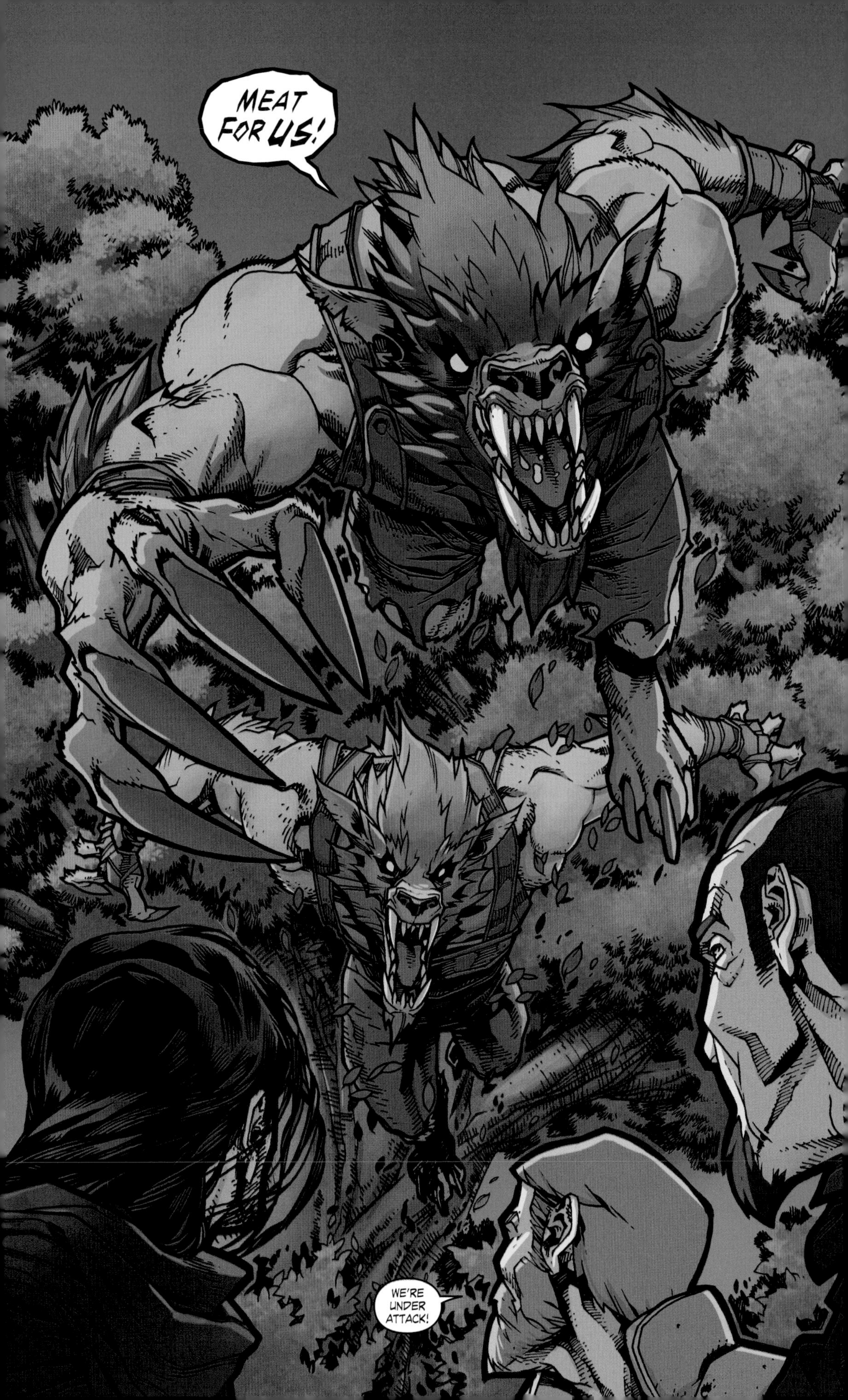
MEAT FOR US!
WE'RE UNDER ATTACK!

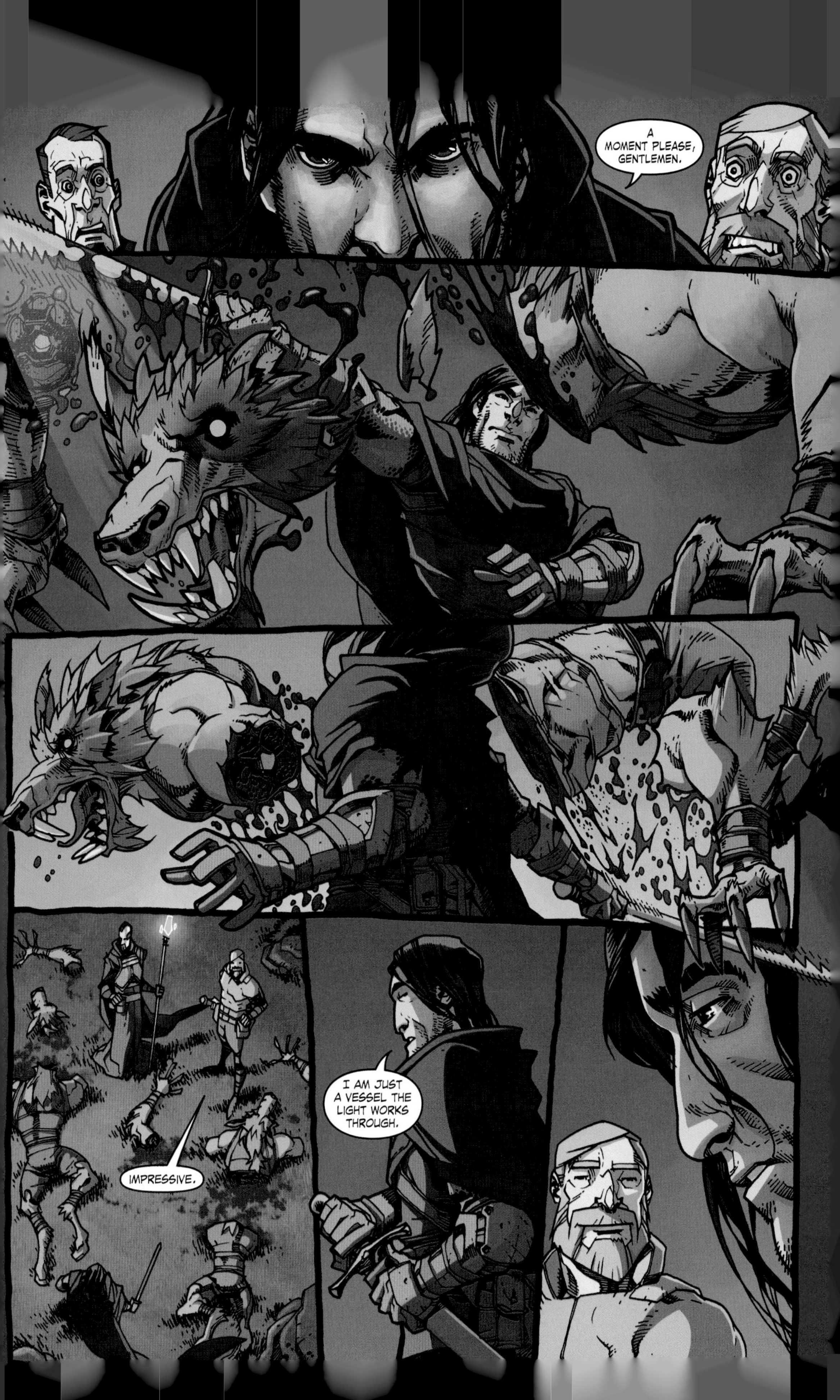
A MOMENT PLEASE, GENTLEMEN.
IMPRESSIVE.
I AM JUST A VESSEL THE LIGHT WORKS THROUGH.

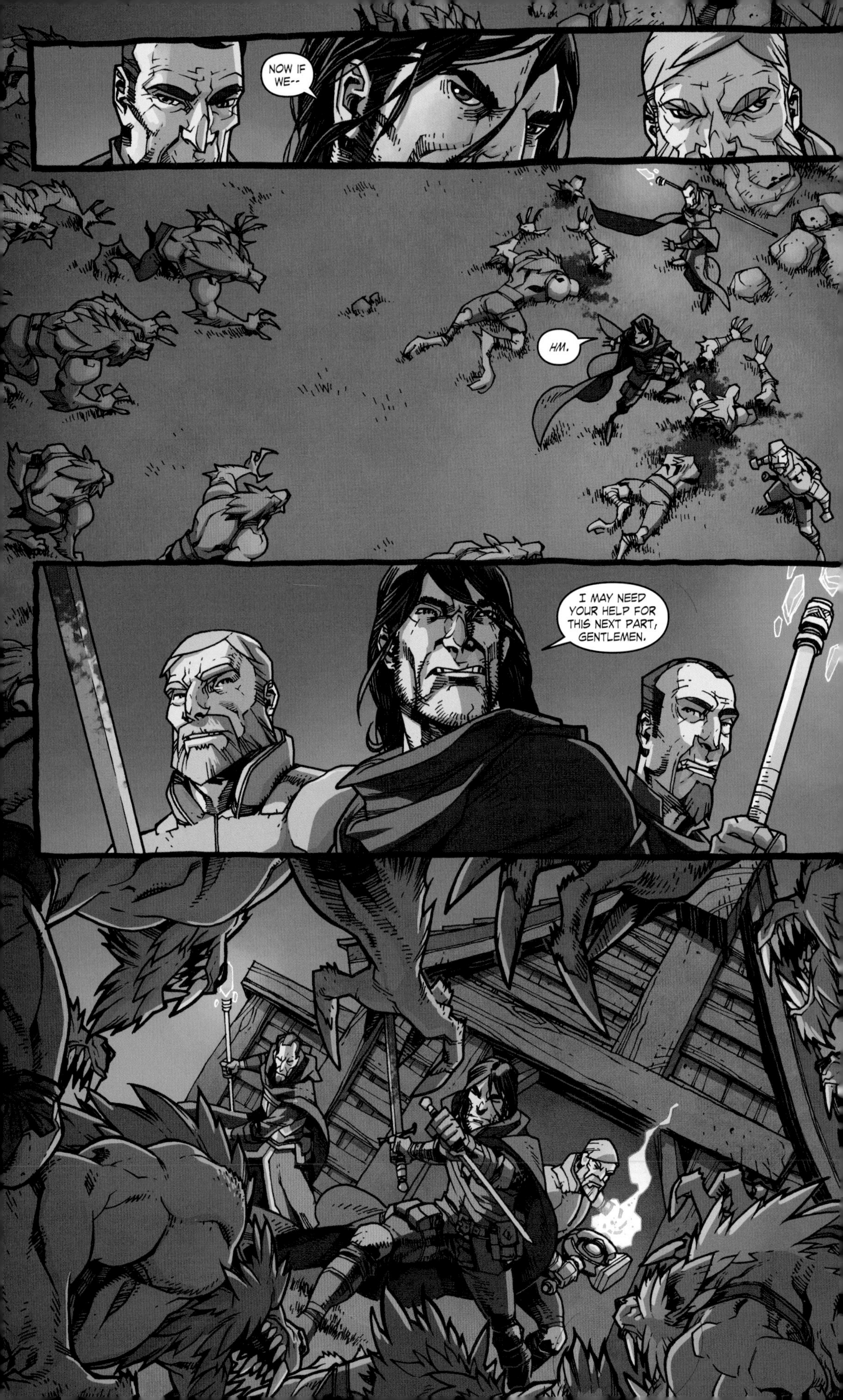
NOW IF WE--
HM.
I MAY NEED YOUR HELP FOR THIS NEXT PART, GENTLEMEN.

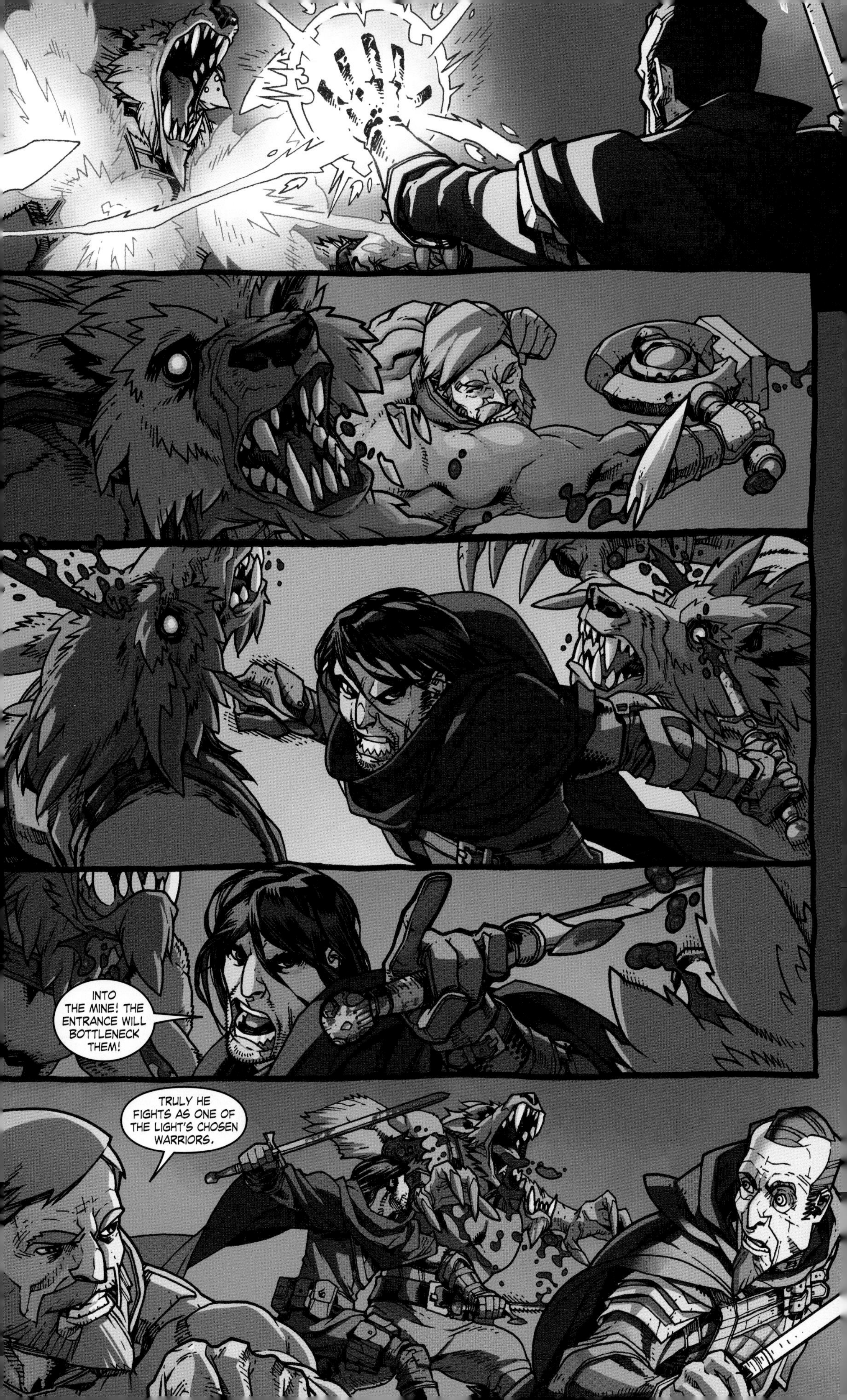
INTO THE MINE! THE ENTRANCE WILL BOTTLENECK THEM!
TRULY HE FIGHTS AS ONE OF THE LIGHT'S CHOSEN WARRIORS.

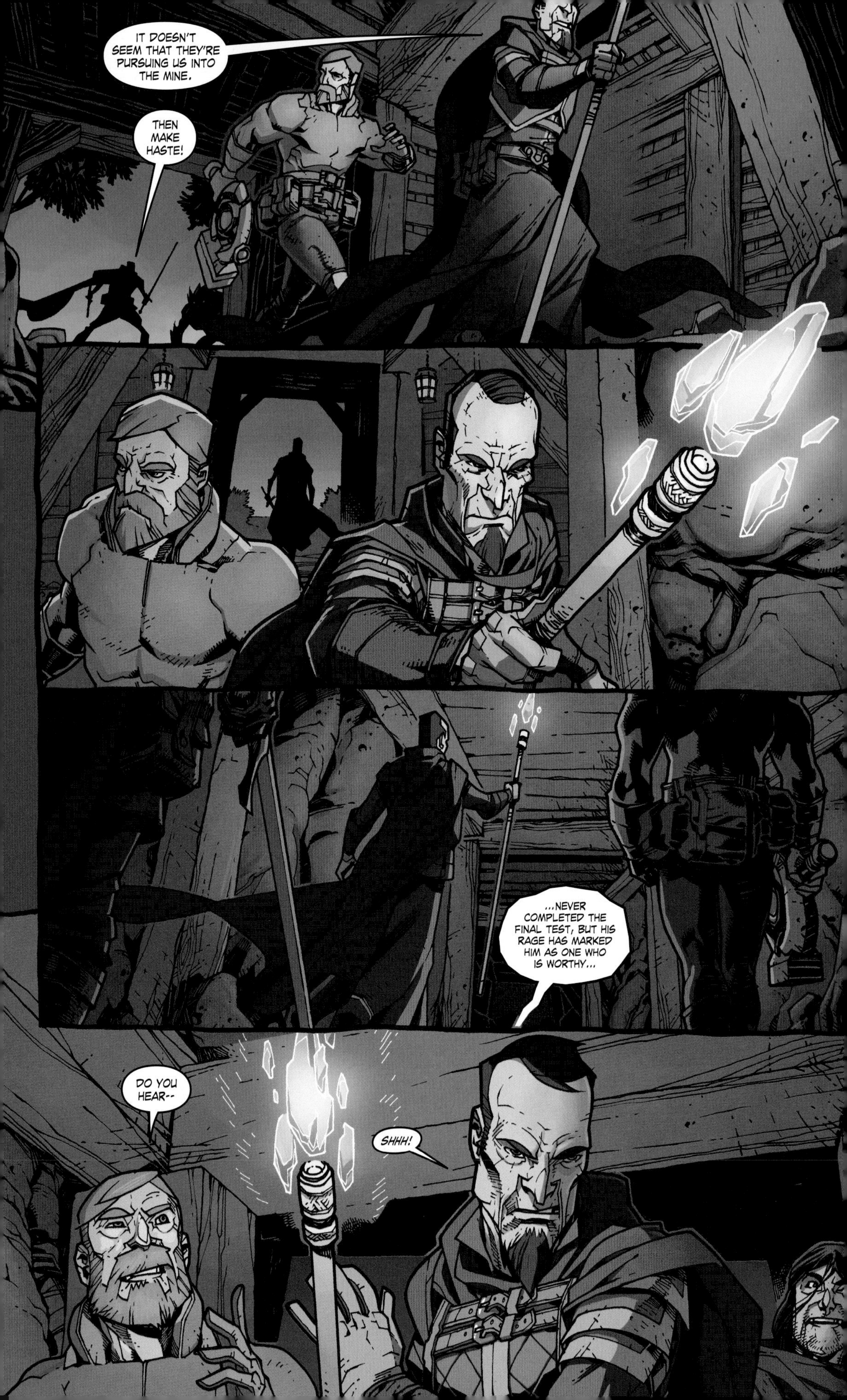
IT DOESN'T SEEM THAT THEY'RE PURSUING US INTO THE MINE.
THEN MAKE HASTE!
...NEVER COMPLETED THE FINAL TEST, BUT HIS RAGE HAS MARKED HIM AS ONE WHO IS WORTHY...
DO YOU HEAR--
SHHH!

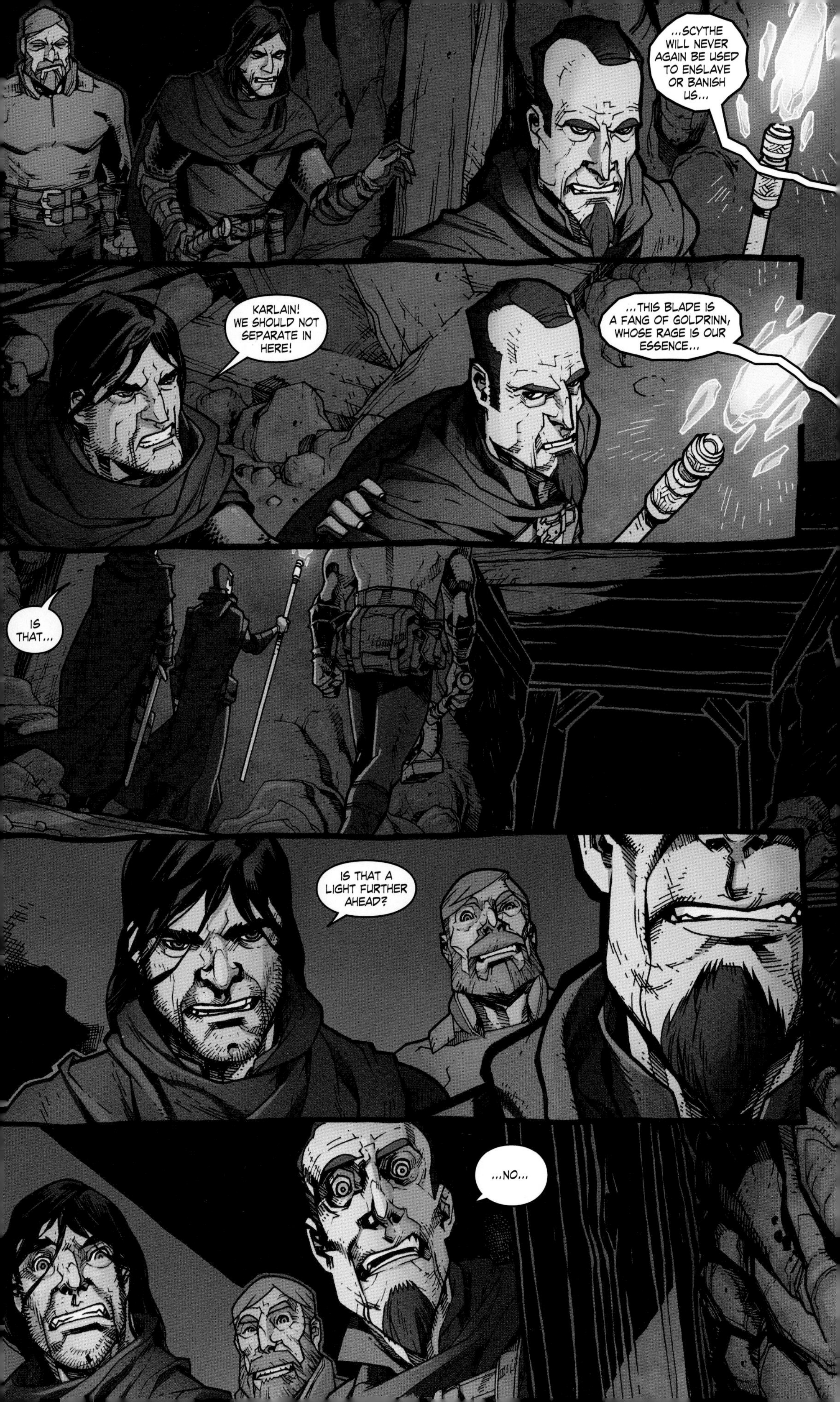
...SCYTHE WILL NEVER AGAIN BE USED TO ENSLAVE OR BANISH US...
KARLAIN! WE SHOULD NOT SEPARATE IN HERE!
...THIS BLADE IS A FANG OF GOLDRINN, WHOSE RAGE IS OUR ESSENCE...
IS THAT...
IS THAT A LIGHT FURTHER AHEAD?
...NO...

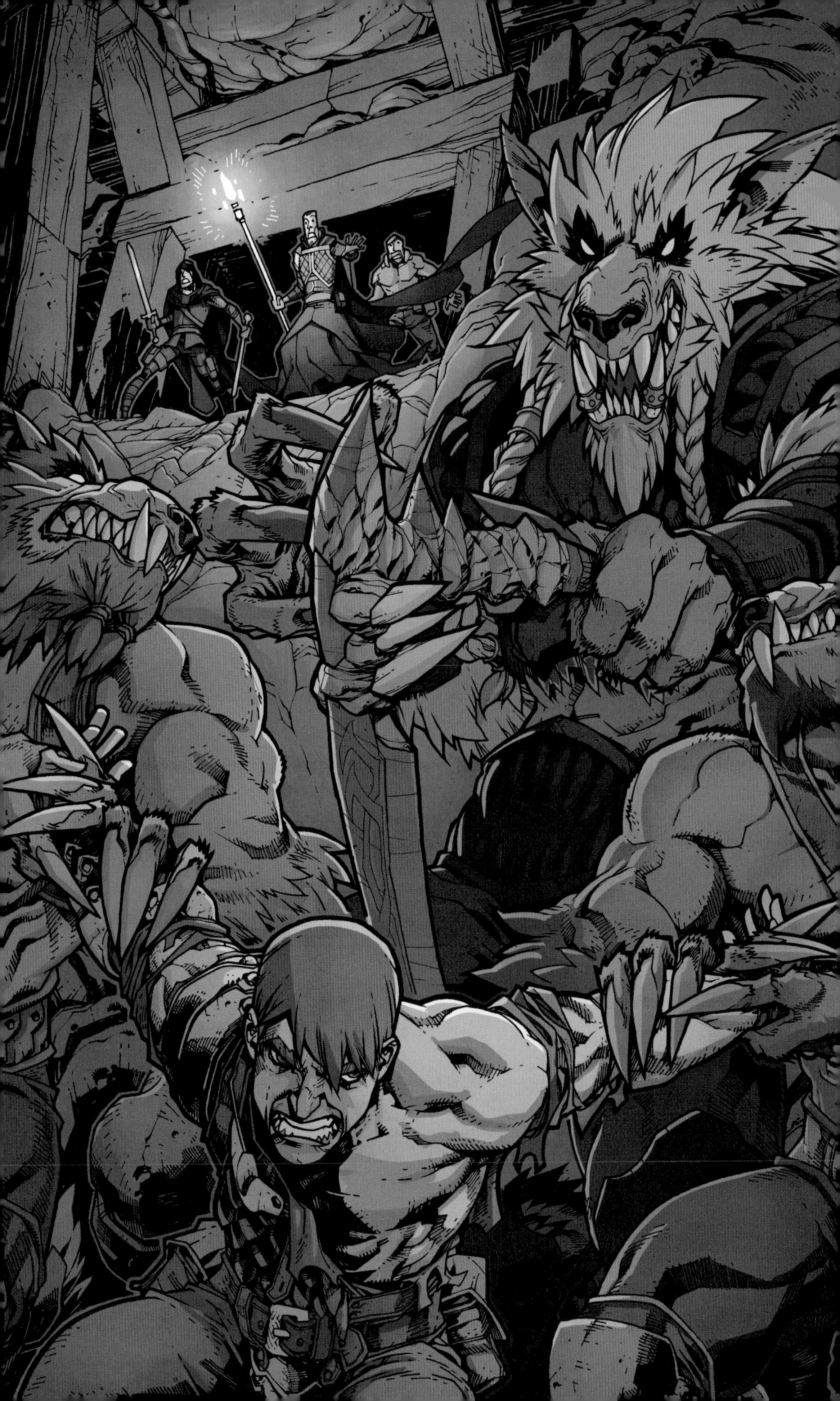

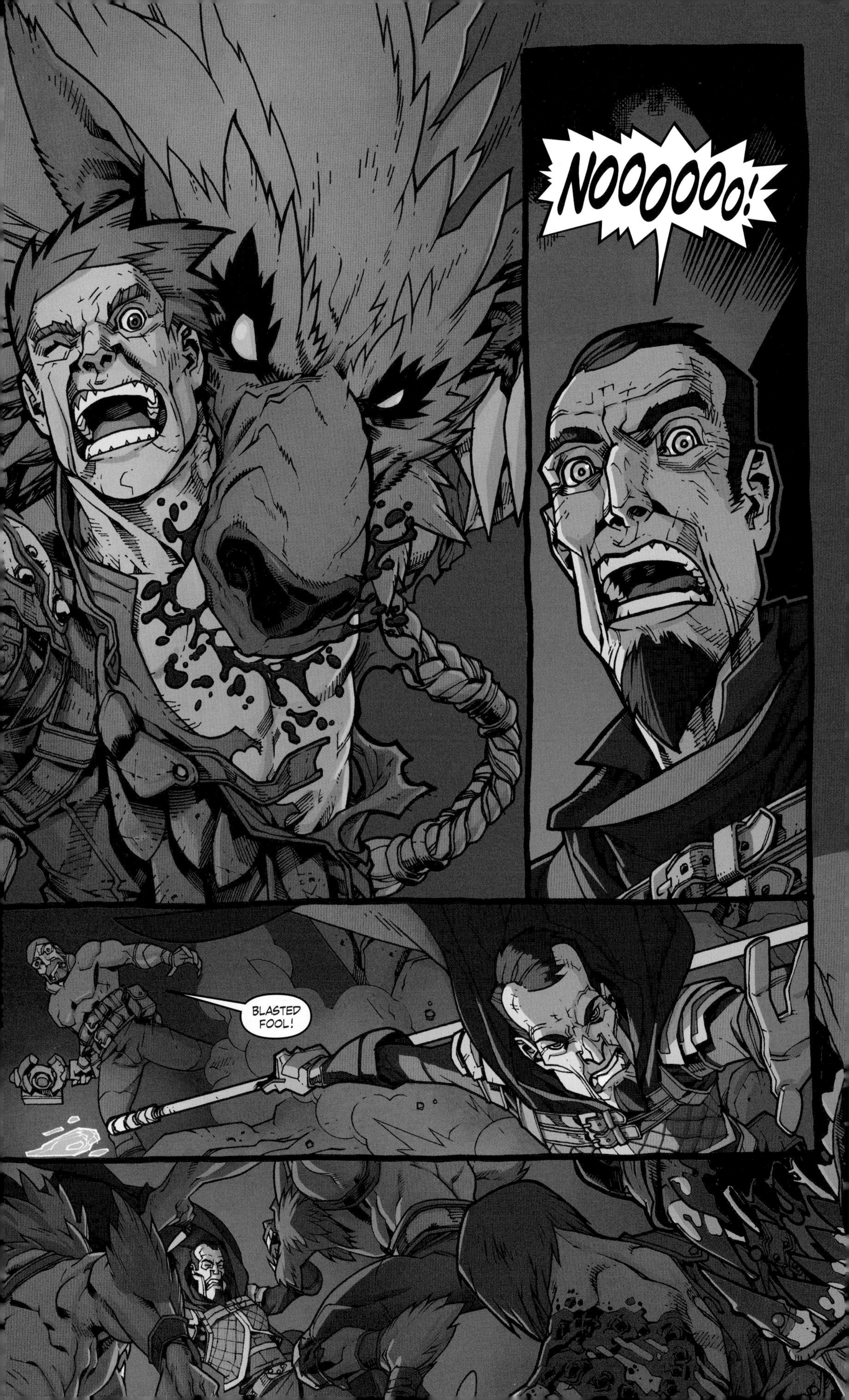
NOOOOOO!
BLASTED FOOL!

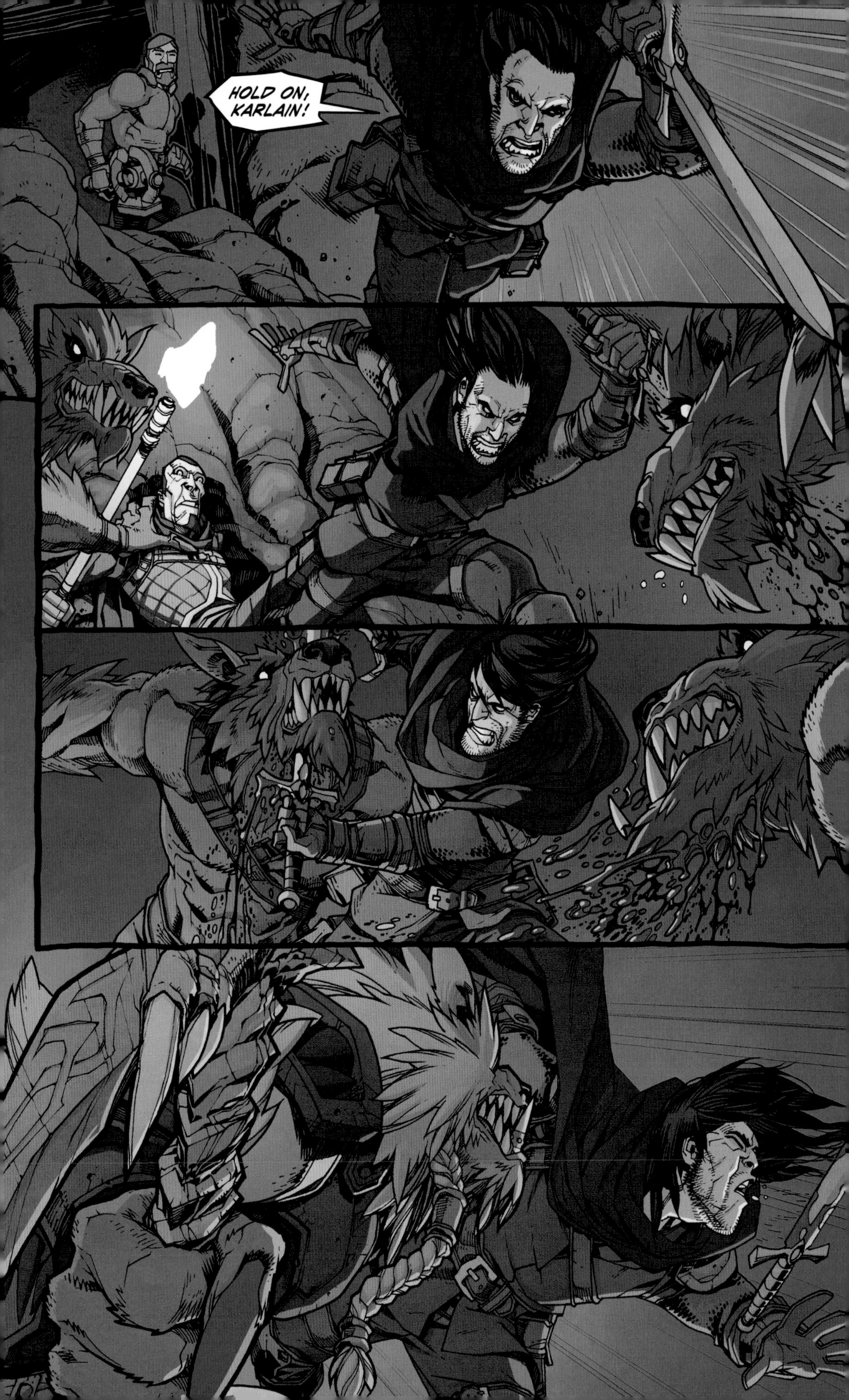
HOLD ON, KARLAIN!

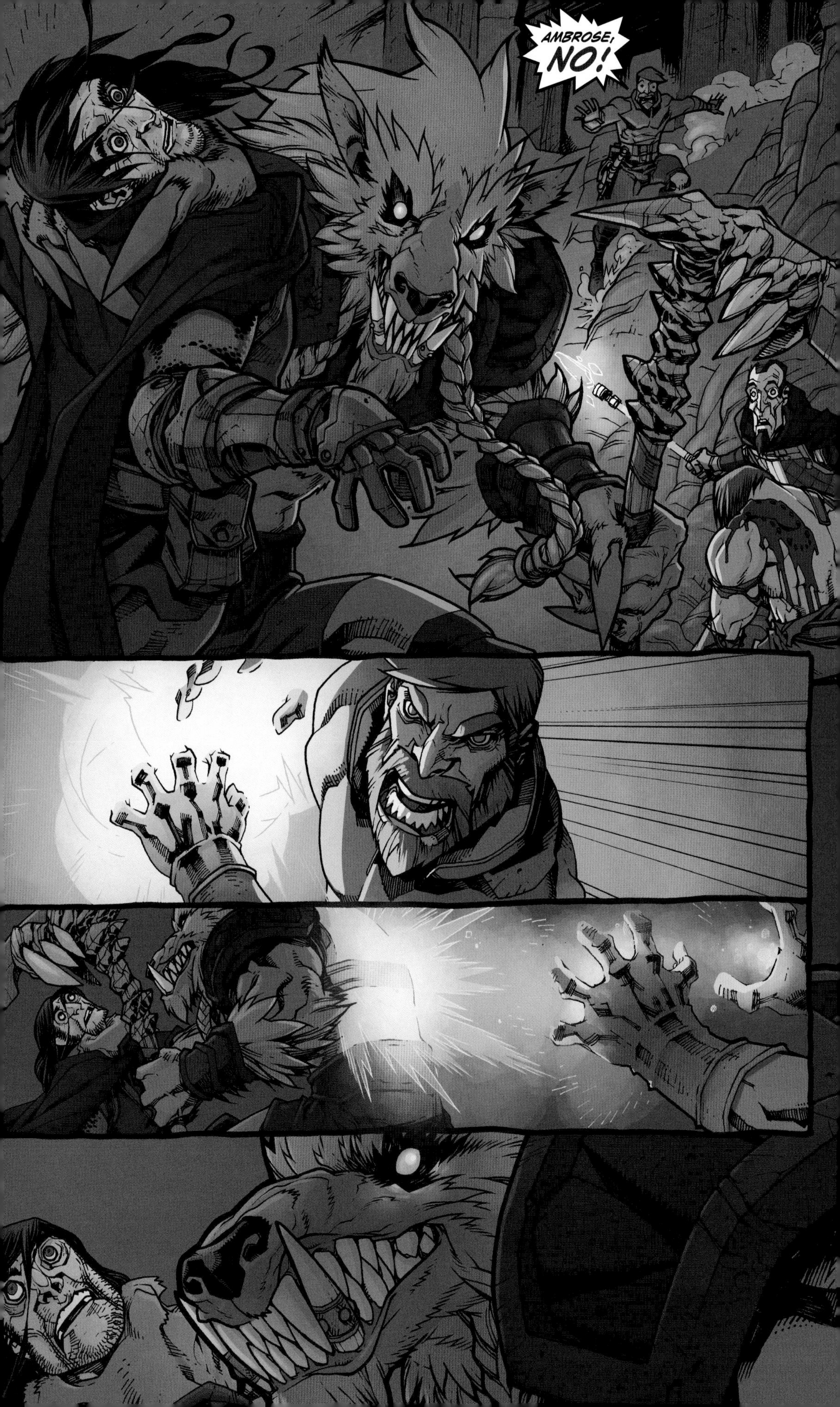
AMBROSE, NO!

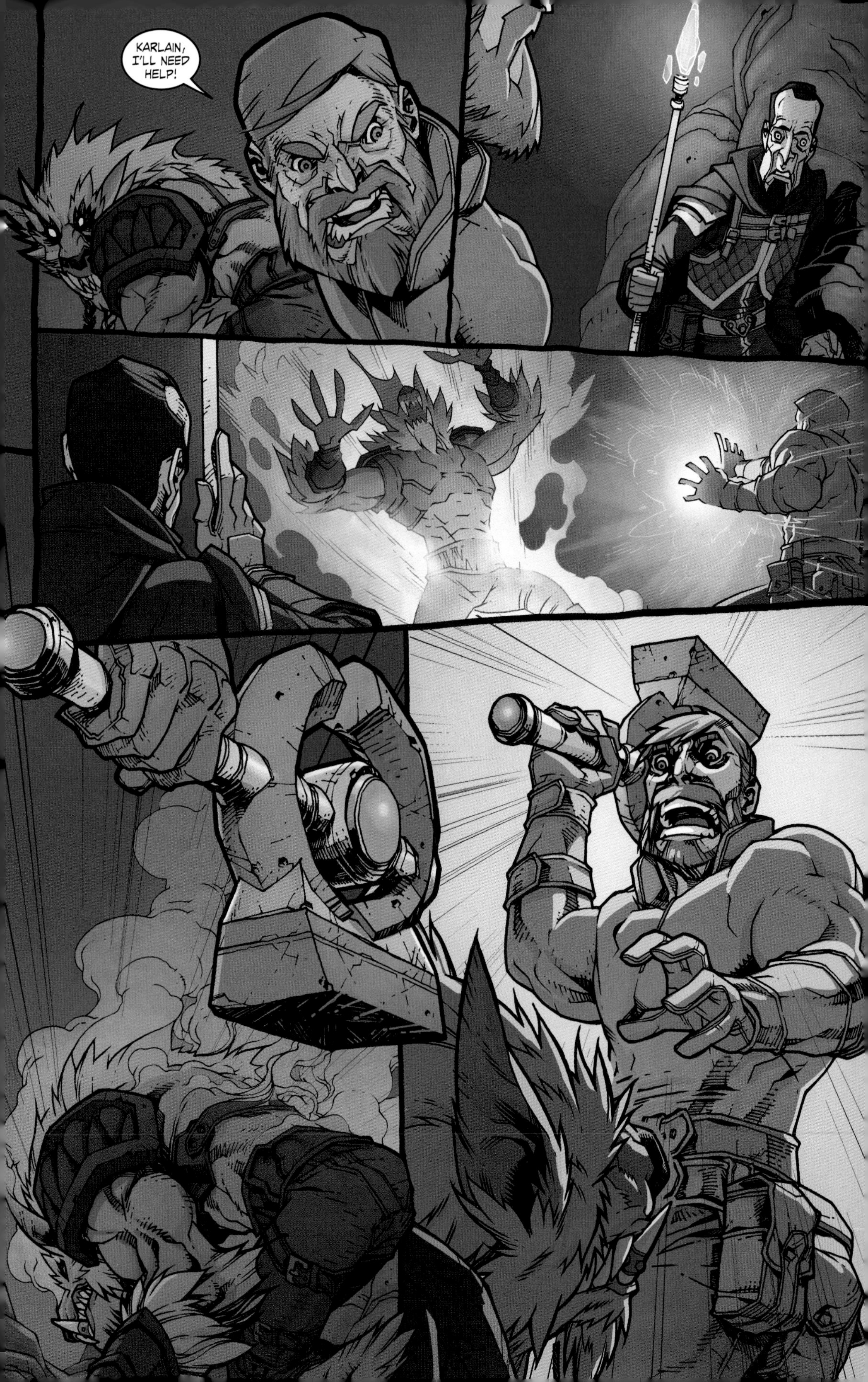
KARLAIN, I'LL NEED HELP!

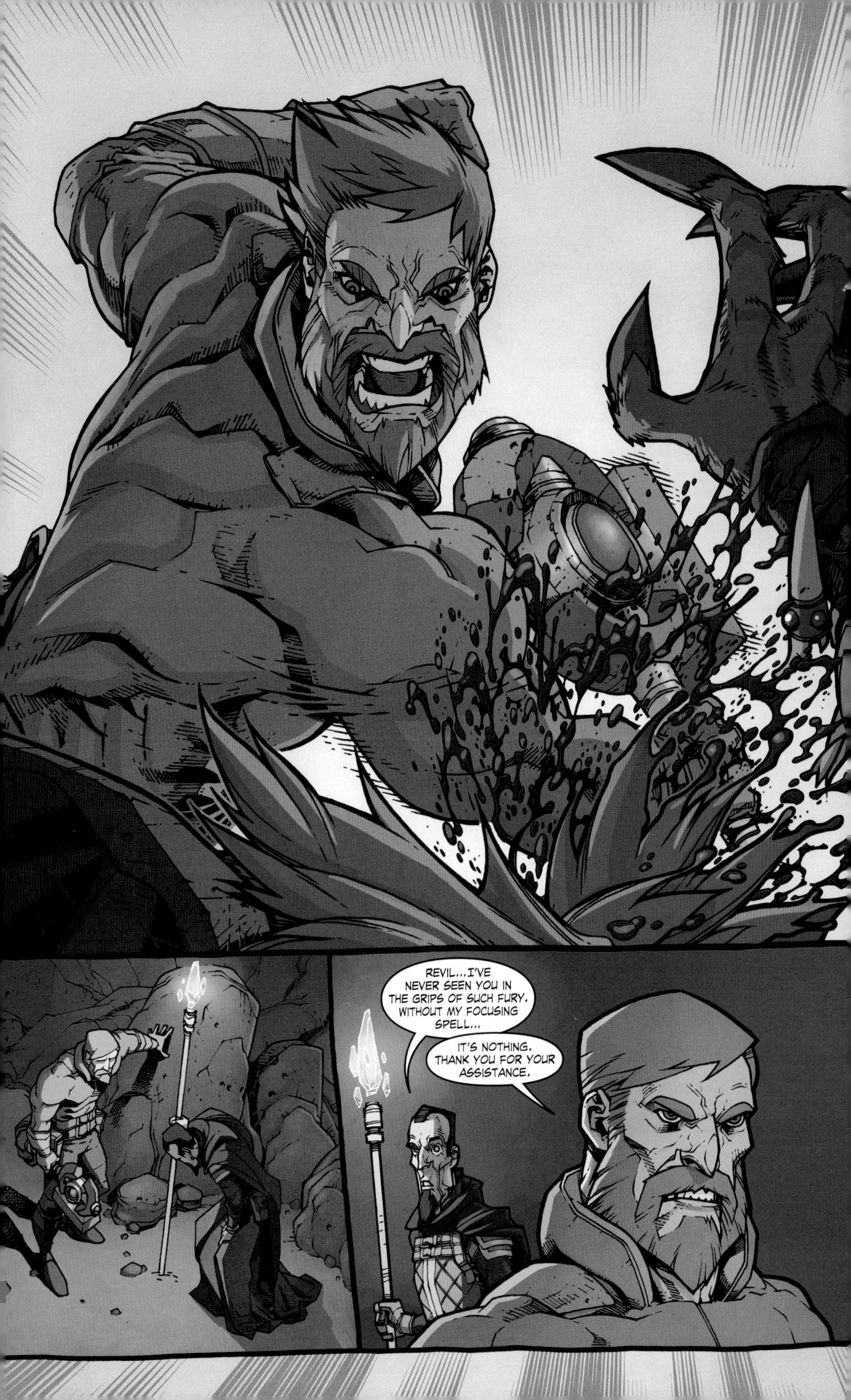
REVIL...I'VE NEVER SEEN YOU IN THE GRIPS OF SUCH FURY. WITHOUT MY FOCUSING SPELL...
IT'S NOTHING. THANK YOU FOR YOUR ASSISTANCE.

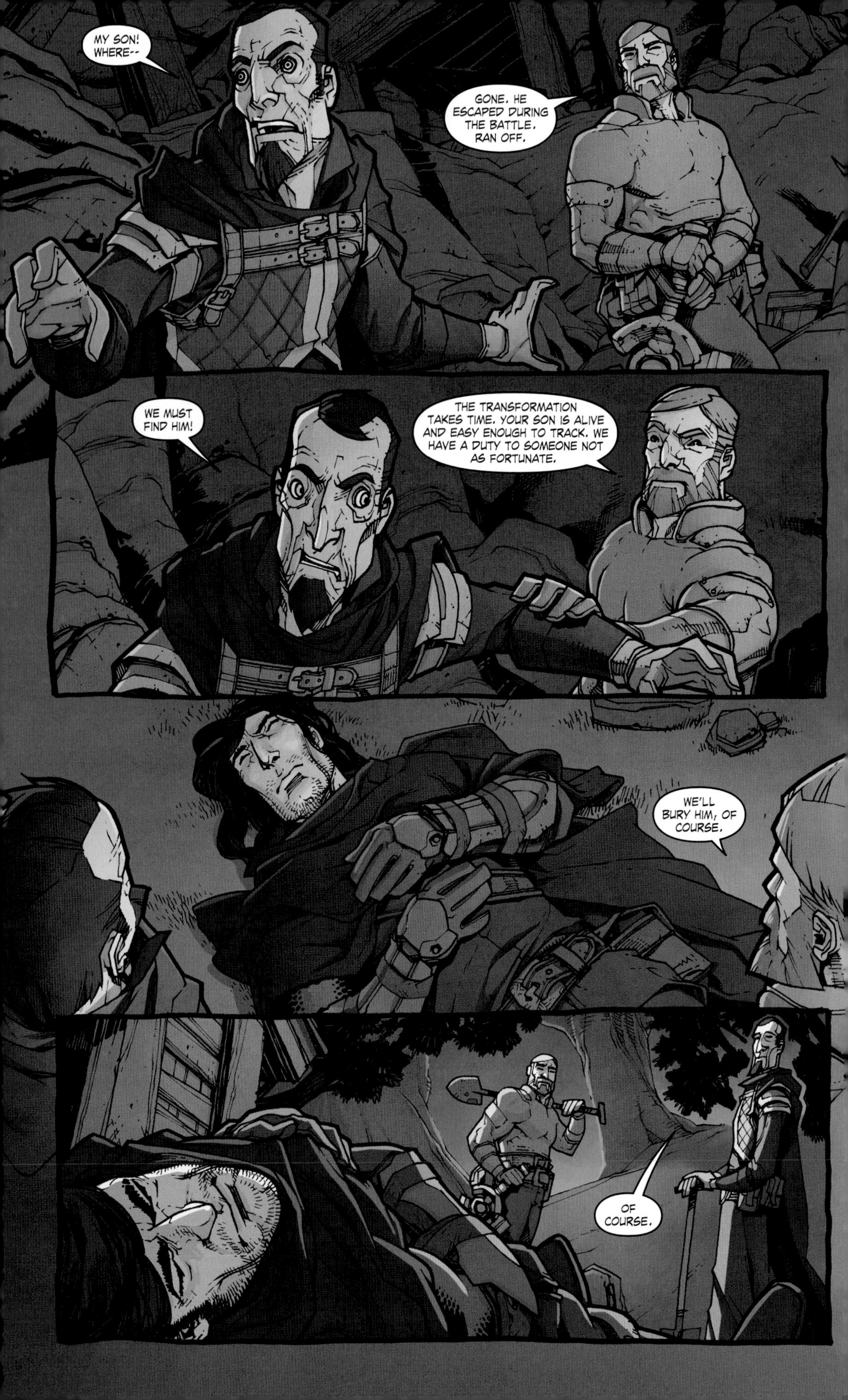
MY SON! WHERE--
GONE. HE ESCAPED DURING THE BATTLE. RAN OFF.
WE MUST FIND HIM!
THE TRANSFORMATION TAKES TIME. YOUR SON IS ALIVE AND EASY ENOUGH TO TRACK. WE HAVE A DUTY TO SOMEONE NOT AS FORTUNATE.
WE'LL BURY HIM, OF COURSE.
OF COURSE.

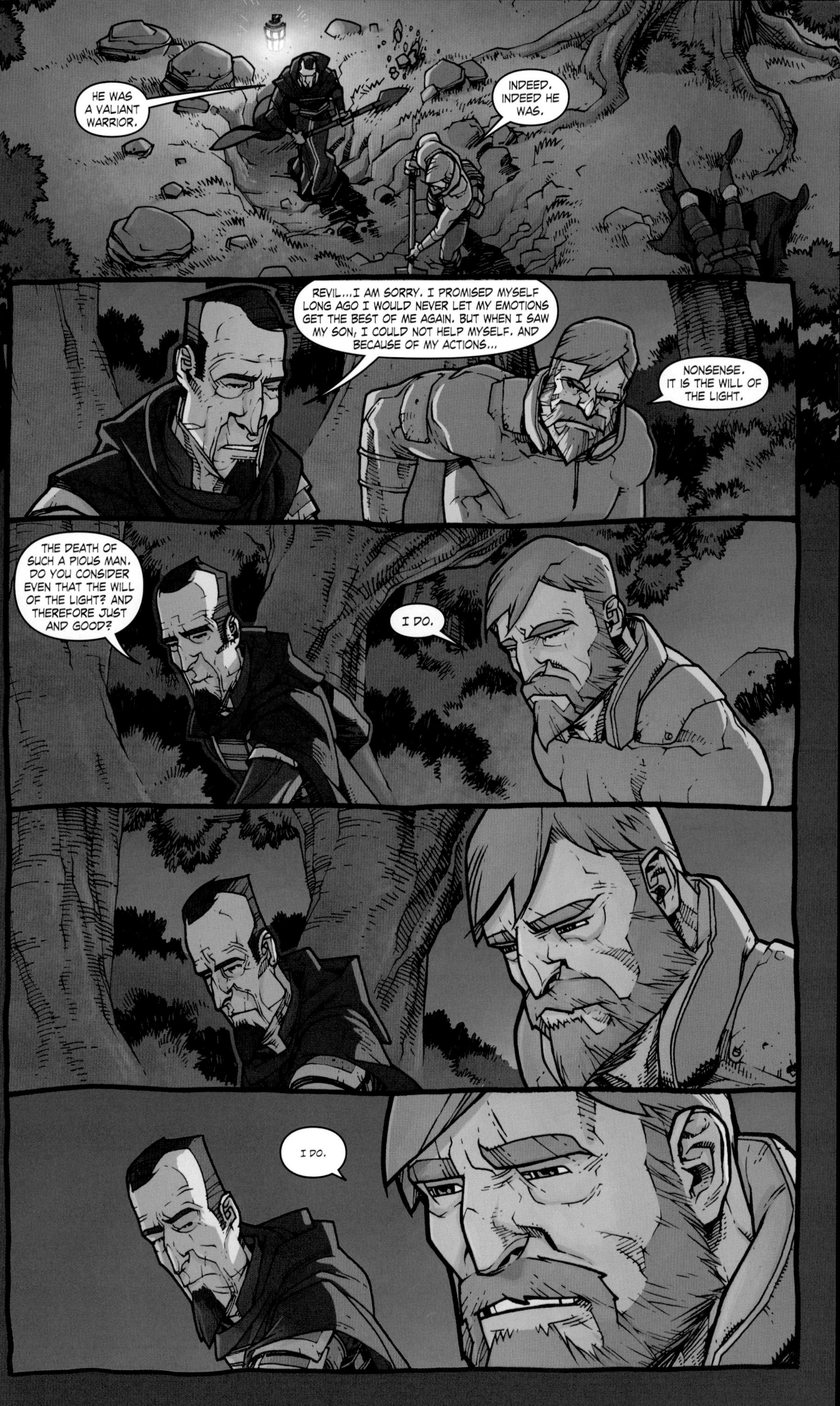

HE WAS A VALIANT WARRIOR.
INDEED. INDEED HE WAS.
REVIL...I AM SORRY. I PROMISED MYSELF LONG AGO I WOULD NEVER LET MY EMOTIONS GET THE BEST OF ME AGAIN. BUT WHEN I SAW MY SON, I COULD NOT HELP MYSELF. AND BECAUSE OF MY ACTIONS...
NONSENSE. IT IS THE WILL OF THE LIGHT.
THE DEATH OF SUCH A PIOUS MAN. DO YOU CONSIDER EVEN THAT THE WILL OF THE LIGHT? AND THEREFORE JUST AND GOOD?
I DO.
I DO.

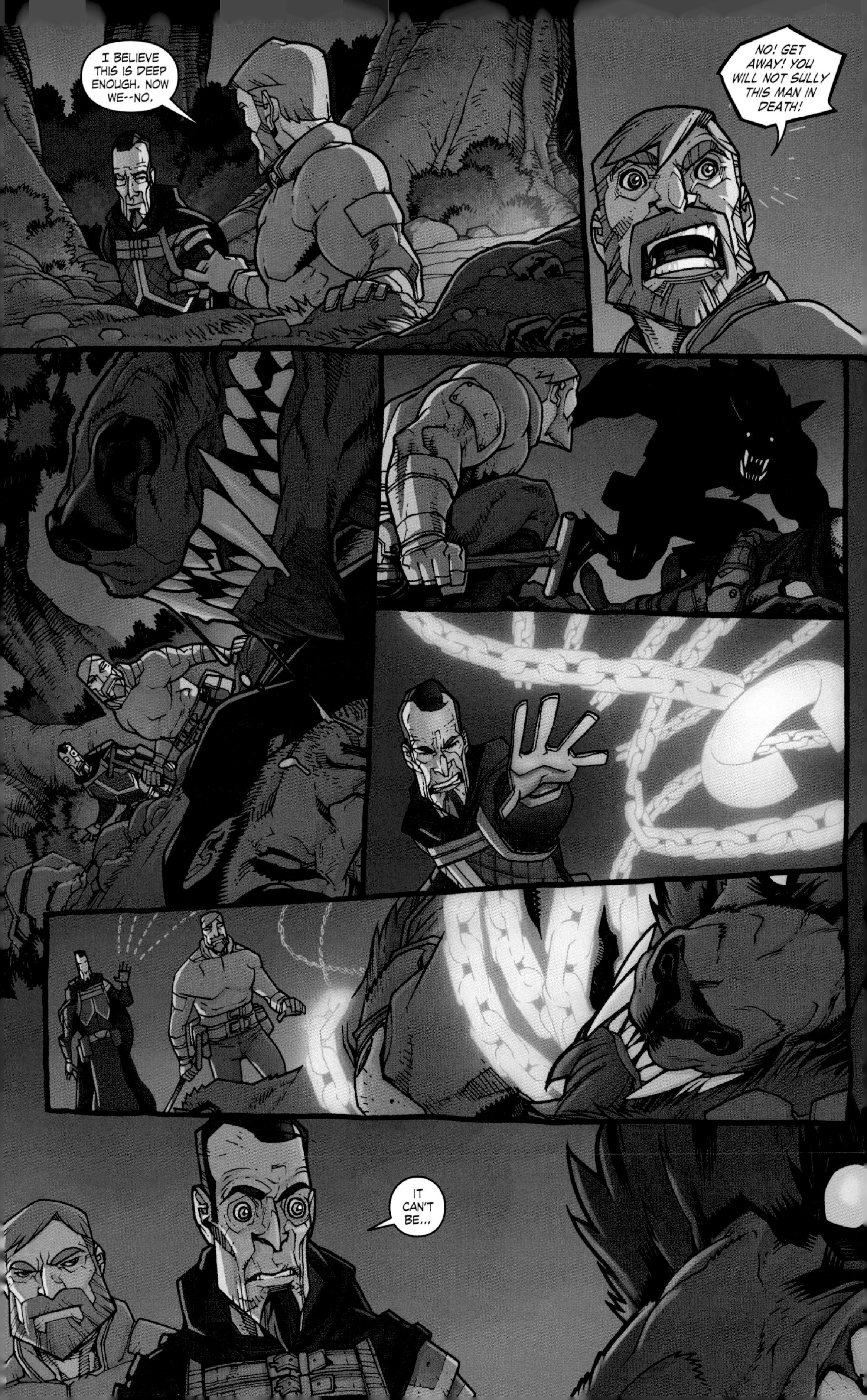

I BELIEVE THIS IS DEEP ENOUGH. NOW WE--NO.
NO! GET AWAY! YOU WILL NOT SULLY THIS MAN IN DEATH!
IT CAN'T BE...

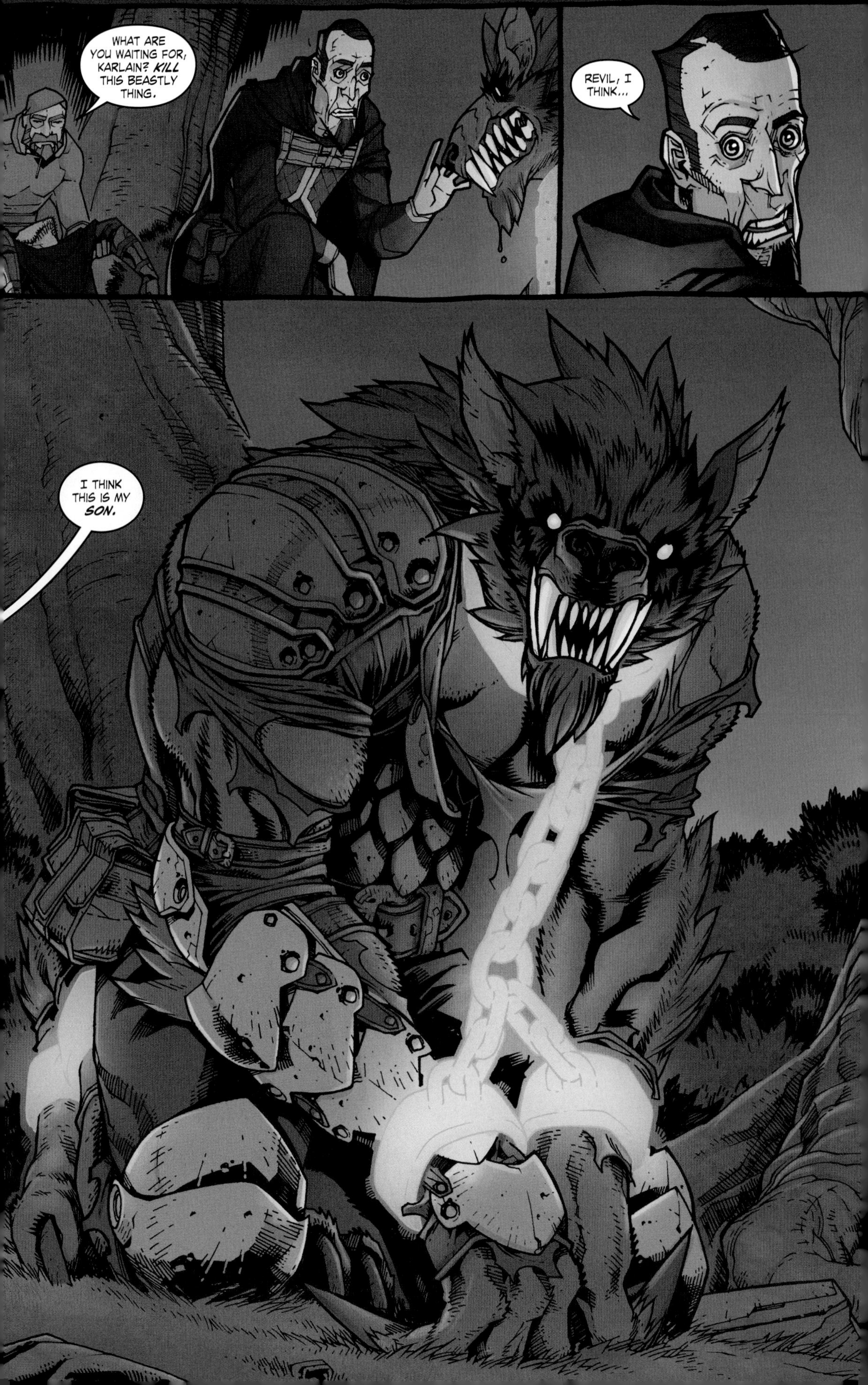
WHAT ARE YOU WAITING FOR, KARLAIN? KILL THIS BEASTLY THING.
REVIL, I THINK...
I THINK THIS IS MY SON.

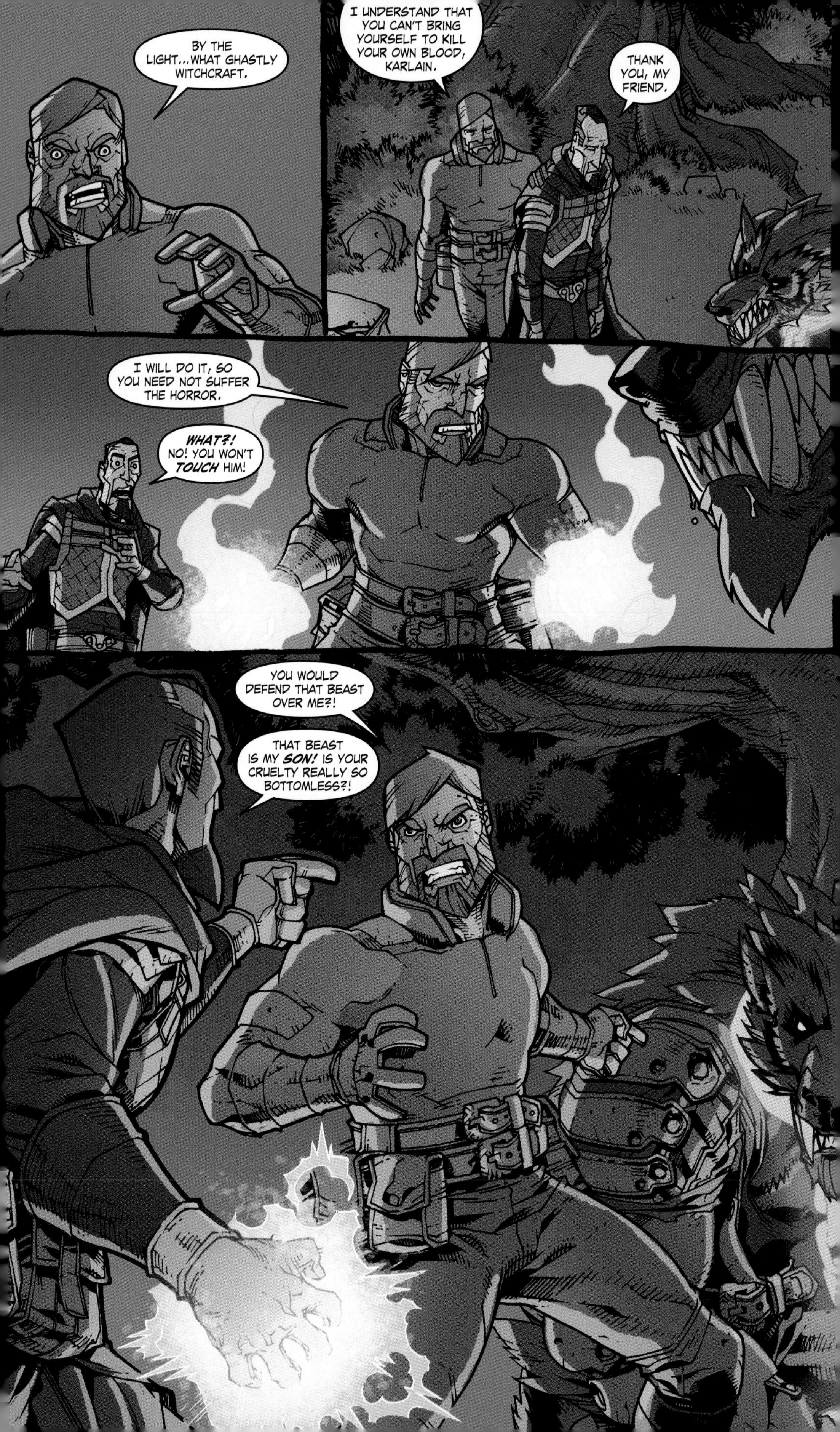
BY THE LIGHT...WHAT GHASTLY WITCHCRAFT.
I UNDERSTAND THAT YOU CAN'T BRING YOURSELF TO KILL YOUR OWN BLOOD, KARLAIN.
THANK YOU, MY FRIEND.
I WILL DO IT, SO YOU NEED NOT SUFFER THE HORROR.
WHAT?! NO! YOU WON'T TOUCH HIM!
YOU WOULD DEFEND THAT BEAST OVER ME?!
THAT BEAST IS MY SON! IS YOUR CRUELTY REALLY SO BOTTOMLESS?!

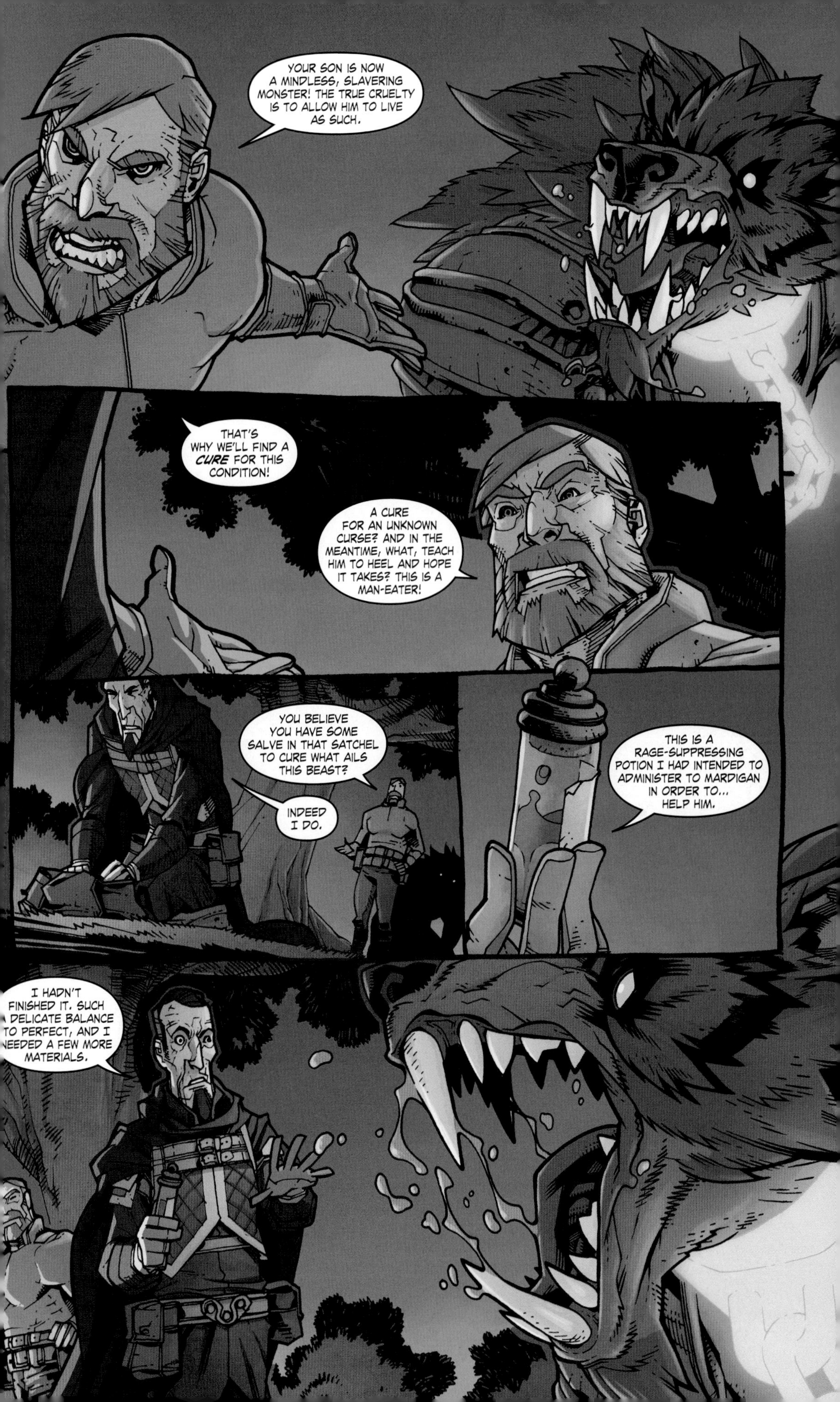
YOUR SON IS NOW A MINDLESS, SLAVERING MONSTER! THE TRUE CRUELTY IS TO ALLOW HIM TO LIVE AS SUCH.
THAT'S WHY WE'LL FIND A CURE FOR THIS CONDITION!
A CURE FOR AN UNKNOWN CURSE? AND IN THE MEANTIME, WHAT, TEACH HIM TO HEEL AND HOPE IT TAKES? THIS IS A MAN-EATER!
YOU BELIEVE YOU HAVE SOME SALVE IN THAT SATCHEL TO CURE WHAT AILS THIS BEAST?
INDEED I DO.
THIS IS A RAGE-SUPPRESSING POTION I HAD INTENDED TO ADMINISTER TO MARDIGAN IN ORDER TO... HELP HIM.
I HADN'T FINISHED IT. SUCH A DELICATE BALANCE TO PERFECT, AND I NEEDED A FEW MORE MATERIALS.

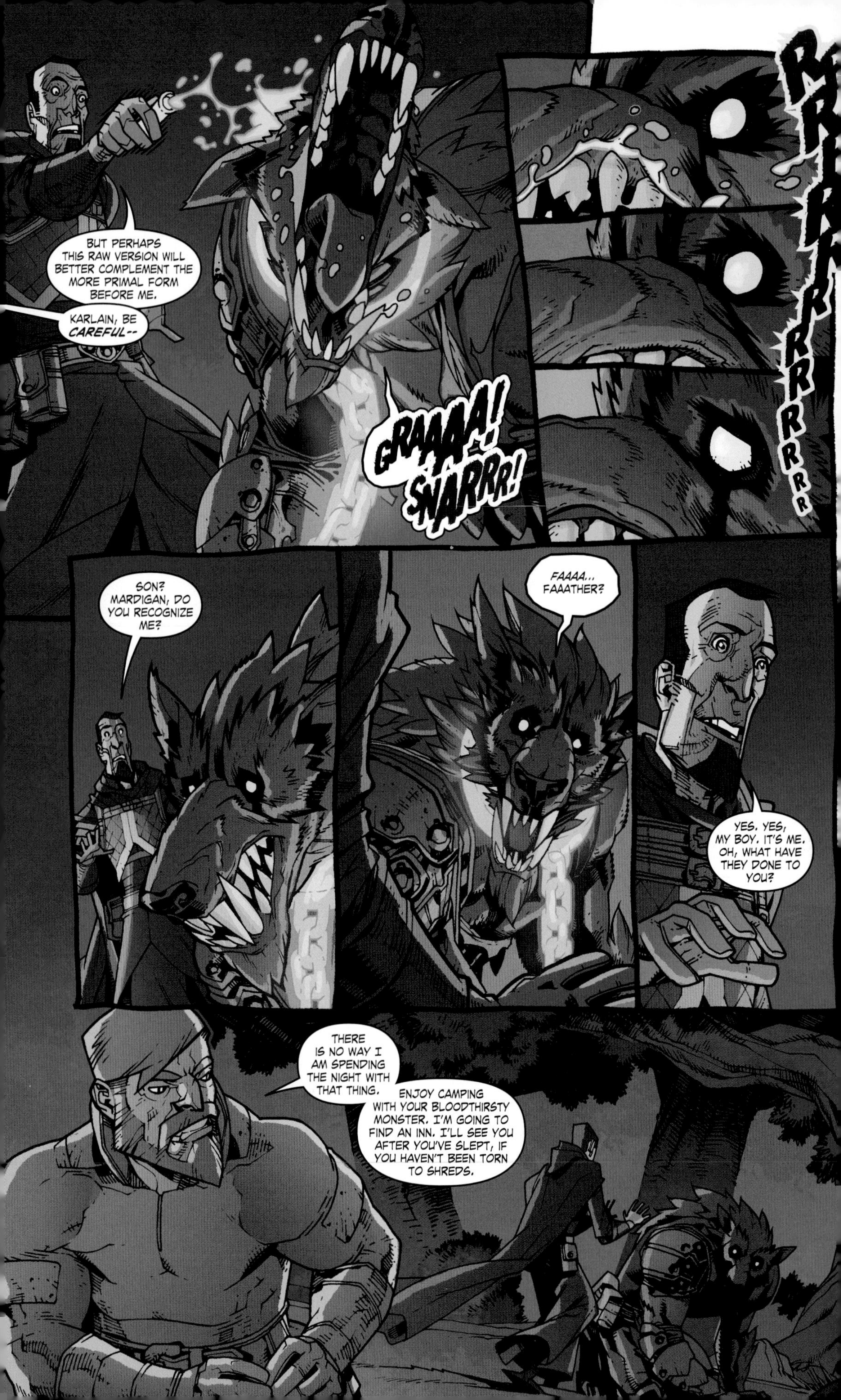
BUT PERHAPS THIS RAW VERSION WILL BETTER COMPLEMENT THE MORE PRIMAL FORM BEFORE ME.
KARLAIN, BE *CAREFUL*--
GRAAAA! SNARRR!
RRRRRRRRRRRR
SON? MARDIGAN, DO YOU RECOGNIZE ME?
FAAAA... FAAATHER?
YES. YES, MY BOY. IT'S ME. OH, WHAT HAVE THEY DONE TO YOU?
THERE IS NO WAY I AM SPENDING THE NIGHT WITH THAT THING.
ENJOY CAMPING WITH YOUR BLOODTHIRSTY MONSTER. I'M GOING TO FIND AN INN. I'LL SEE YOU AFTER YOU'VE SLEPT, IF YOU HAVEN'T BEEN TORN TO SHREDS.

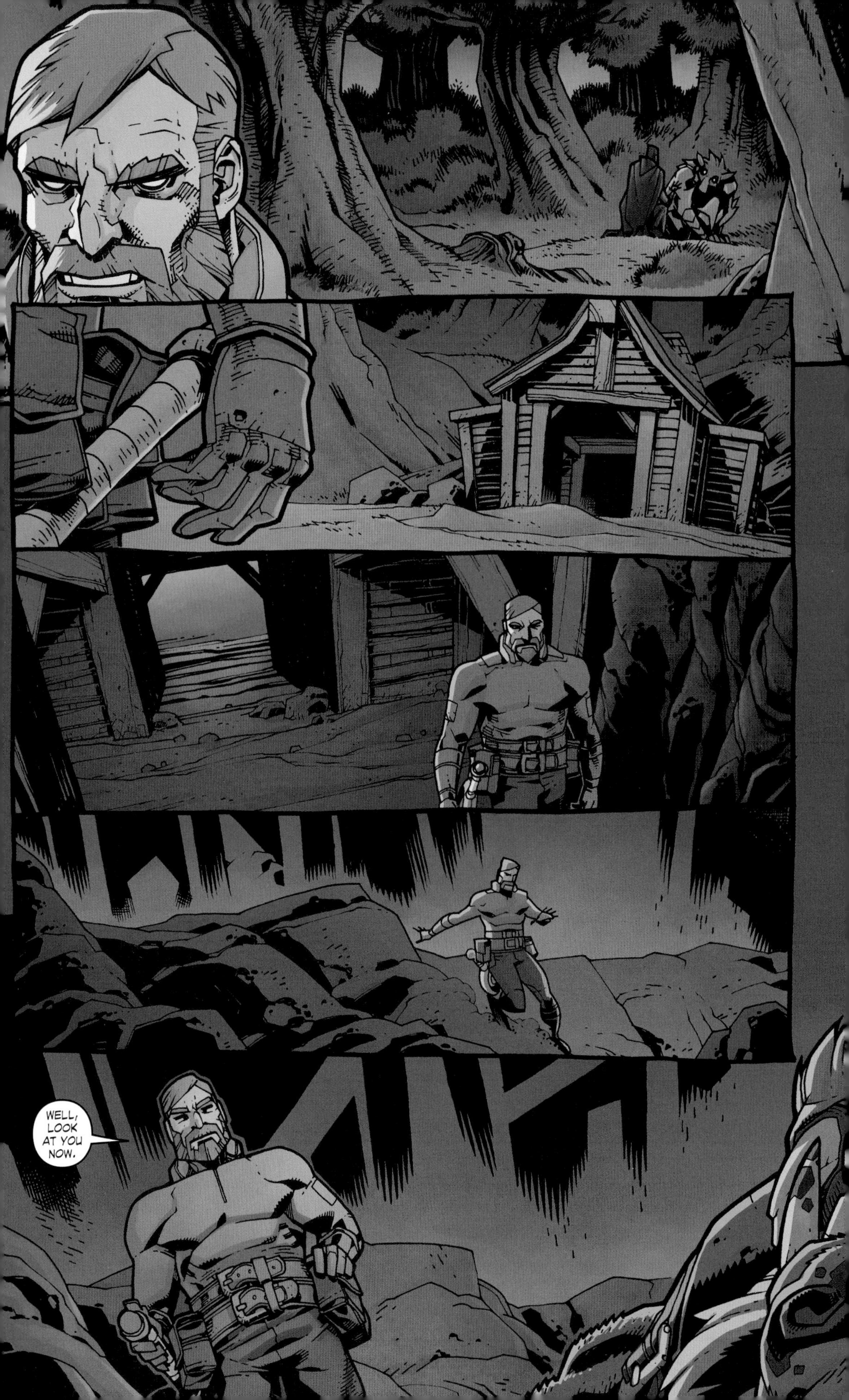
WELL, LOOK AT YOU NOW.

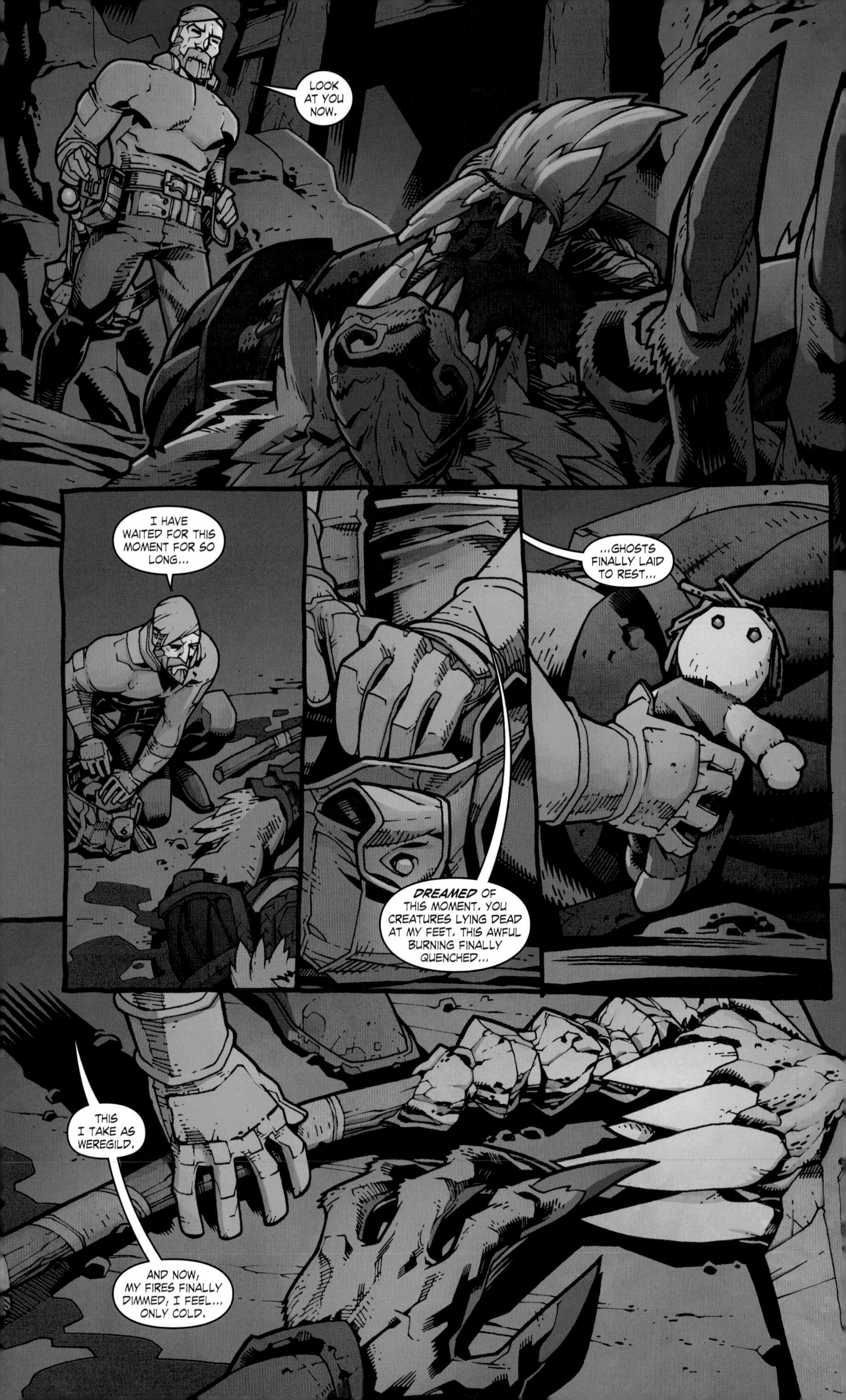
LOOK AT YOU NOW.
I HAVE WAITED FOR THIS MOMENT FOR SO LONG...
DREAMED OF THIS MOMENT. YOU CREATURES LYING DEAD AT MY FEET. THIS AWFUL BURNING FINALLY QUENCHED...
...GHOSTS FINALLY LAID TO REST...
THIS I TAKE AS WEREGILD.
AND NOW, MY FIRES FINALLY DIMMED, I FEEL... ONLY COLD.

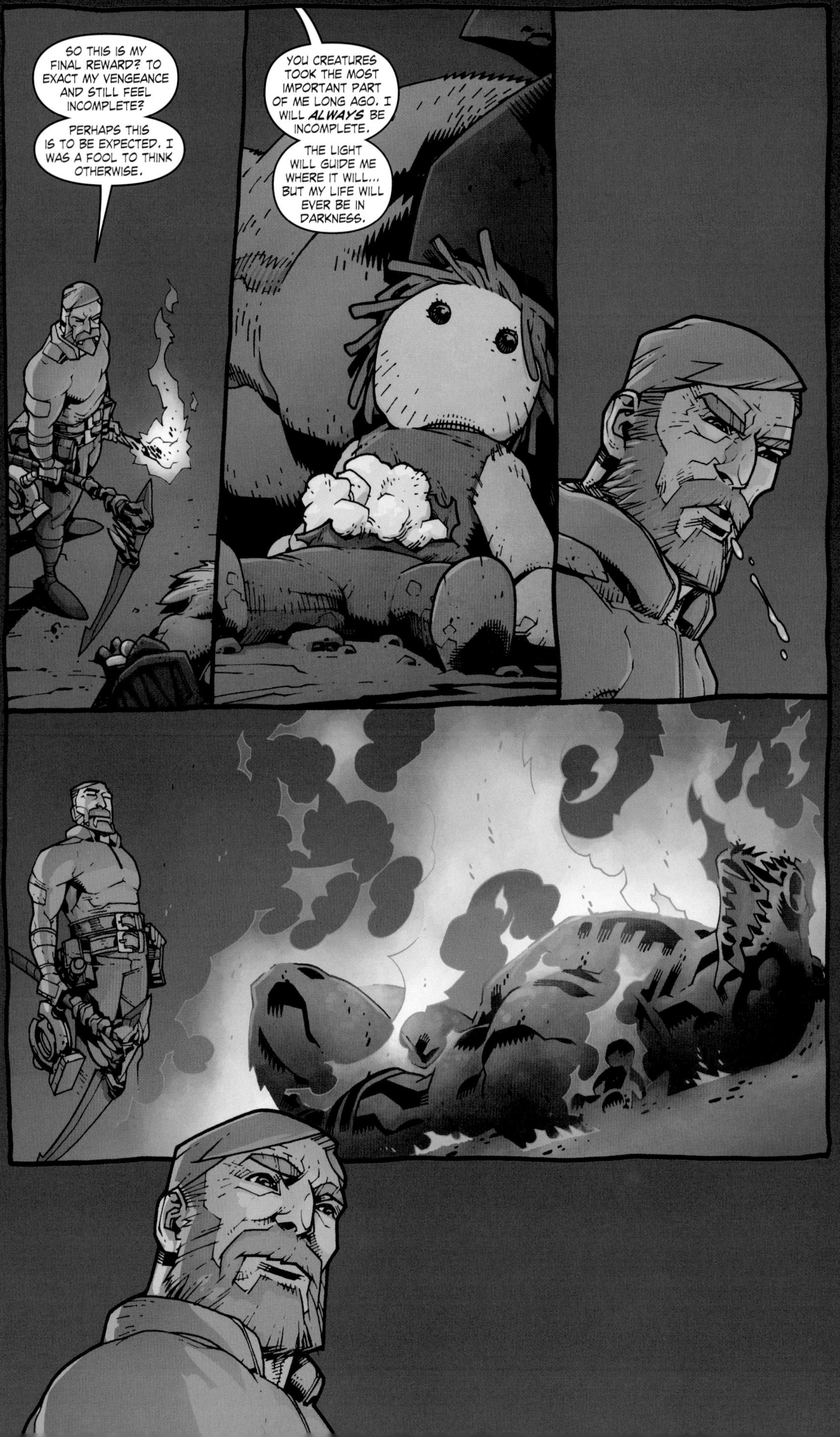
SO THIS IS MY FINAL REWARD? TO EXACT MY VENGEANCE AND STILL FEEL INCOMPLETE?
PERHAPS THIS IS TO BE EXPECTED. I WAS A FOOL TO THINK OTHERWISE.
YOU CREATURES TOOK THE MOST IMPORTANT PART OF ME LONG AGO. I WILL *ALWAYS* BE INCOMPLETE.
THE LIGHT WILL GUIDE ME WHERE IT WILL... BUT MY LIFE WILL EVER BE IN DARKNESS.

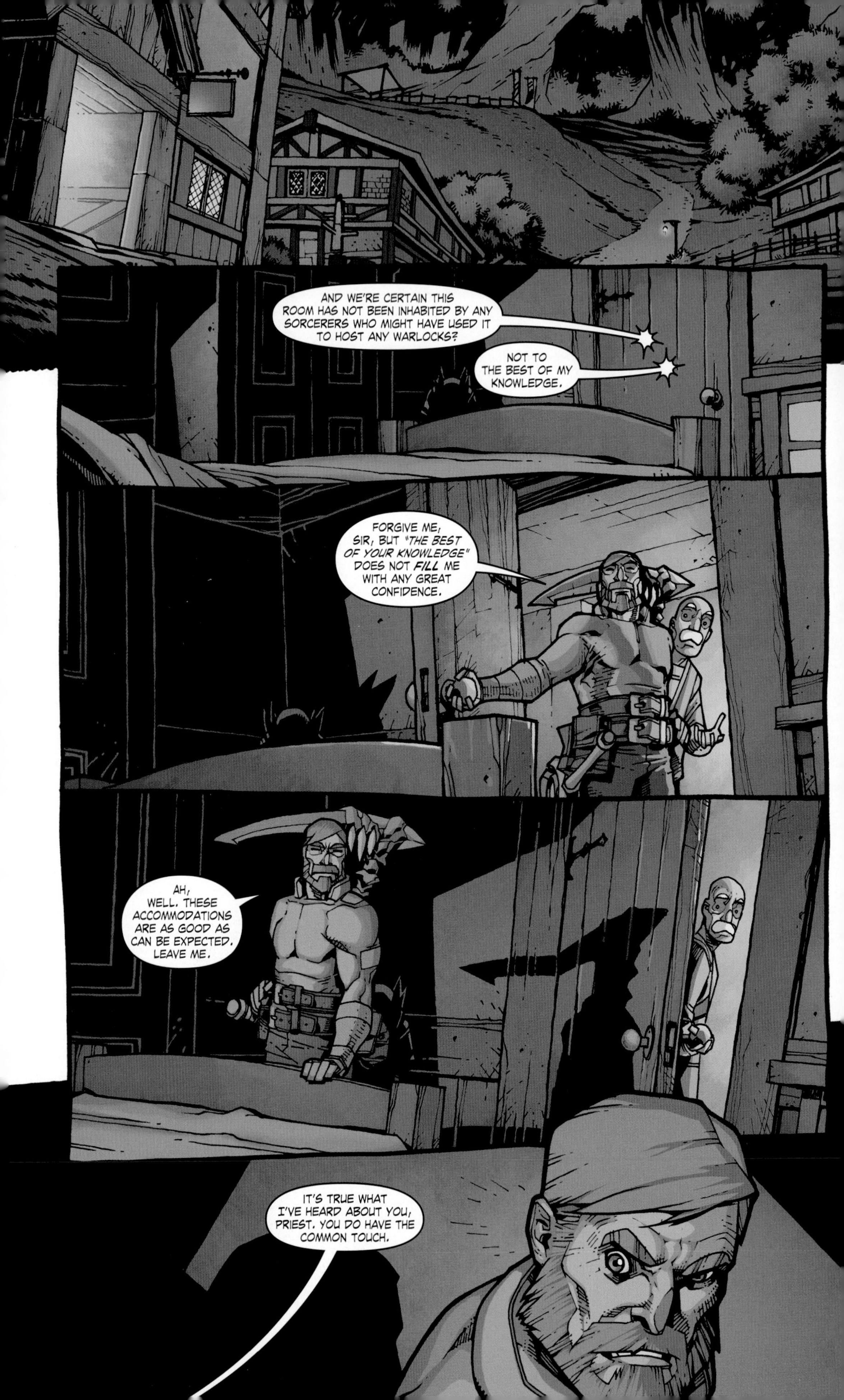
AND WE'RE CERTAIN THIS ROOM HAS NOT BEEN INHABITED BY ANY SORCERERS WHO MIGHT HAVE USED IT TO HOST ANY WARLOCKS?
NOT TO THE BEST OF MY KNOWLEDGE.
FORGIVE ME, SIR, BUT "THE BEST OF YOUR KNOWLEDGE" DOES NOT FILL ME WITH ANY GREAT CONFIDENCE.
AH, WELL. THESE ACCOMMODATIONS ARE AS GOOD AS CAN BE EXPECTED. LEAVE ME.
IT'S TRUE WHAT I'VE HEARD ABOUT YOU, PRIEST. YOU DO HAVE THE COMMON TOUCH.

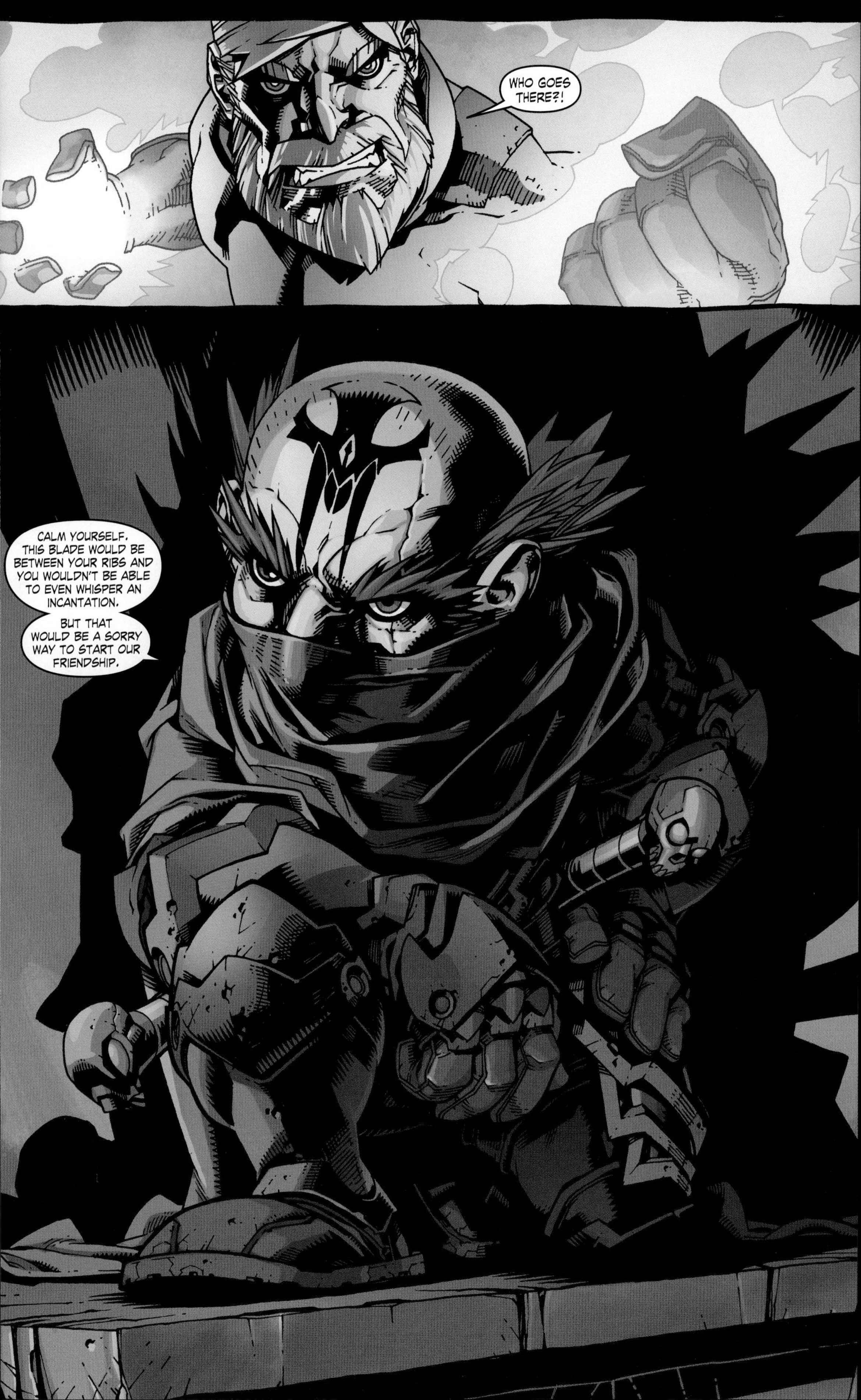
WHO GOES THERE?!
CALM YOURSELF. THIS BLADE WOULD BE BETWEEN YOUR RIBS AND YOU WOULDN'T BE ABLE TO EVEN WHISPER AN INCANTATION.
BUT THAT WOULD BE A SORRY WAY TO START OUR FRIENDSHIP.

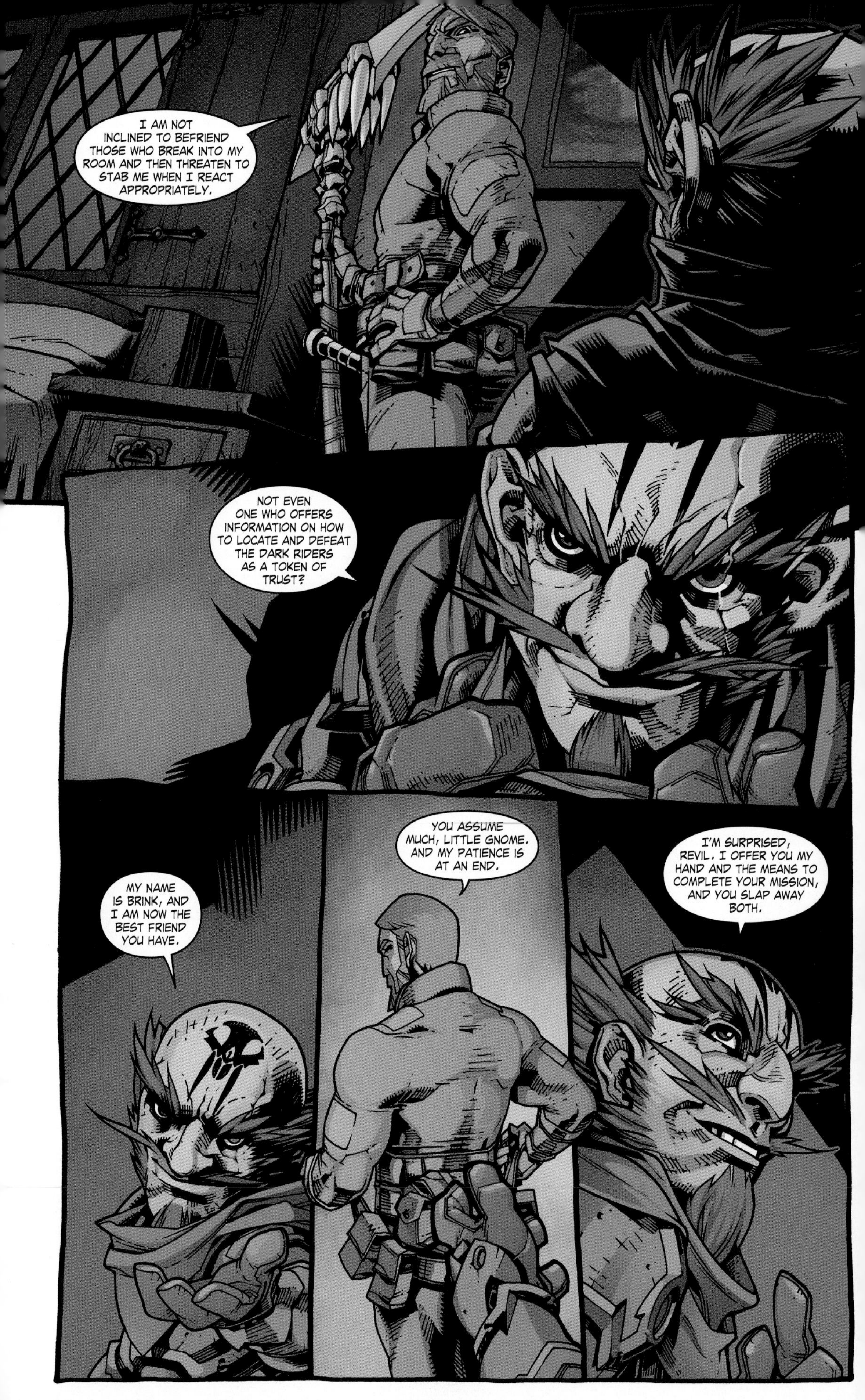
I AM NOT INCLINED TO BEFRIEND THOSE WHO BREAK INTO MY ROOM AND THEN THREATEN TO STAB ME WHEN I REACT APPROPRIATELY.
NOT EVEN ONE WHO OFFERS INFORMATION ON HOW TO LOCATE AND DEFEAT THE DARK RIDERS AS A TOKEN OF TRUST?
MY NAME IS BRINK, AND I AM NOW THE BEST FRIEND YOU HAVE.
YOU ASSUME MUCH, LITTLE GNOME. AND MY PATIENCE IS AT AN END.
I'M SURPRISED, REVIL. I OFFER YOU MY HAND AND THE MEANS TO COMPLETE YOUR MISSION, AND YOU SLAP AWAY BOTH.

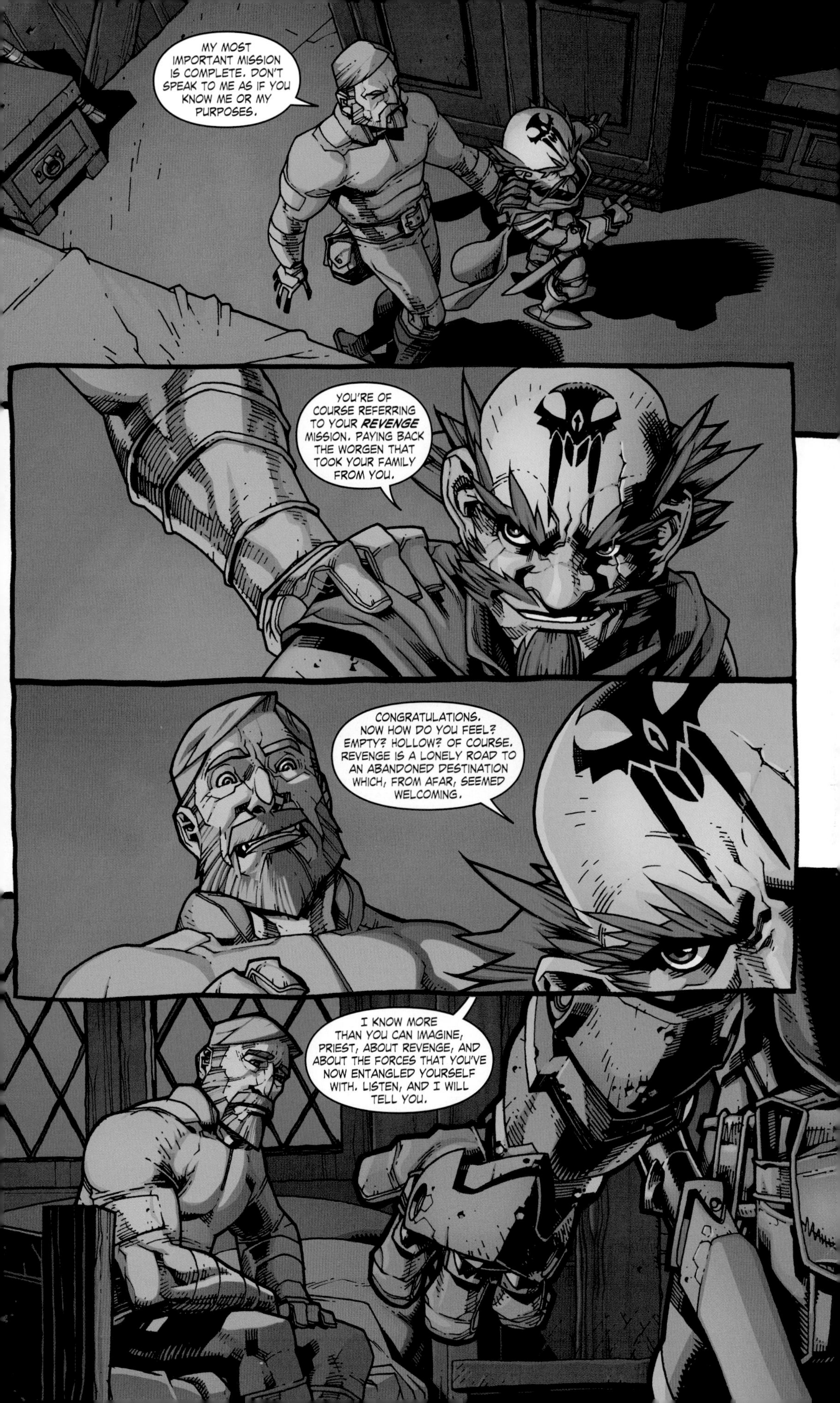

MY MOST IMPORTANT MISSION IS COMPLETE. DON'T SPEAK TO ME AS IF YOU KNOW ME OR MY PURPOSES.
YOU'RE OF COURSE REFERRING TO YOUR ***REVENGE*** MISSION. PAYING BACK THE WORGEN THAT TOOK YOUR FAMILY FROM YOU.
CONGRATULATIONS. NOW HOW DO YOU FEEL? EMPTY? HOLLOW? OF COURSE. REVENGE IS A LONELY ROAD TO AN ABANDONED DESTINATION WHICH, FROM AFAR, SEEMED WELCOMING.
I KNOW MORE THAN YOU CAN IMAGINE, PRIEST, ABOUT REVENGE, AND ABOUT THE FORCES THAT YOU'VE NOW ENTANGLED YOURSELF WITH. LISTEN, AND I WILL TELL YOU.

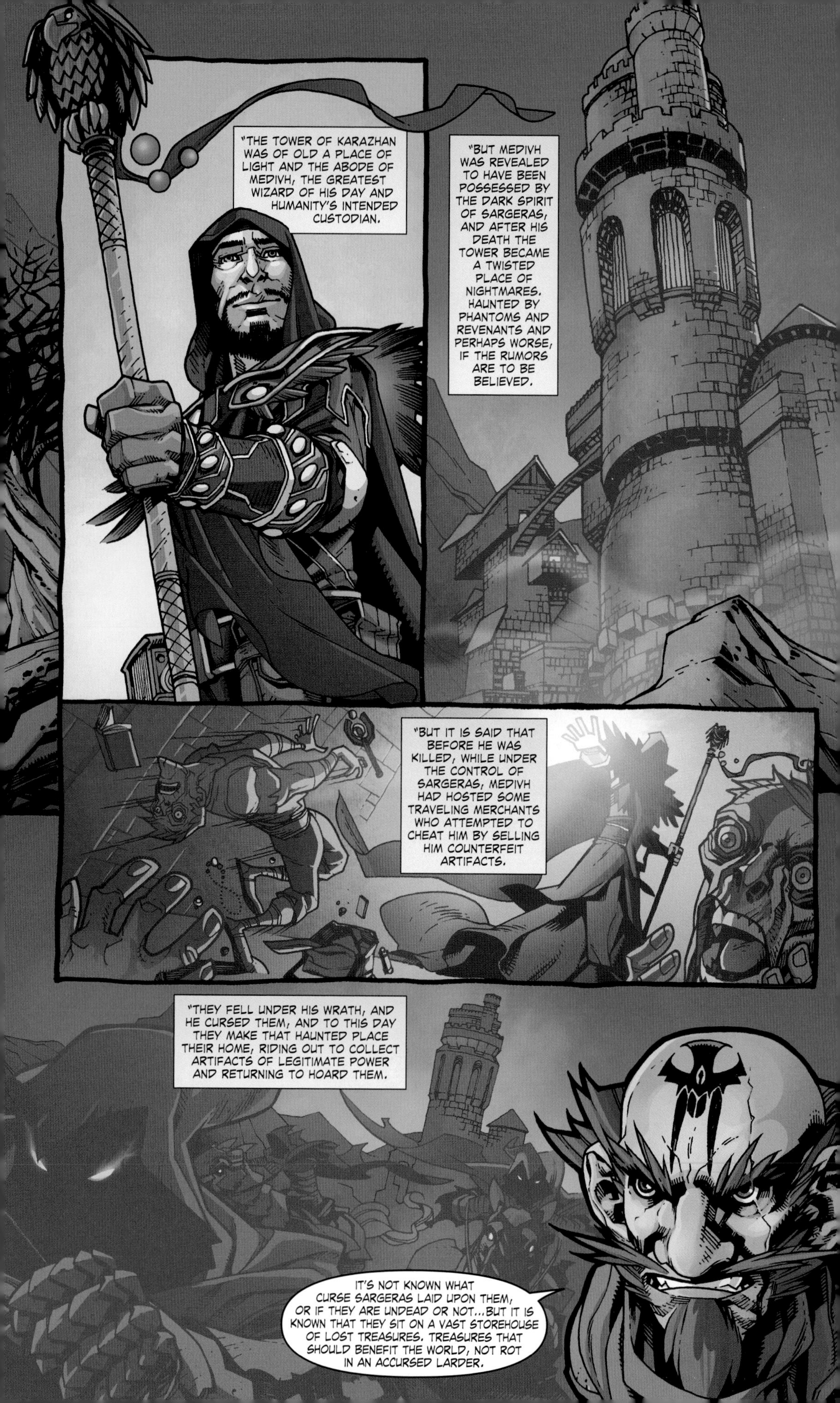
"THE TOWER OF KARAZHAN WAS OF OLD A PLACE OF LIGHT AND THE ABODE OF MEDIVH, THE GREATEST WIZARD OF HIS DAY AND HUMANITY'S INTENDED CUSTODIAN.
"BUT MEDIVH WAS REVEALED TO HAVE BEEN POSSESSED BY THE DARK SPIRIT OF SARGERAS, AND AFTER HIS DEATH THE TOWER BECAME A TWISTED PLACE OF NIGHTMARES. HAUNTED BY PHANTOMS AND REVENANTS AND PERHAPS WORSE, IF THE RUMORS ARE TO BE BELIEVED.
"BUT IT IS SAID THAT BEFORE HE WAS KILLED, WHILE UNDER THE CONTROL OF SARGERAS, MEDIVH HAD HOSTED SOME TRAVELING MERCHANTS WHO ATTEMPTED TO CHEAT HIM BY SELLING HIM COUNTERFEIT ARTIFACTS.
"THEY FELL UNDER HIS WRATH, AND HE CURSED THEM, AND TO THIS DAY THEY MAKE THAT HAUNTED PLACE THEIR HOME, RIDING OUT TO COLLECT ARTIFACTS OF LEGITIMATE POWER AND RETURNING TO HOARD THEM.
IT'S NOT KNOWN WHAT CURSE SARGERAS LAID UPON THEM, OR IF THEY ARE UNDEAD OR NOT...BUT IT IS KNOWN THAT THEY SIT ON A VAST STOREHOUSE OF LOST TREASURES. TREASURES THAT SHOULD BENEFIT THE WORLD, NOT ROT IN AN ACCURSED LARDER.

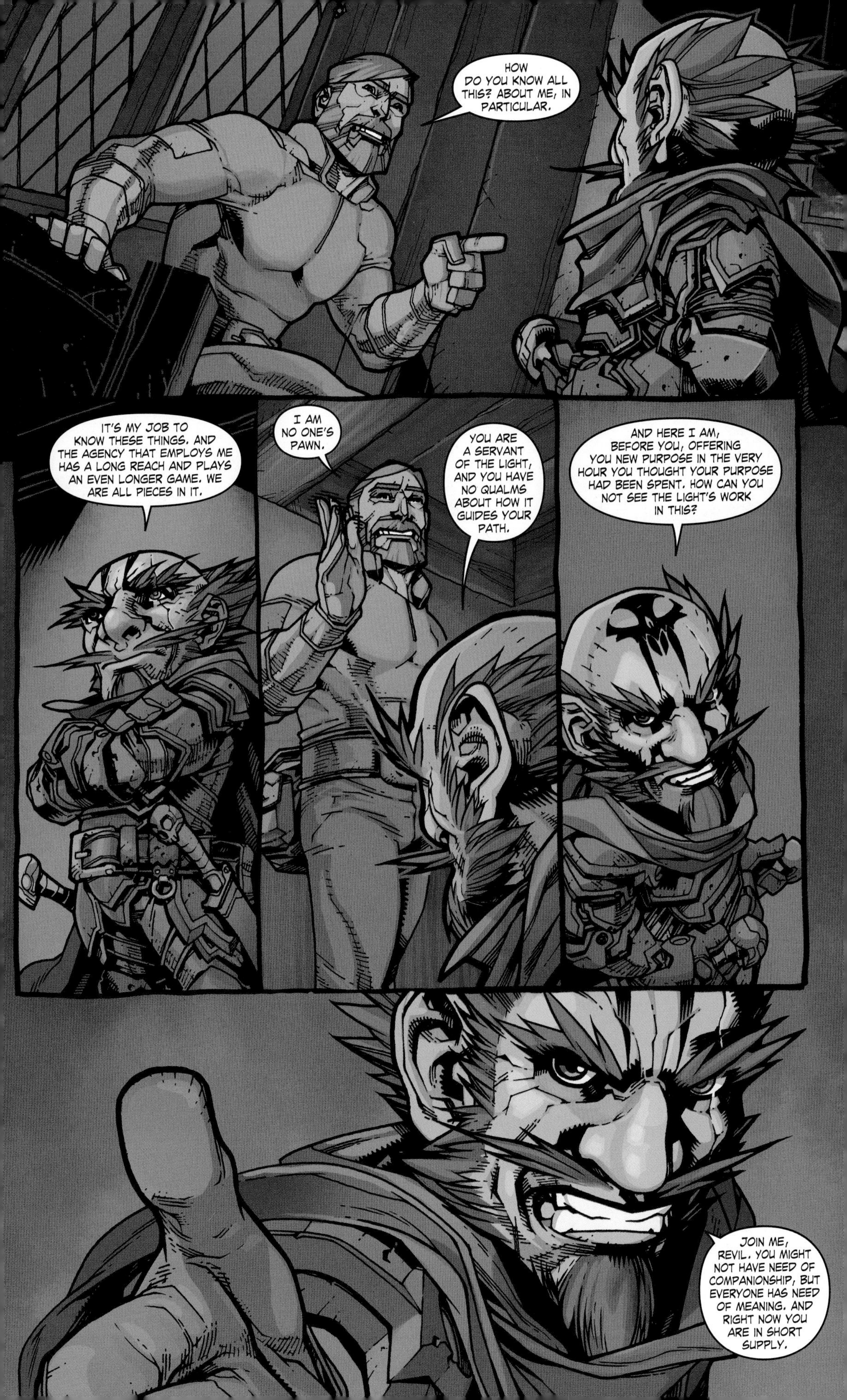
HOW DO YOU KNOW ALL THIS? ABOUT ME, IN PARTICULAR.
IT'S MY JOB TO KNOW THESE THINGS. AND THE AGENCY THAT EMPLOYS ME HAS A LONG REACH AND PLAYS AN EVEN LONGER GAME. WE ARE ALL PIECES IN IT.
I AM NO ONE'S PAWN.
YOU ARE A SERVANT OF THE LIGHT, AND YOU HAVE NO QUALMS ABOUT HOW IT GUIDES YOUR PATH.
AND HERE I AM, BEFORE YOU, OFFERING YOU NEW PURPOSE IN THE VERY HOUR YOU THOUGHT YOUR PURPOSE HAD BEEN SPENT. HOW CAN YOU NOT SEE THE LIGHT'S WORK IN THIS?
JOIN ME, REVIL. YOU MIGHT NOT HAVE NEED OF COMPANIONSHIP, BUT EVERYONE HAS NEED OF MEANING. AND RIGHT NOW YOU ARE IN SHORT SUPPLY.

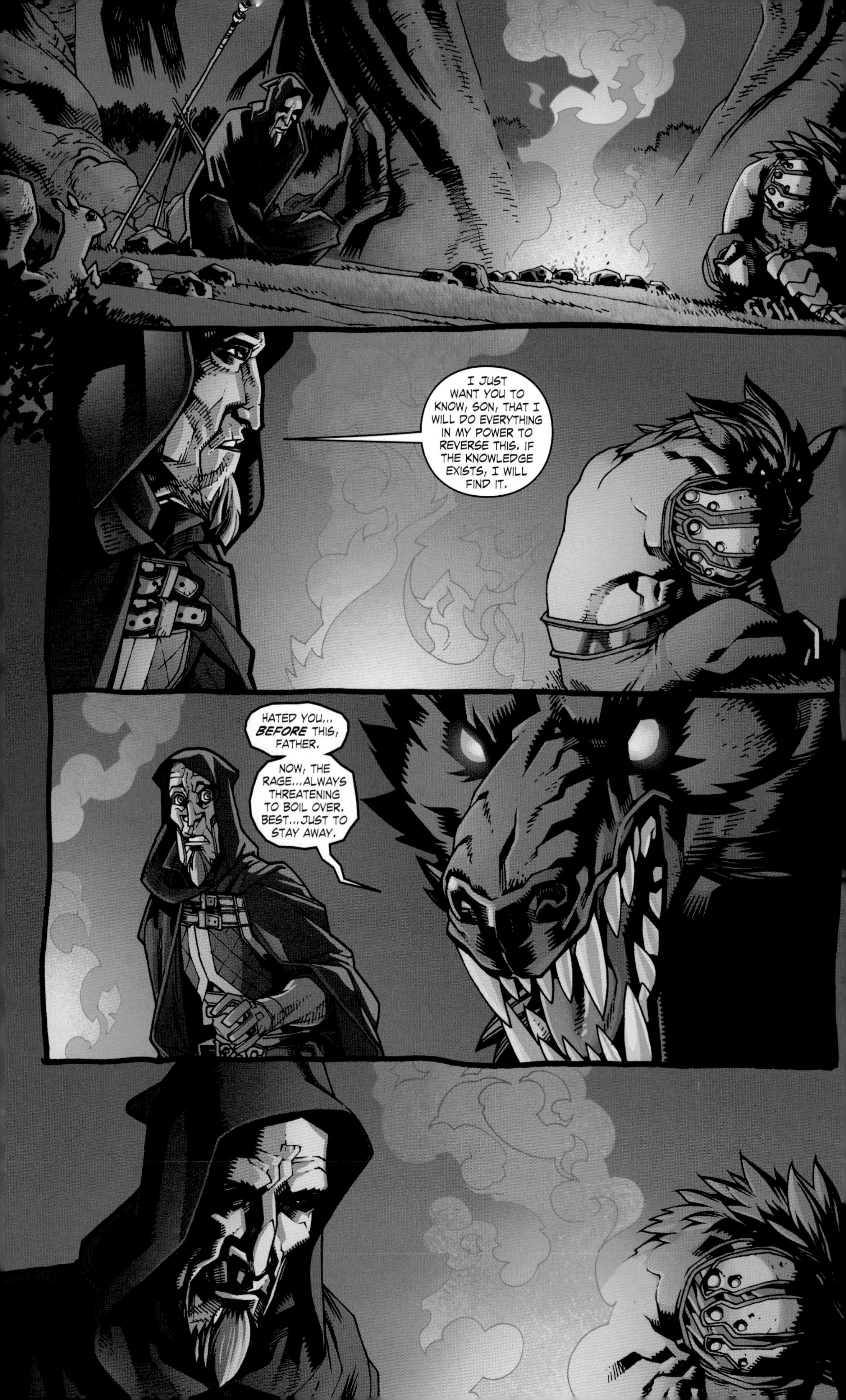
I JUST WANT YOU TO KNOW, SON, THAT I WILL DO EVERYTHING IN MY POWER TO REVERSE THIS. IF THE KNOWLEDGE EXISTS, I WILL FIND IT.
HATED YOU... *BEFORE* THIS, FATHER.
NOW, THE RAGE...ALWAYS THREATENING TO BOIL OVER. BEST...JUST TO STAY AWAY.

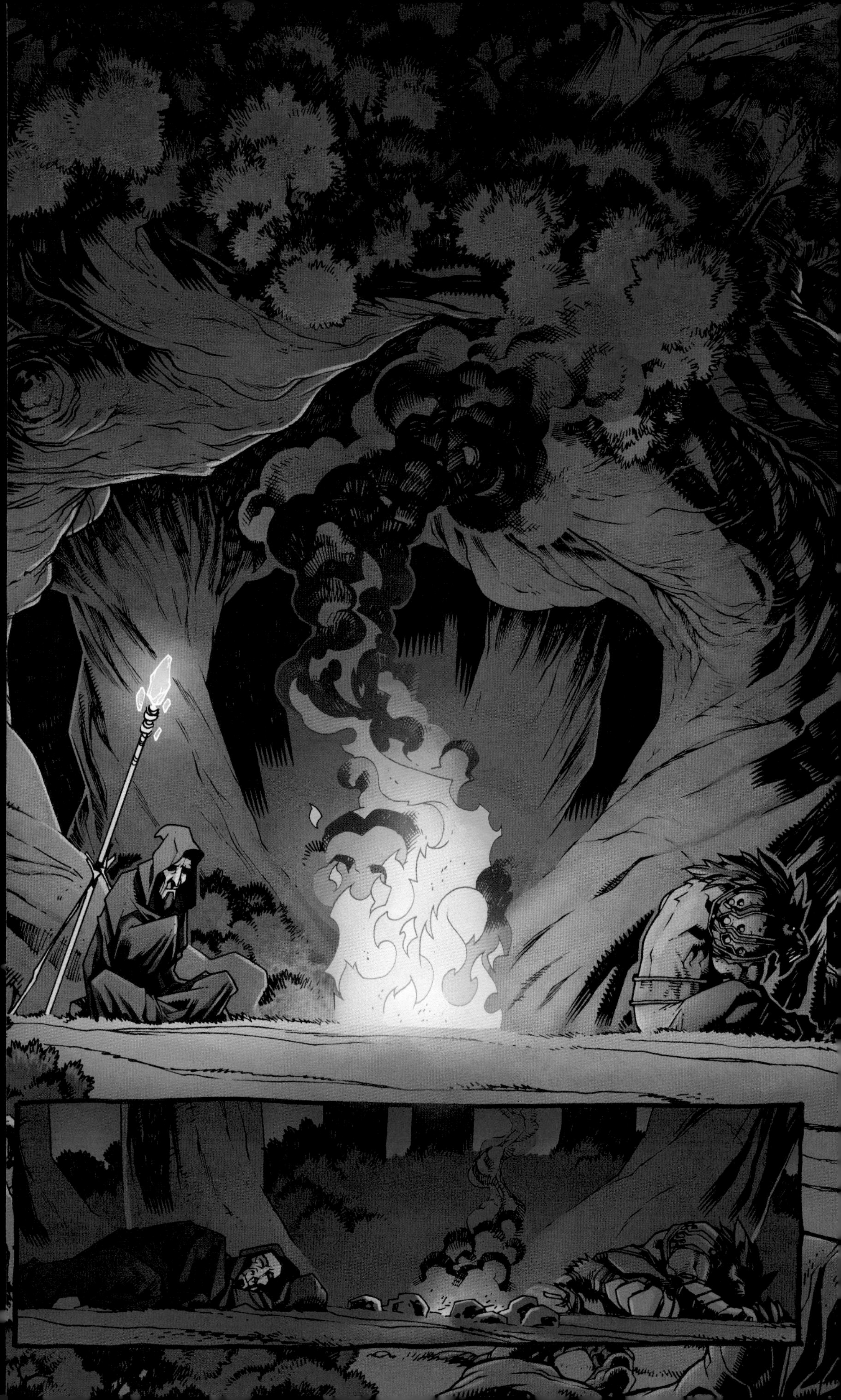

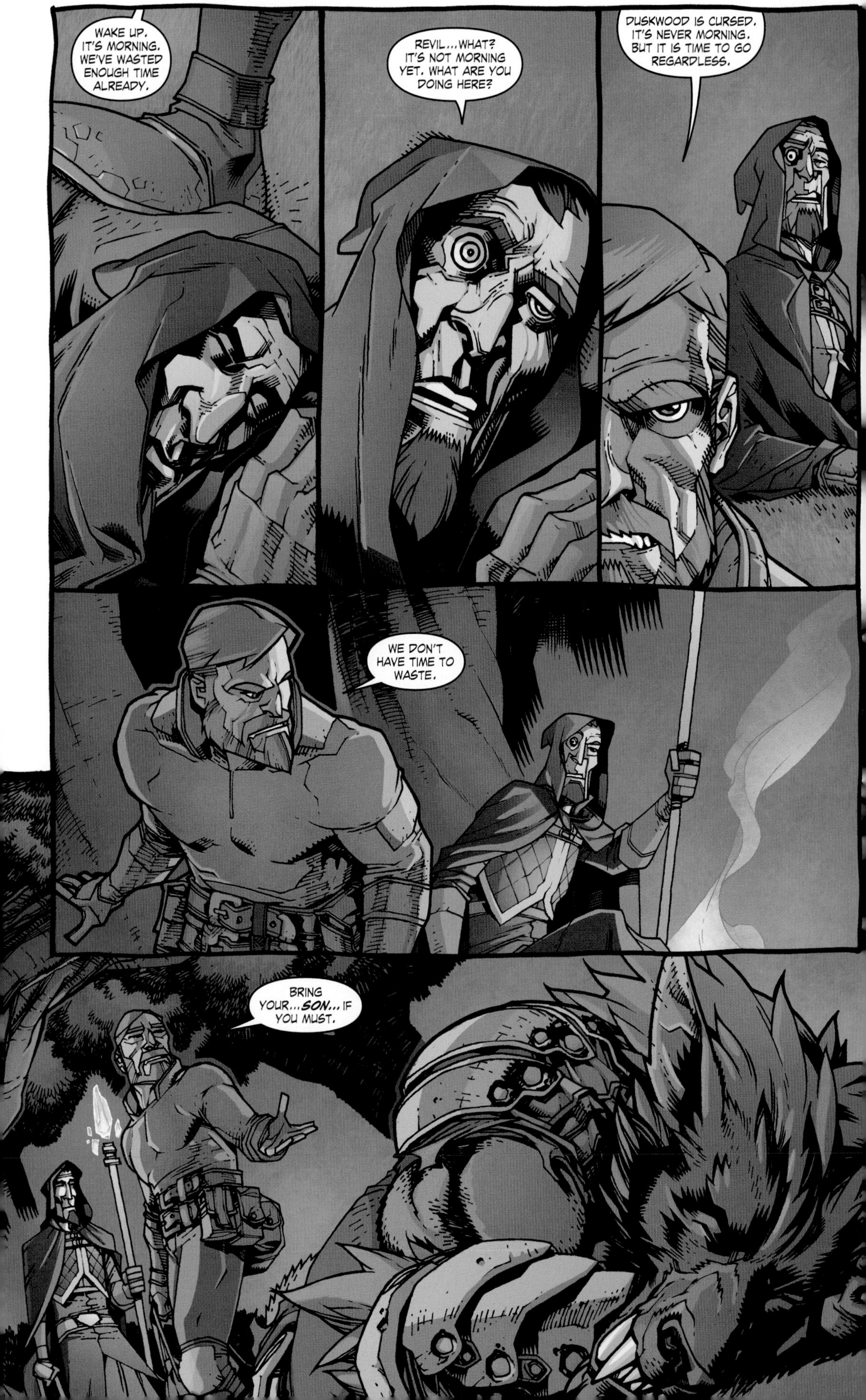

WAKE UP. IT'S MORNING. WE'VE WASTED ENOUGH TIME ALREADY.
REVIL...WHAT? IT'S NOT MORNING YET. WHAT ARE YOU DOING HERE?
DUSKWOOD IS CURSED. IT'S NEVER MORNING. BUT IT IS TIME TO GO REGARDLESS.
WE DON'T HAVE TIME TO WASTE.
BRING YOUR...**SON**... IF YOU MUST.

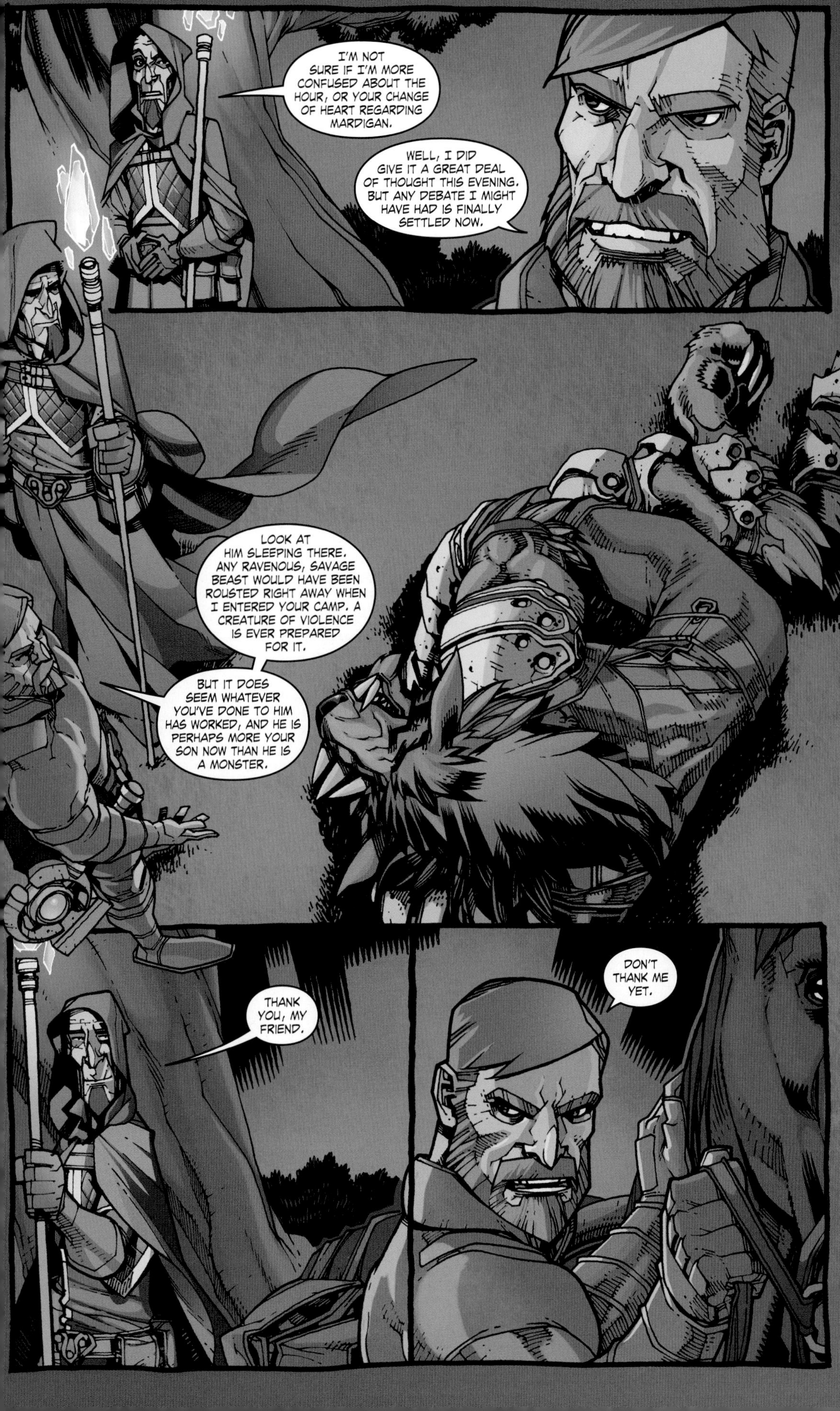
I'M NOT SURE IF I'M MORE CONFUSED ABOUT THE HOUR, OR YOUR CHANGE OF HEART REGARDING MARDIGAN.
WELL, I DID GIVE IT A GREAT DEAL OF THOUGHT THIS EVENING. BUT ANY DEBATE I MIGHT HAVE HAD IS FINALLY SETTLED NOW.
LOOK AT HIM SLEEPING THERE. ANY RAVENOUS, SAVAGE BEAST WOULD HAVE BEEN ROUSTED RIGHT AWAY WHEN I ENTERED YOUR CAMP. A CREATURE OF VIOLENCE IS EVER PREPARED FOR IT.
BUT IT DOES SEEM WHATEVER YOU'VE DONE TO HIM HAS WORKED, AND HE IS PERHAPS MORE YOUR SON NOW THAN HE IS A MONSTER.
THANK YOU, MY FRIEND.
DON'T THANK ME YET.

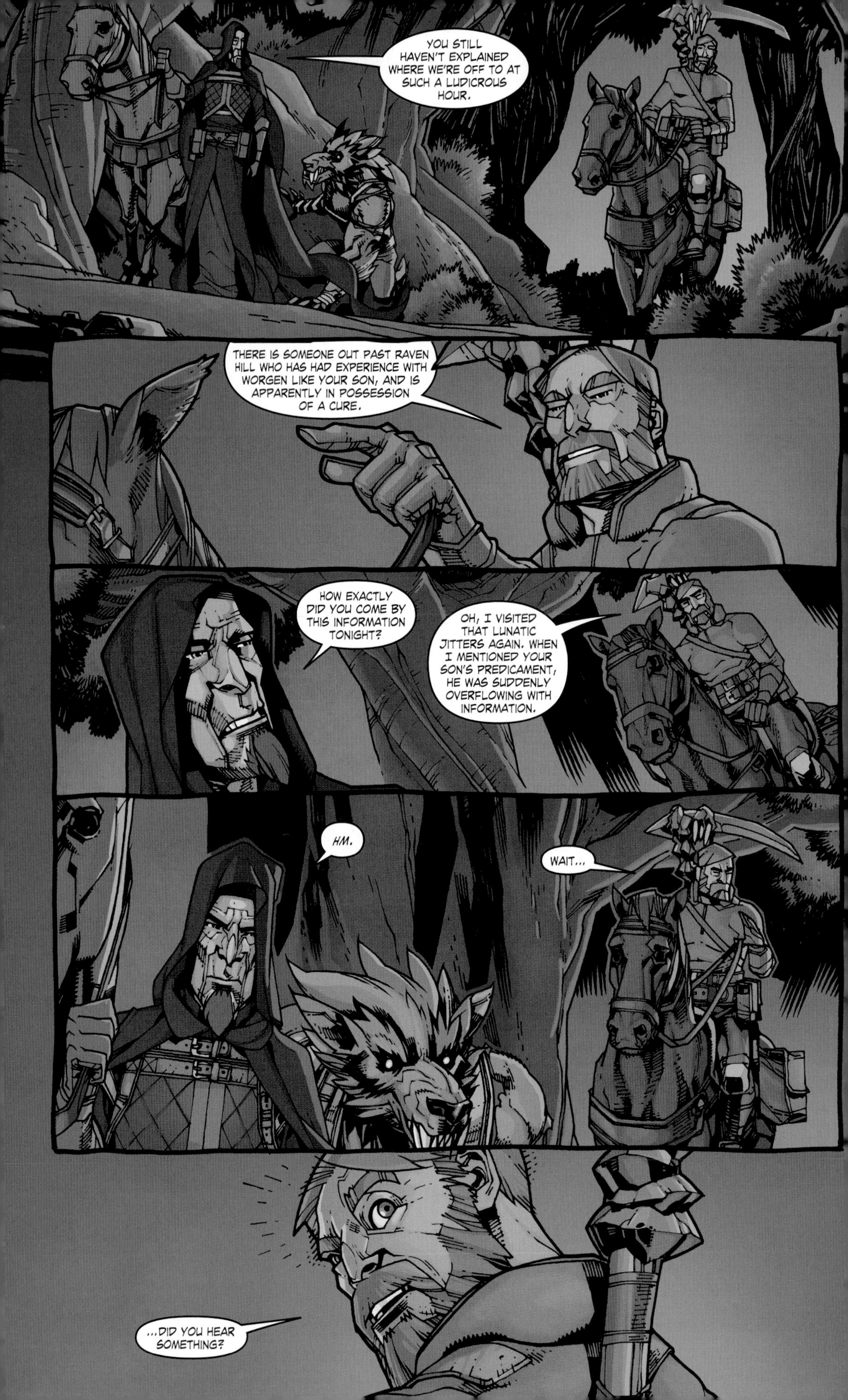
YOU STILL HAVEN'T EXPLAINED WHERE WE'RE OFF TO AT SUCH A LUDICROUS HOUR.
THERE IS SOMEONE OUT PAST RAVEN HILL WHO HAS HAD EXPERIENCE WITH WORGEN LIKE YOUR SON, AND IS APPARENTLY IN POSSESSION OF A CURE.
HOW EXACTLY DID YOU COME BY THIS INFORMATION TONIGHT?
OH, I VISITED THAT LUNATIC JITTERS AGAIN. WHEN I MENTIONED YOUR SON'S PREDICAMENT, HE WAS SUDDENLY OVERFLOWING WITH INFORMATION.
HM.
WAIT...
...DID YOU HEAR SOMETHING?

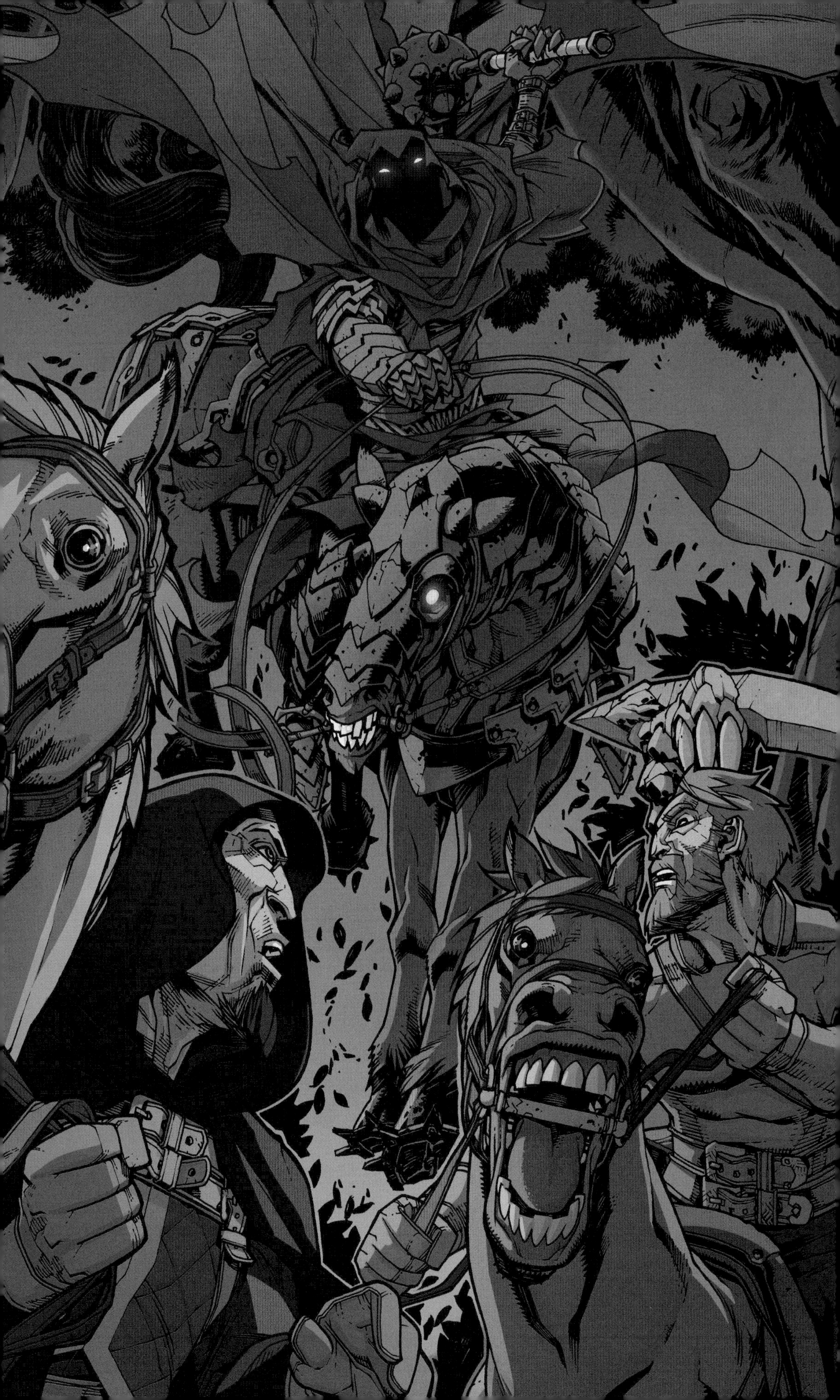

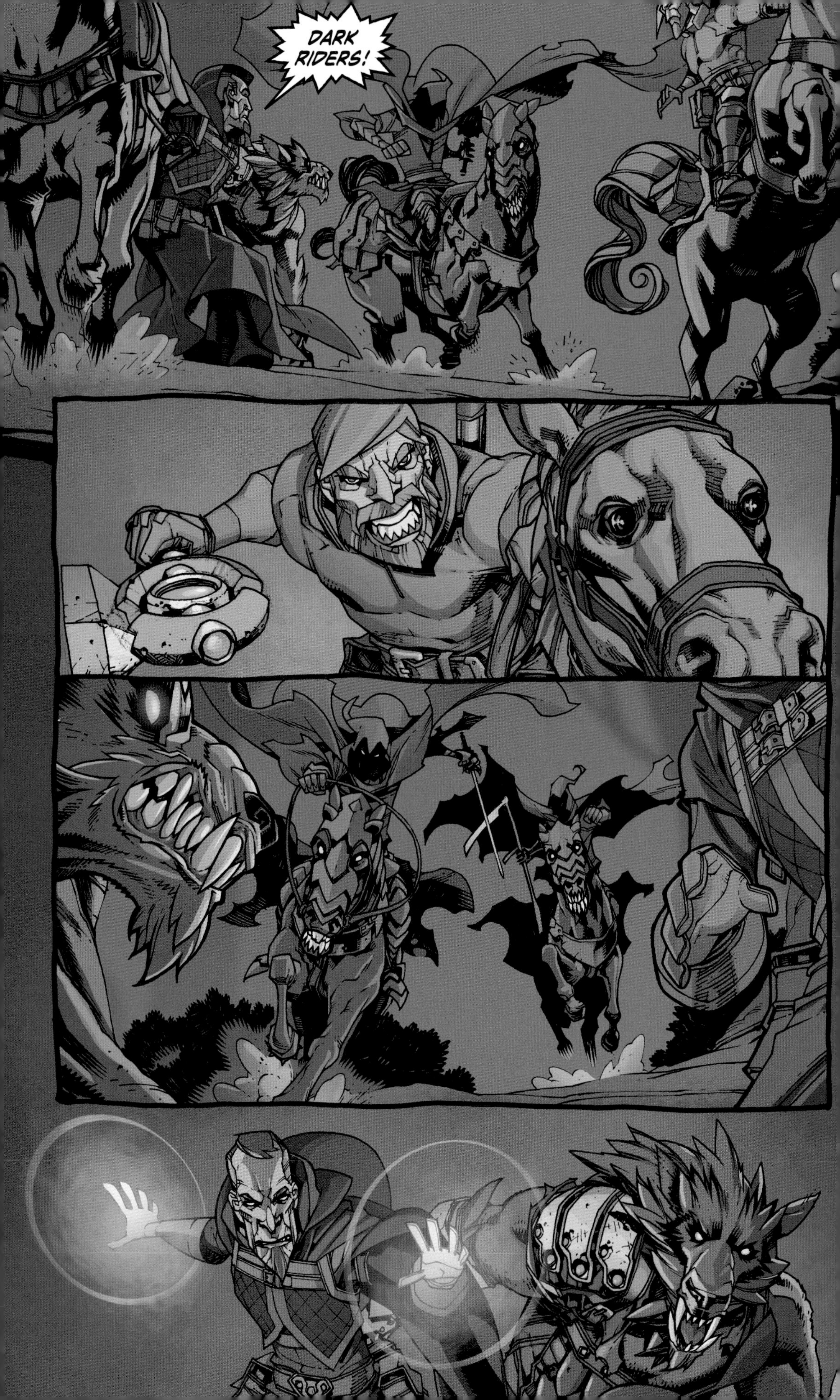
DARK RIDERS!

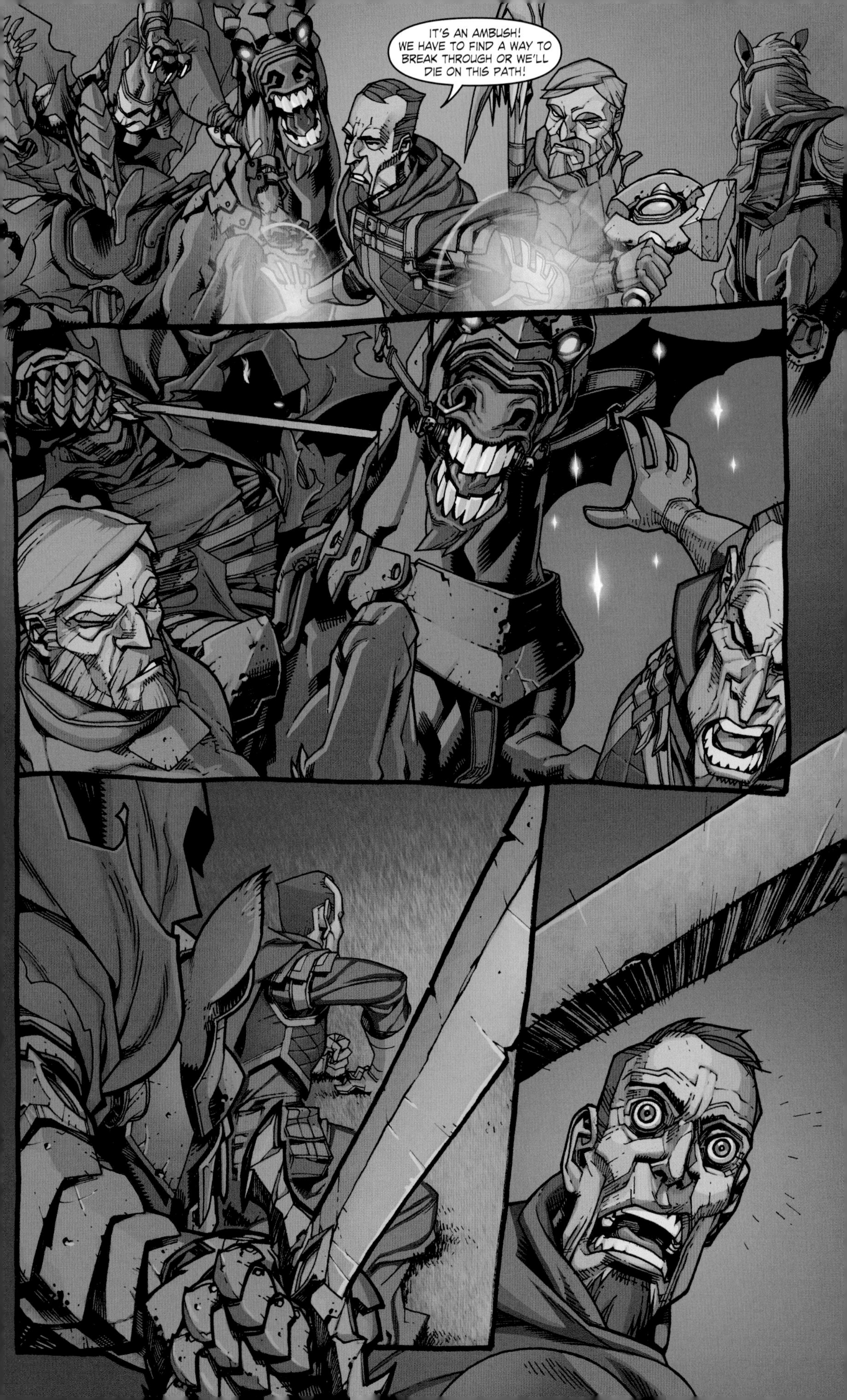
IT'S AN AMBUSH! WE HAVE TO FIND A WAY TO BREAK THROUGH OR WE'LL DIE ON THIS PATH!

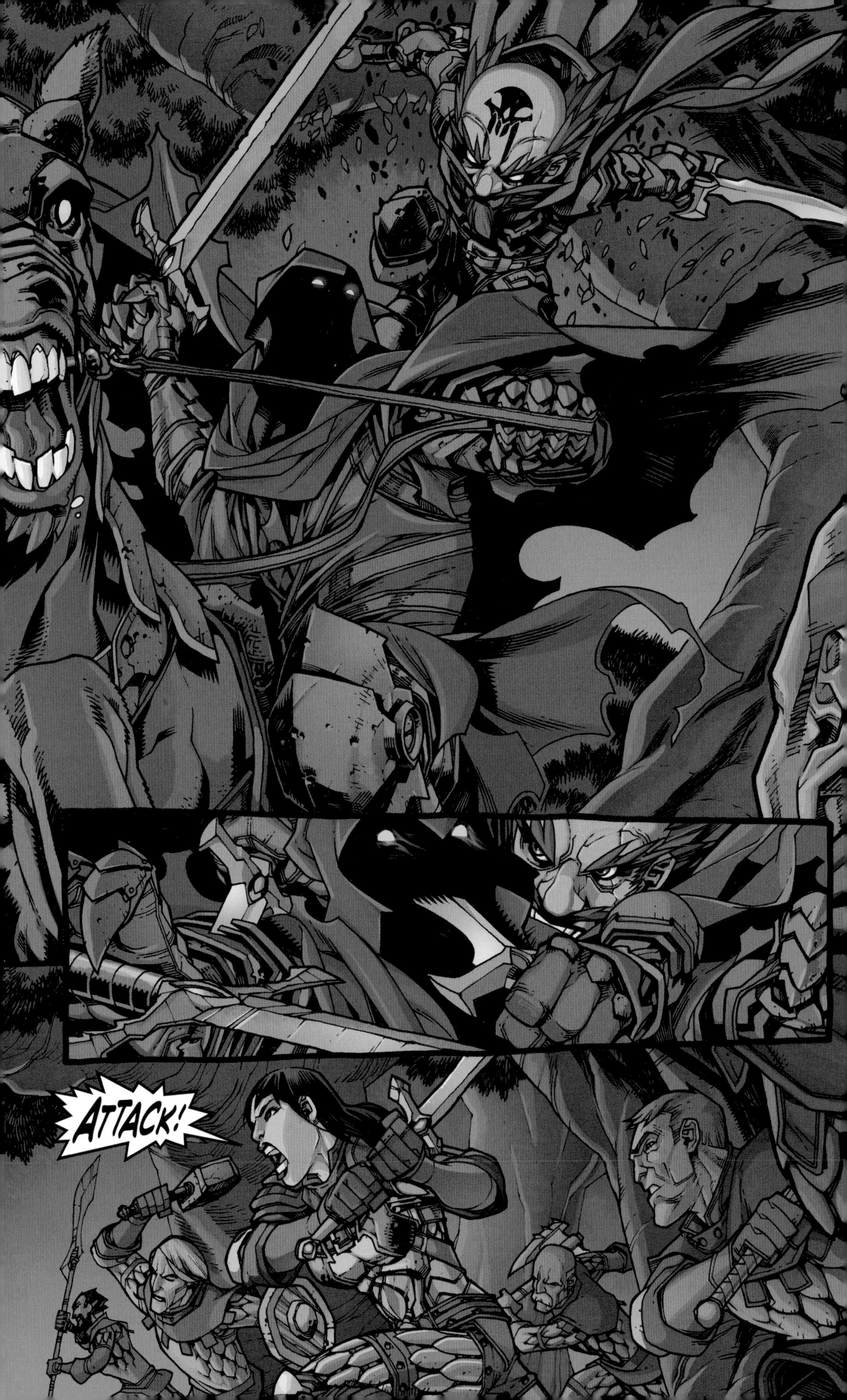
ATTACK!

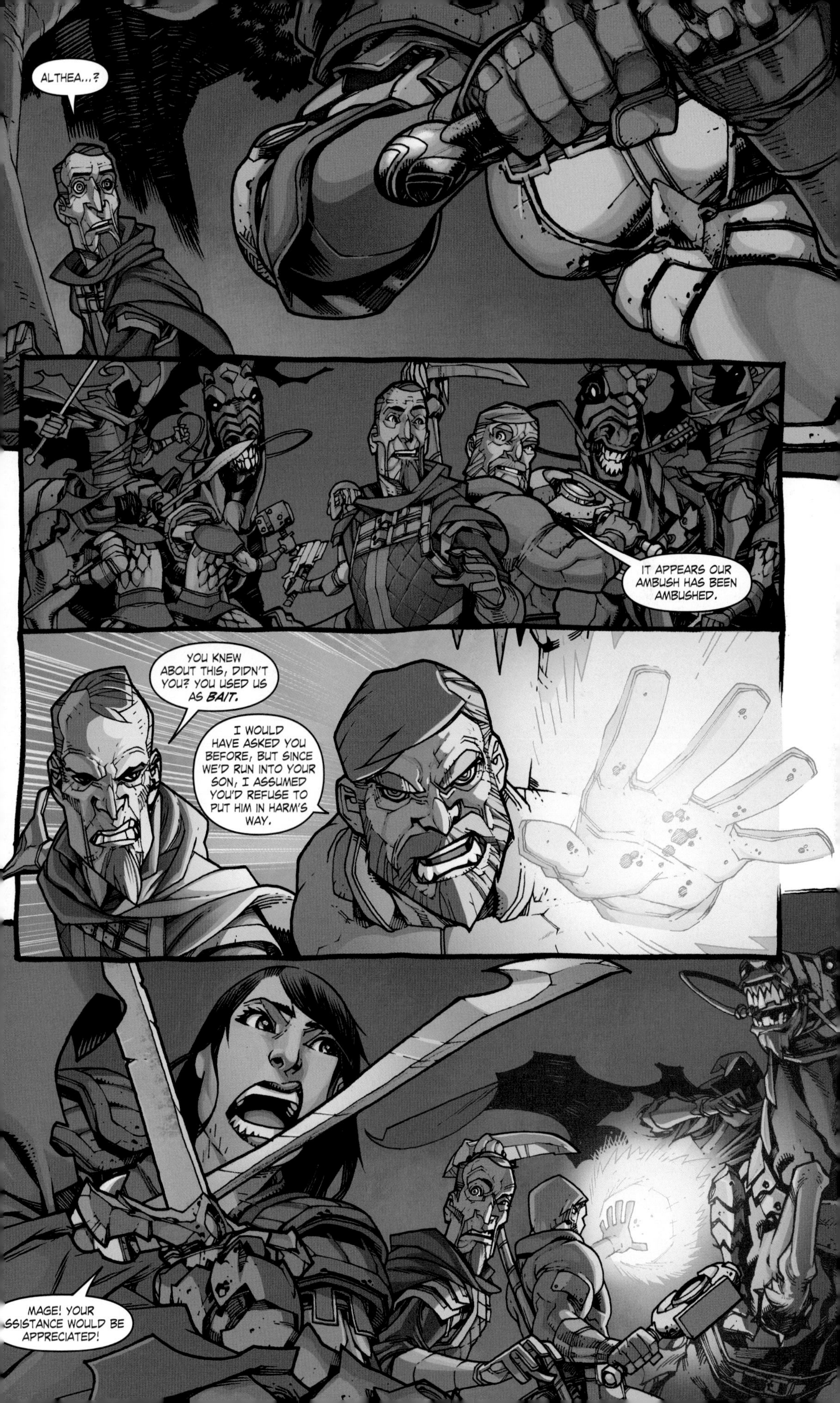

ALTHEA...?
IT APPEARS OUR AMBUSH HAS BEEN AMBUSHED.
YOU KNEW ABOUT THIS, DIDN'T YOU? YOU USED US AS BAIT.
I WOULD HAVE ASKED YOU BEFORE, BUT SINCE WE'D RUN INTO YOUR SON, I ASSUMED YOU'D REFUSE TO PUT HIM IN HARM'S WAY.
MAGE! YOUR SSISTANCE WOULD BE APPRECIATED!

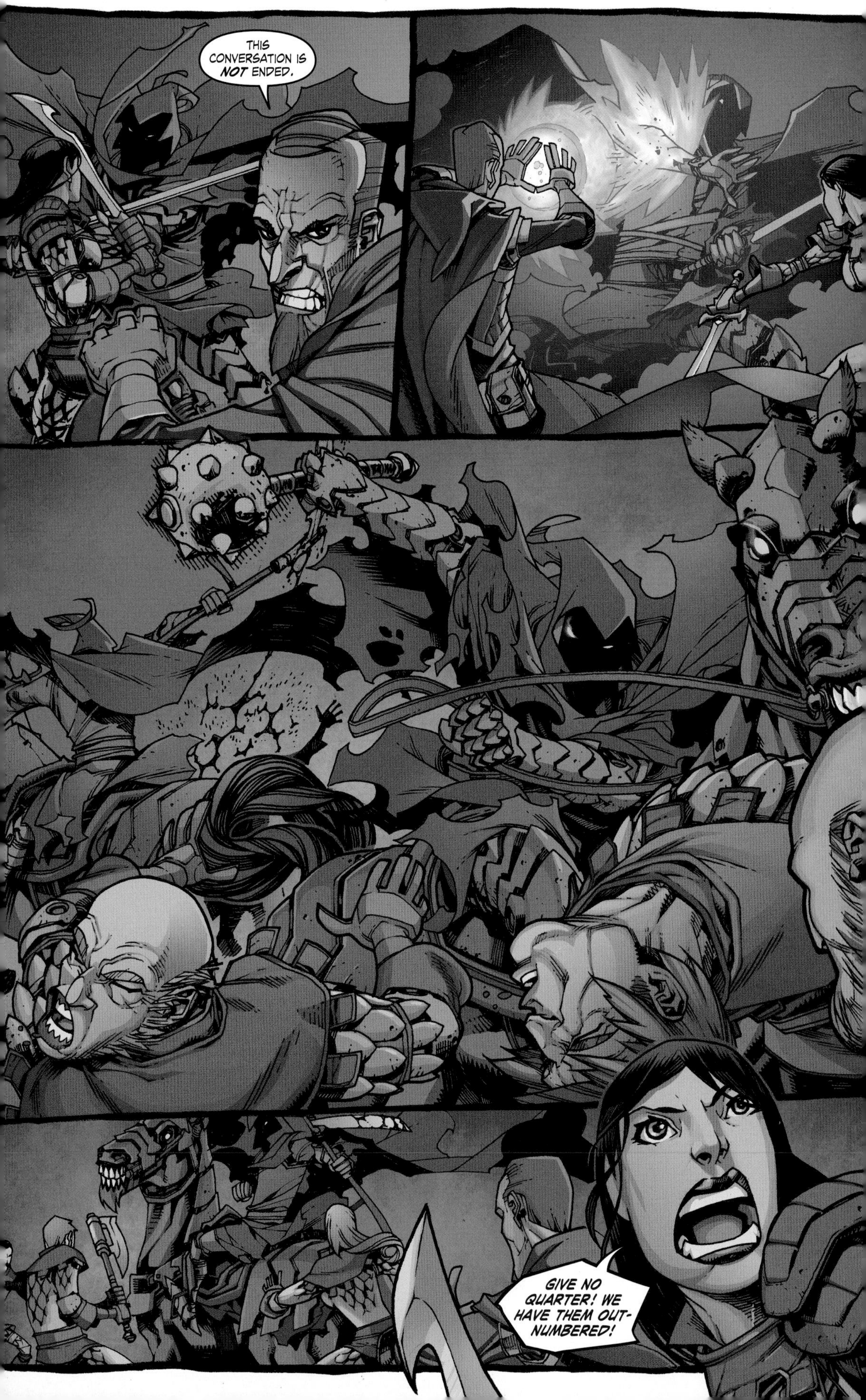
THIS CONVERSATION IS NOT ENDED.
GIVE NO QUARTER! WE HAVE THEM OUT-NUMBERED!

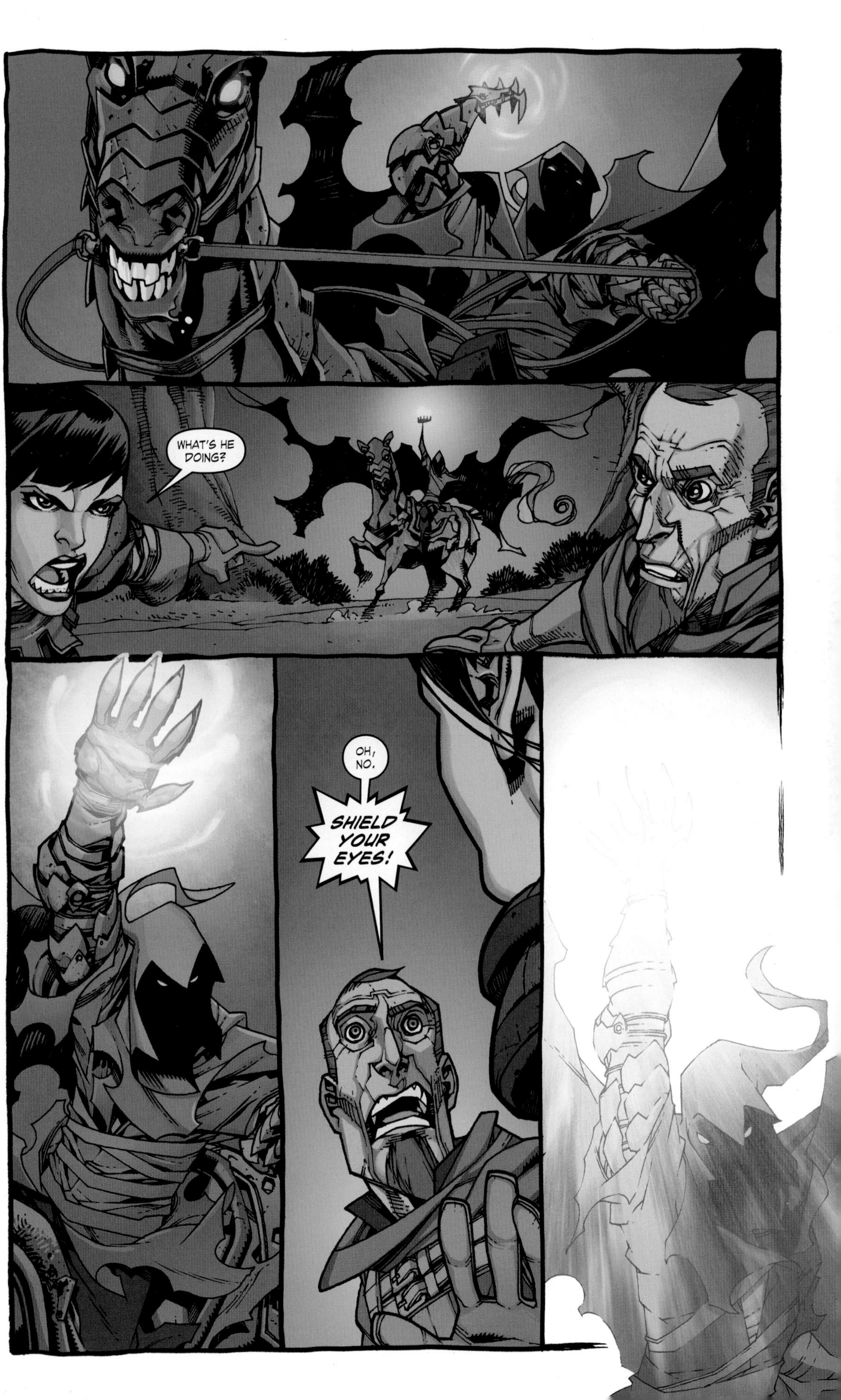
WHAT'S HE DOING?
OH, NO.
SHIELD YOUR EYES!

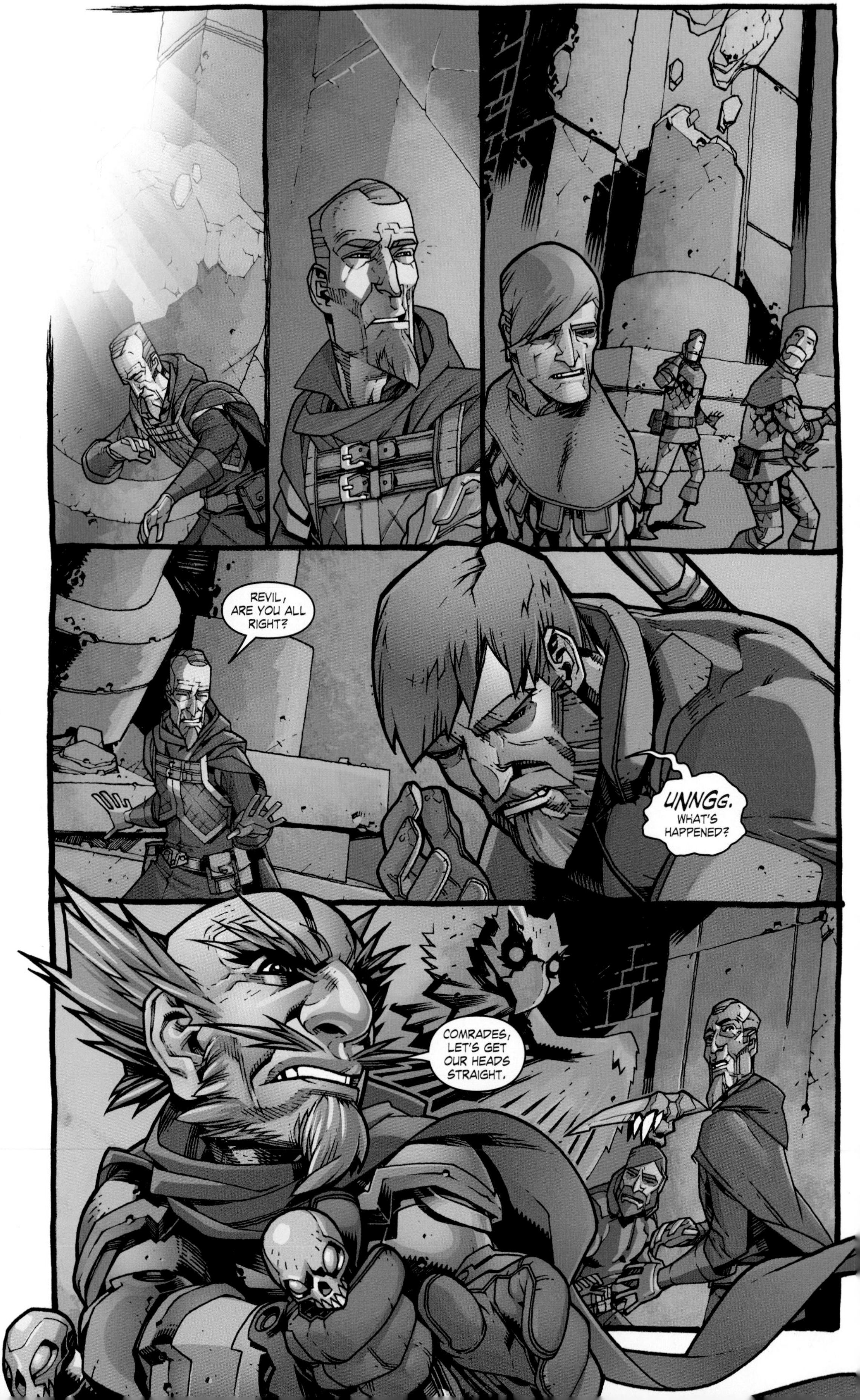
REVIL, ARE YOU ALL RIGHT?
UNNGG. WHAT'S HAPPENED?
COMRADES, LET'S GET OUR HEADS STRAIGHT.

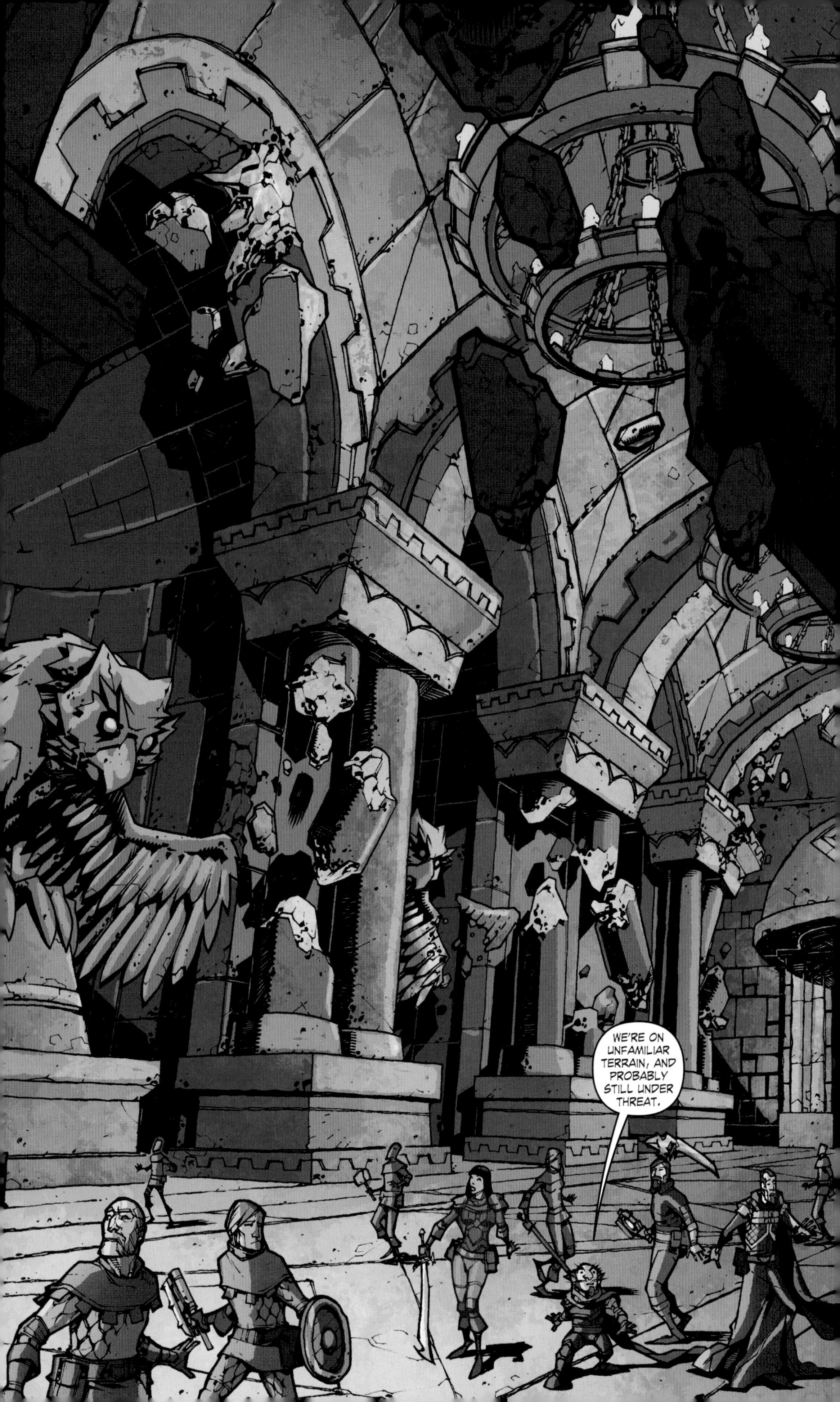
WE'RE ON UNFAMILIAR TERRAIN, AND PROBABLY STILL UNDER THREAT.

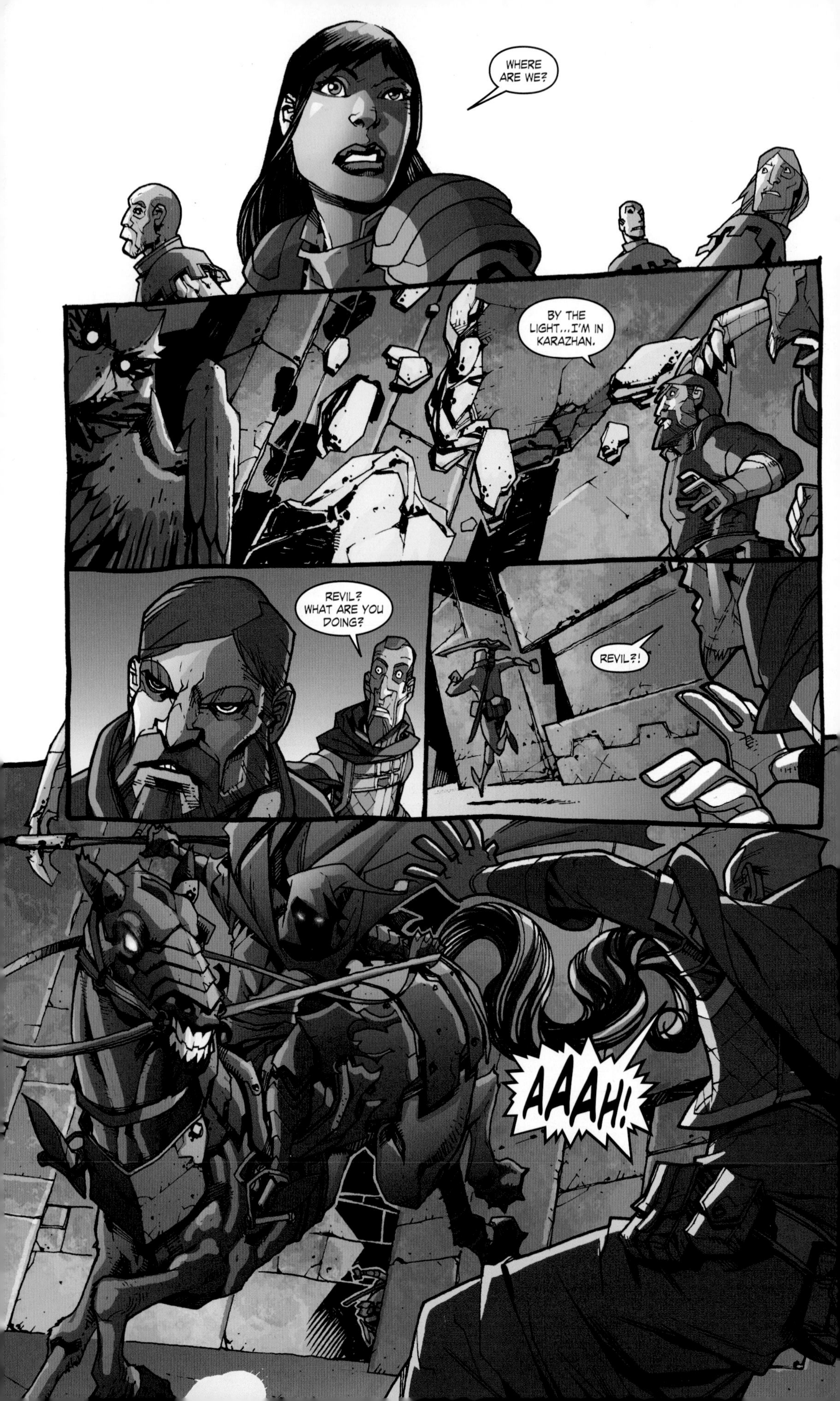
WHERE ARE WE?
BY THE LIGHT...I'M IN KARAZHAN.
REVIL? WHAT ARE YOU DOING?
REVIL?!
AAAH!

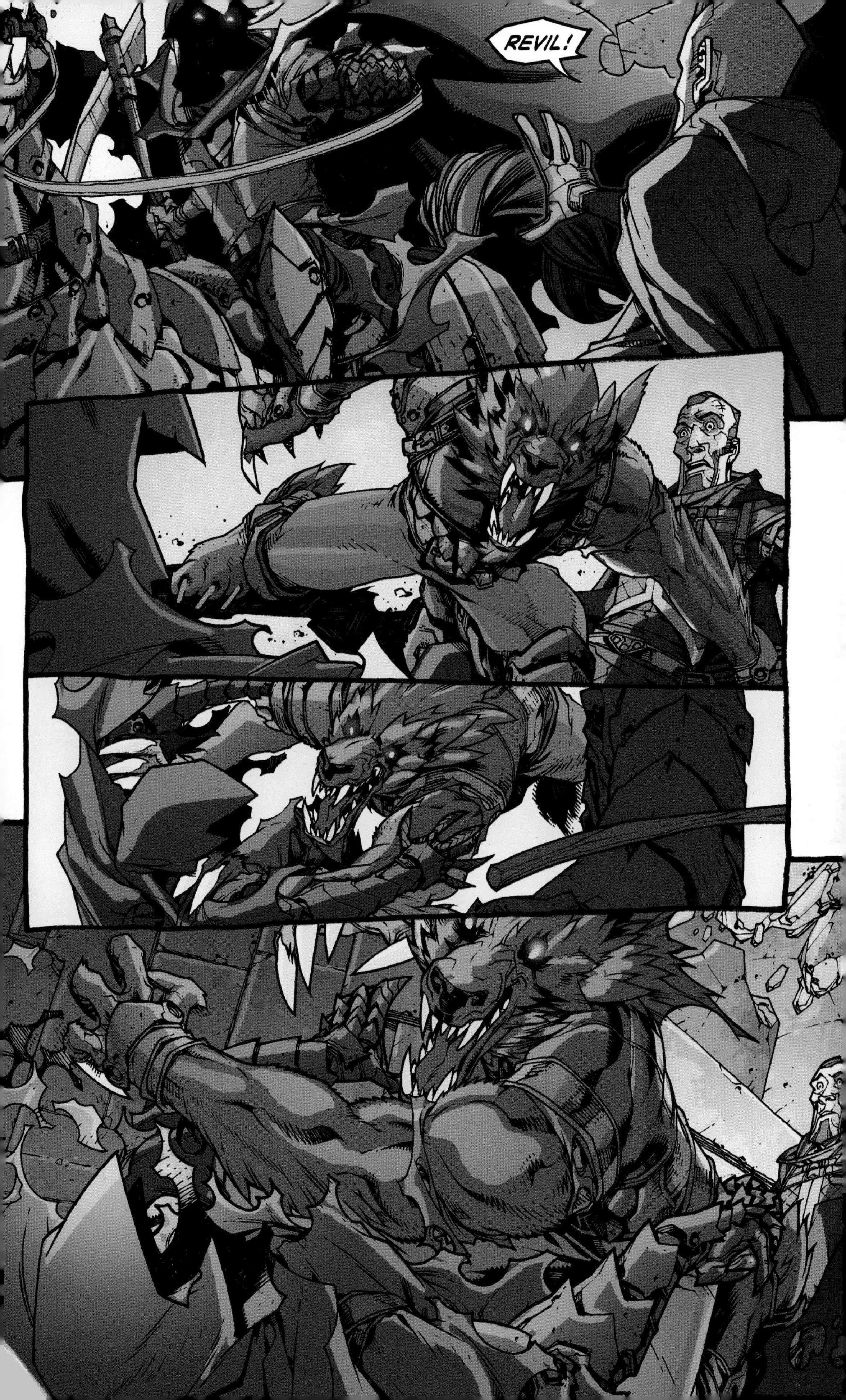
REVIL!

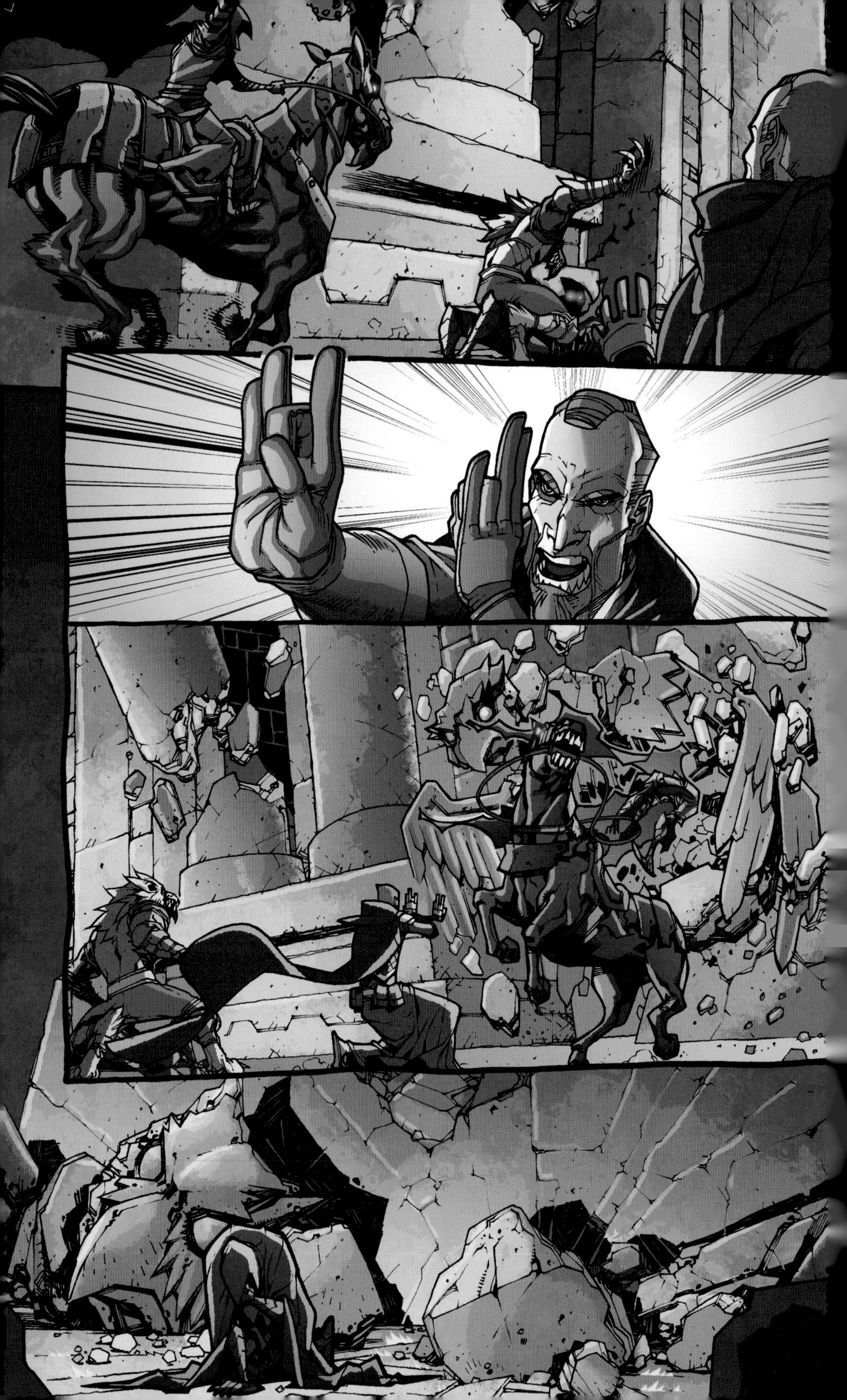

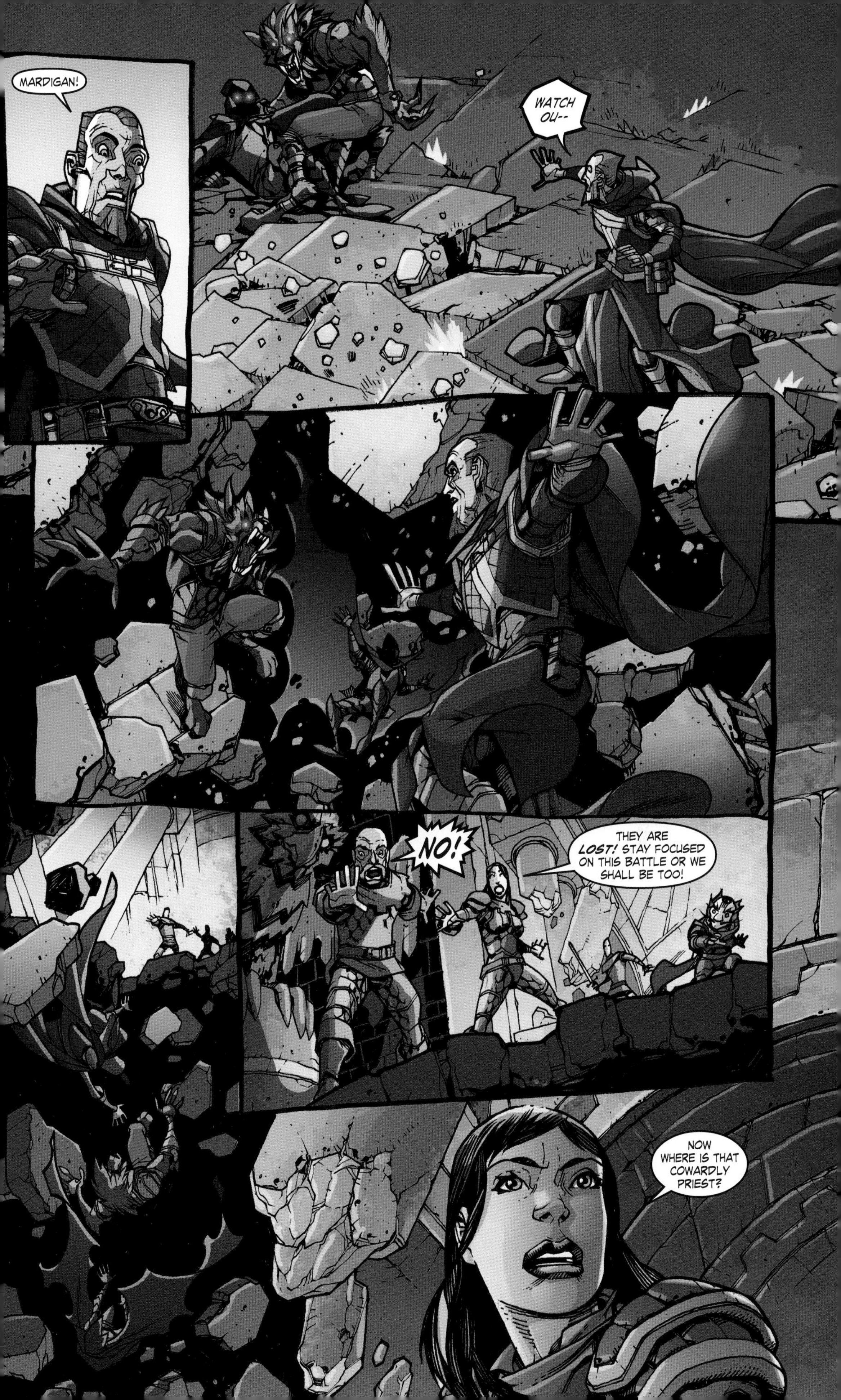

MARDIGAN!
WATCH OU--
NO!
THEY ARE *LOST!* STAY FOCUSED ON THIS BATTLE OR WE SHALL BE TOO!
NOW WHERE IS THAT COWARDLY PRIEST?

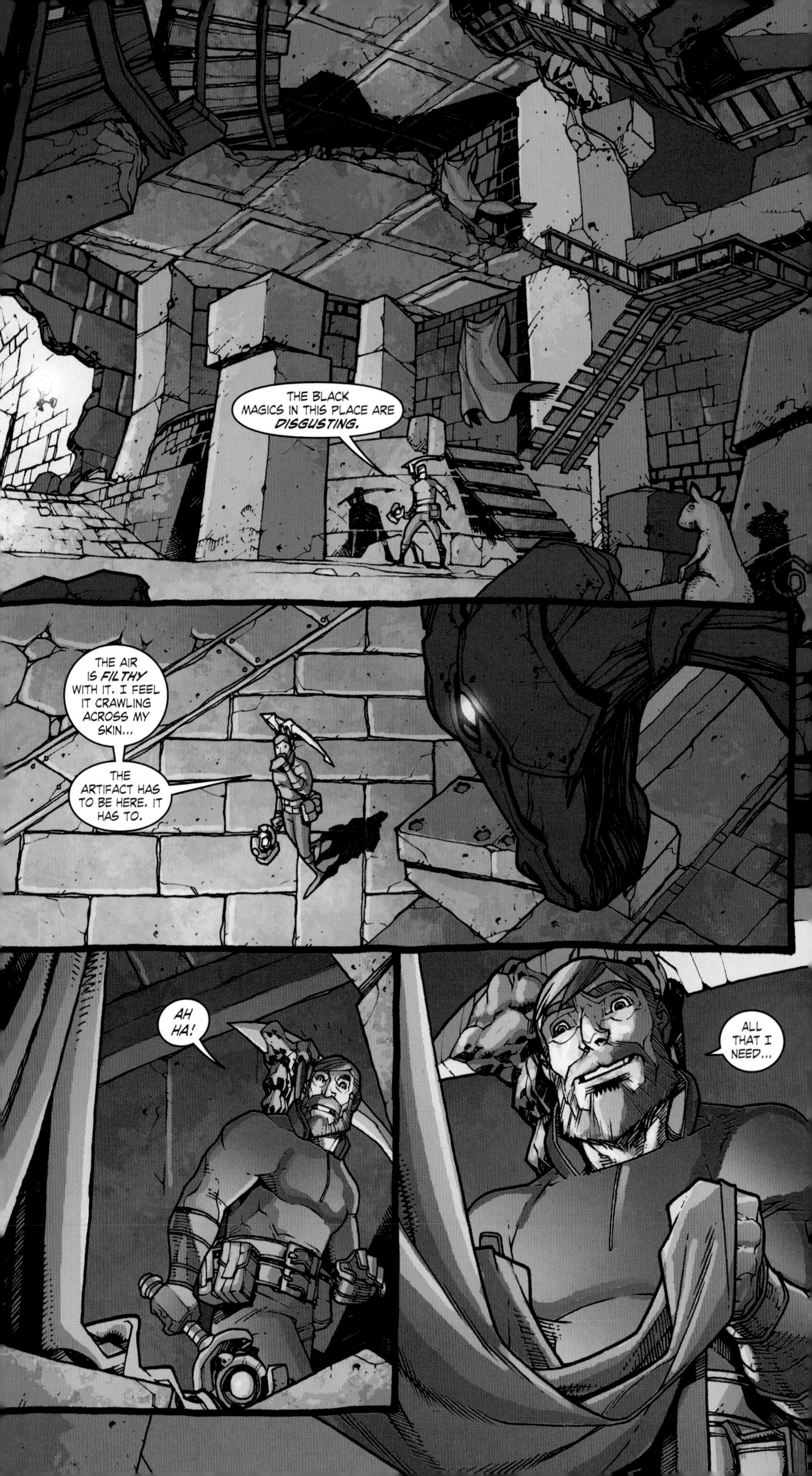
THE BLACK MAGICS IN THIS PLACE ARE DISGUSTING.
THE AIR IS FILTHY WITH IT. I FEEL IT CRAWLING ACROSS MY SKIN...
THE ARTIFACT HAS TO BE HERE. IT HAS TO.
AH HA!
ALL THAT I NEED...

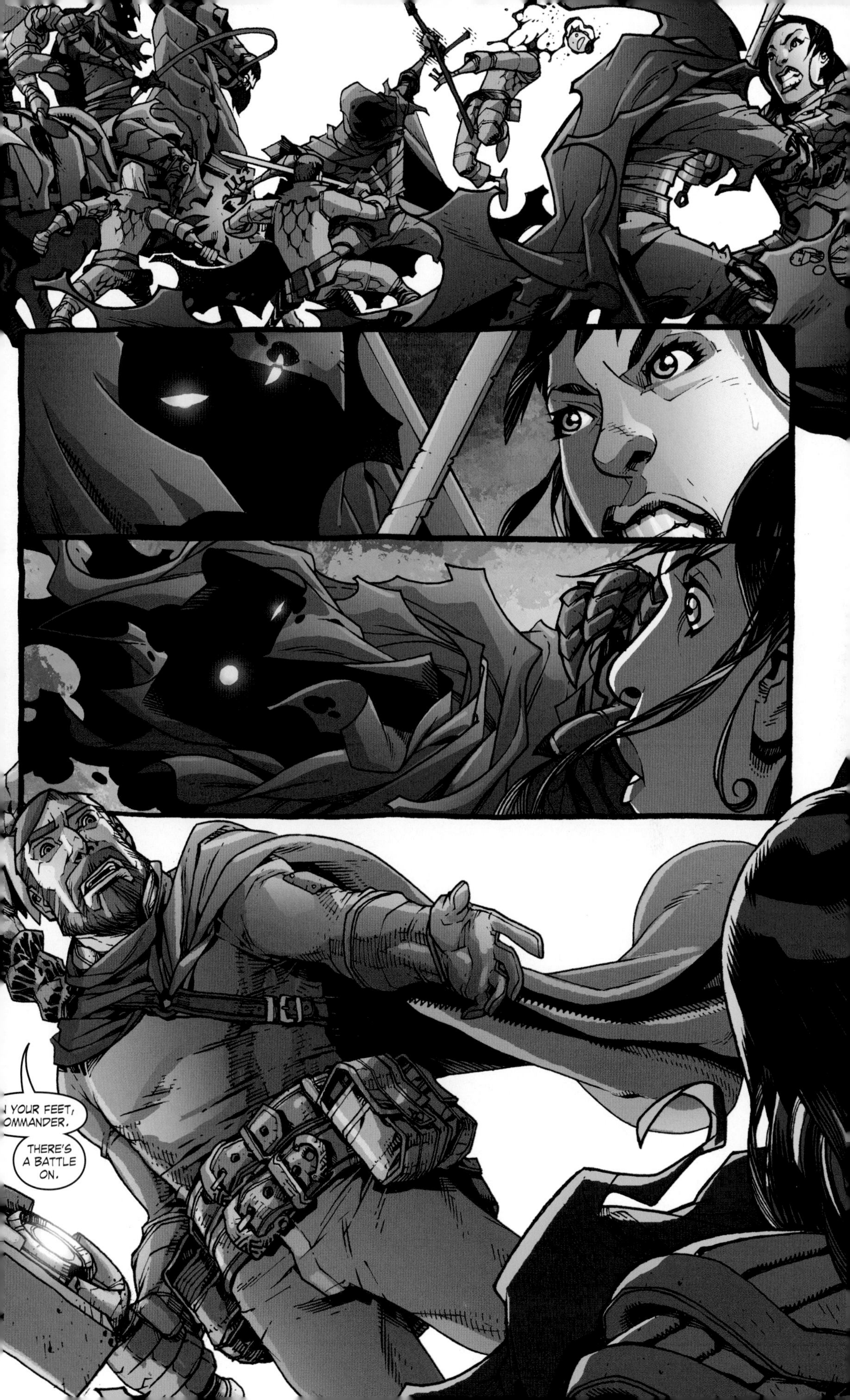
N YOUR FEET, OMMANDER.
THERE'S A BATTLE ON.

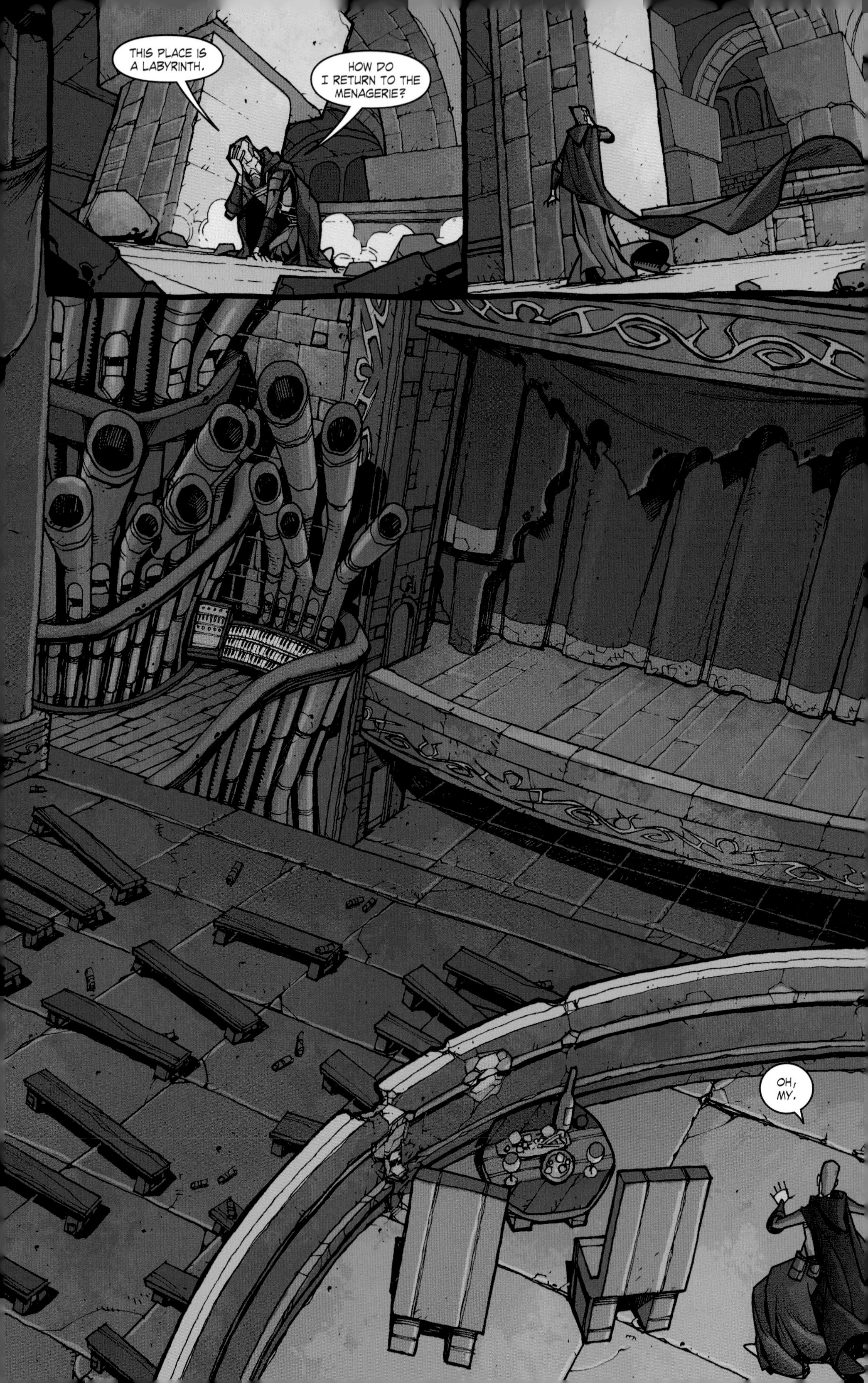
THIS PLACE IS A LABYRINTH.
HOW DO I RETURN TO THE MENAGERIE?
OH, MY.

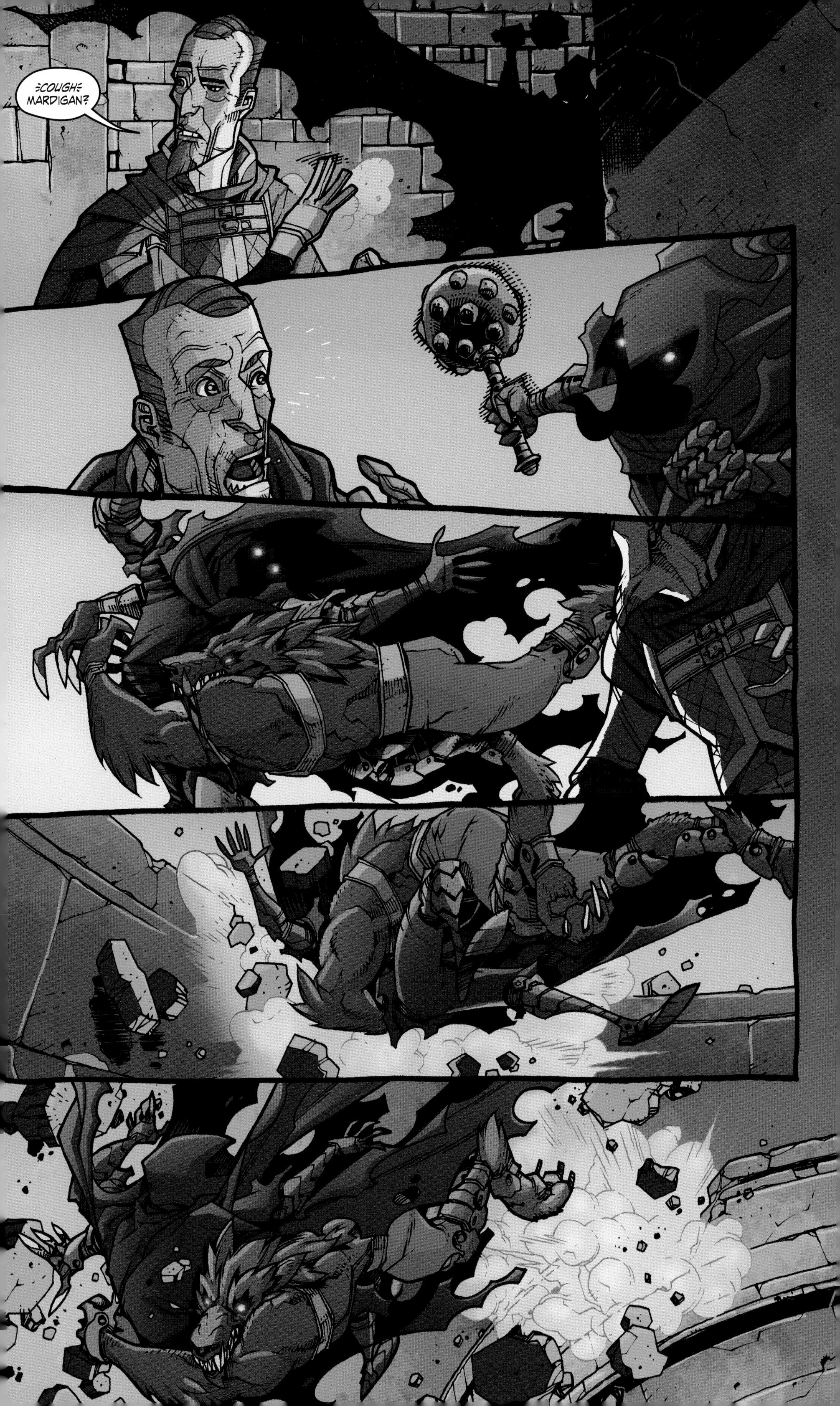

=COUGH= MARDIGAN?

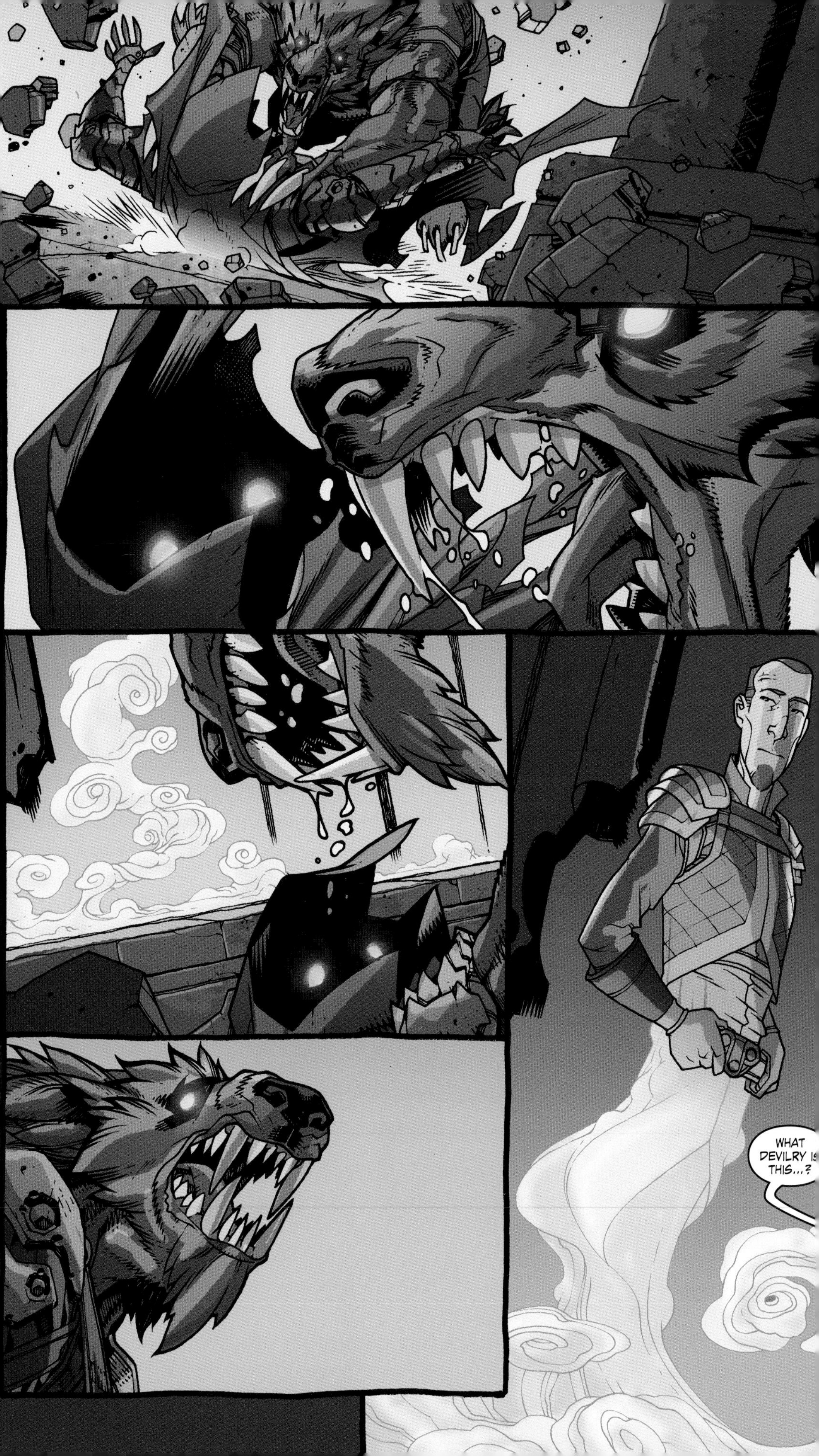
WHAT DEVILRY IS THIS...?

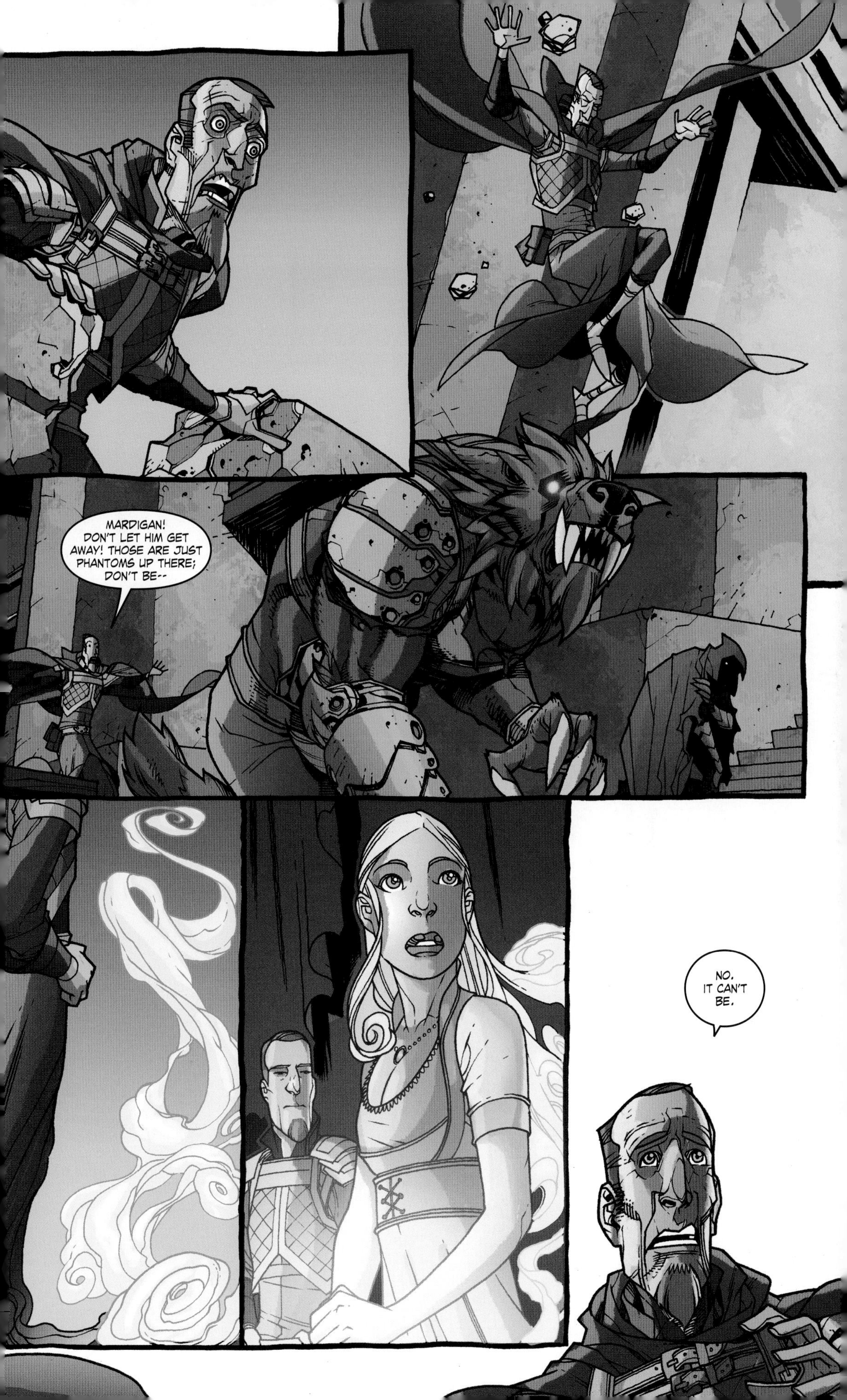
MARDIGAN! DON'T LET HIM GET AWAY! THOSE ARE JUST PHANTOMS UP THERE; DON'T BE--
NO. IT CAN'T BE.

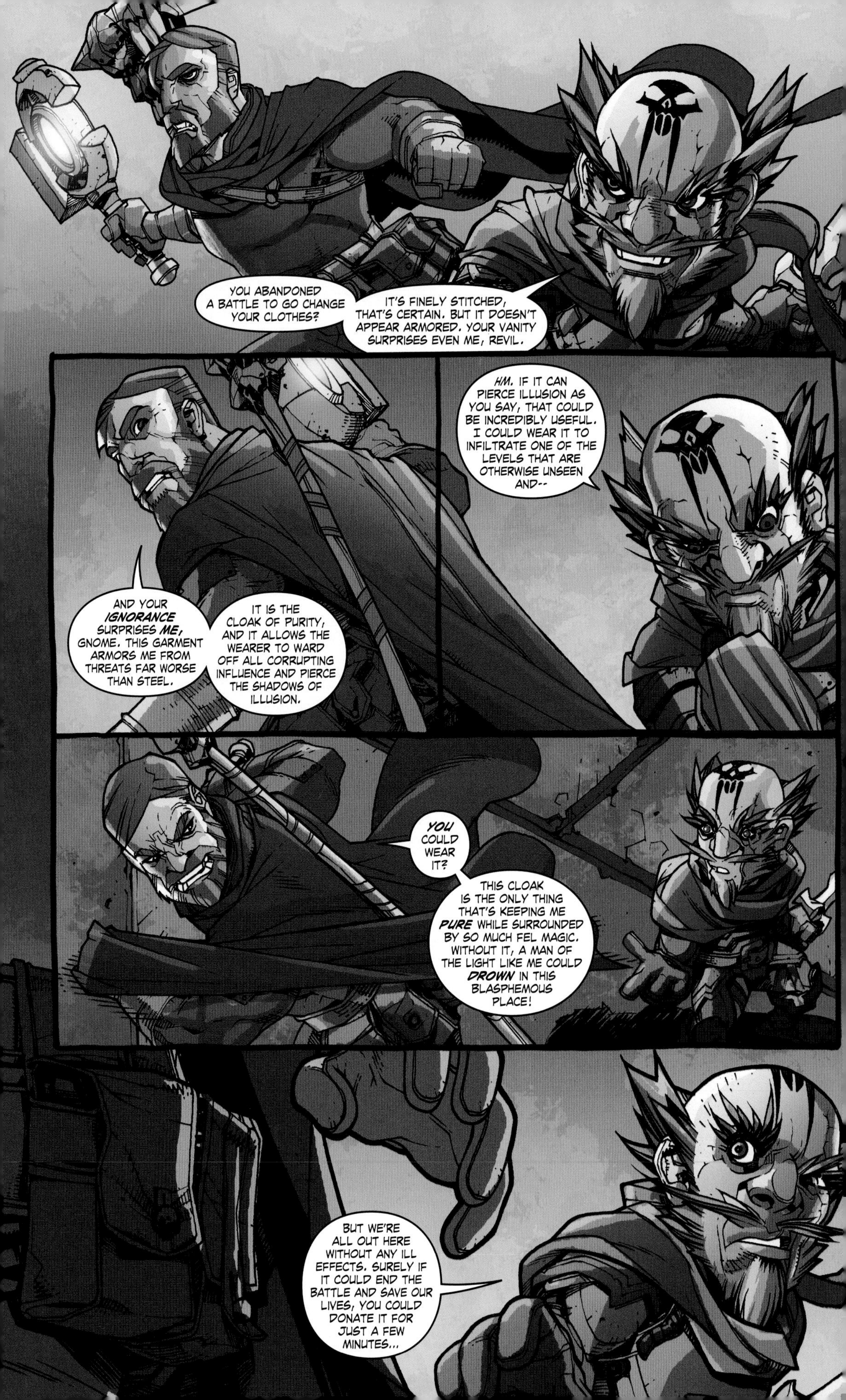
YOU ABANDONED A BATTLE TO GO CHANGE YOUR CLOTHES?
IT'S FINELY STITCHED, THAT'S CERTAIN. BUT IT DOESN'T APPEAR ARMORED. YOUR VANITY SURPRISES EVEN ME, REVIL.
AND YOUR *IGNORANCE* SURPRISES *ME,* GNOME. THIS GARMENT ARMORS ME FROM THREATS FAR WORSE THAN STEEL.
IT IS THE CLOAK OF PURITY, AND IT ALLOWS THE WEARER TO WARD OFF ALL CORRUPTING INFLUENCE AND PIERCE THE SHADOWS OF ILLUSION.
HM. IF IT CAN PIERCE ILLUSION AS YOU SAY, THAT COULD BE INCREDIBLY USEFUL. I COULD WEAR IT TO INFILTRATE ONE OF THE LEVELS THAT ARE OTHERWISE UNSEEN AND--
YOU COULD WEAR IT?
THIS CLOAK IS THE ONLY THING THAT'S KEEPING ME *PURE* WHILE SURROUNDED BY SO MUCH FEL MAGIC. WITHOUT IT, A MAN OF THE LIGHT LIKE ME COULD *DROWN* IN THIS BLASPHEMOUS PLACE!
BUT WE'RE ALL OUT HERE WITHOUT ANY ILL EFFECTS. SURELY IF IT COULD END THE BATTLE AND SAVE OUR LIVES, YOU COULD DONATE IT FOR JUST A FEW MINUTES...

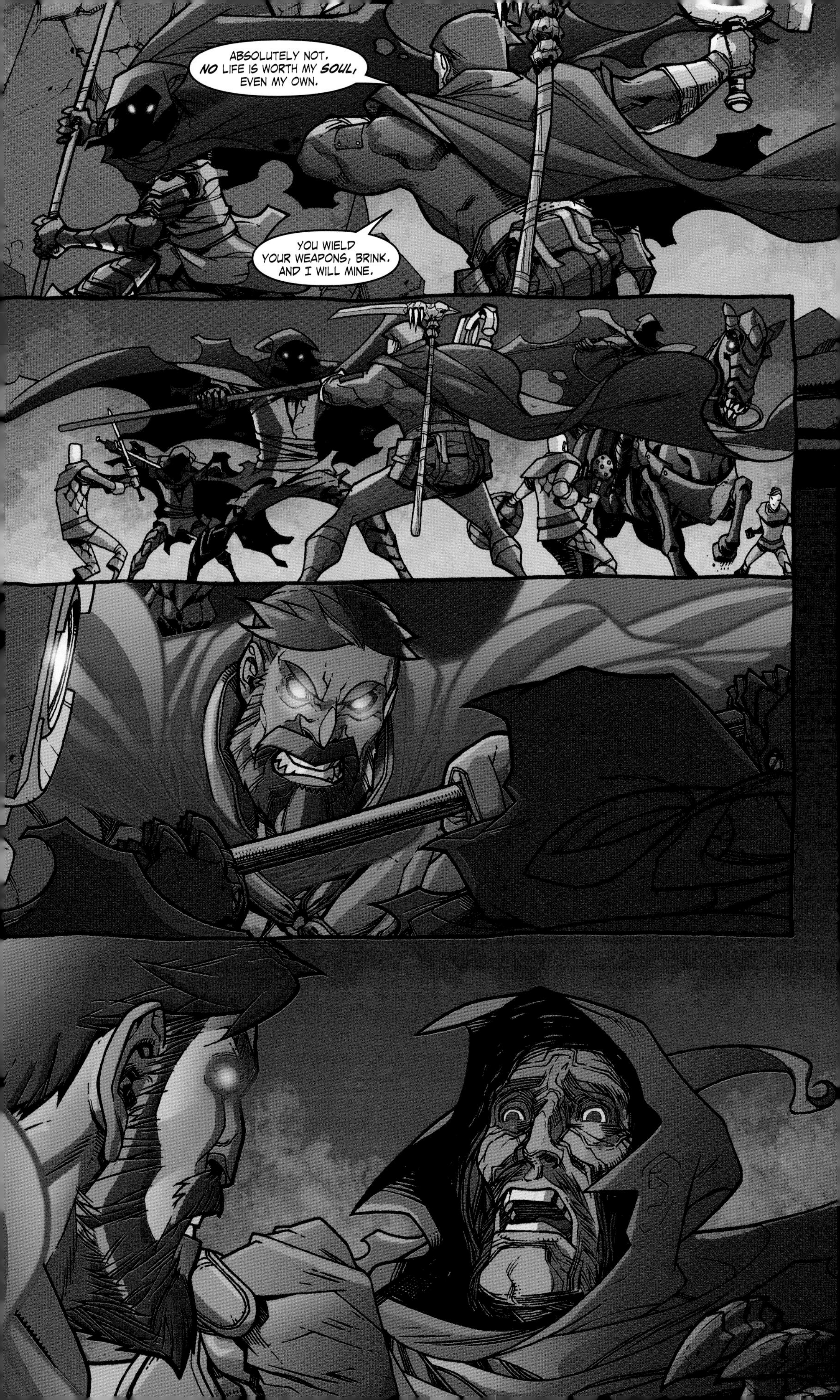
ABSOLUTELY NOT. *NO* LIFE IS WORTH MY *SOUL*, EVEN MY OWN.
YOU WIELD YOUR WEAPONS, BRINK. AND I WILL MINE.

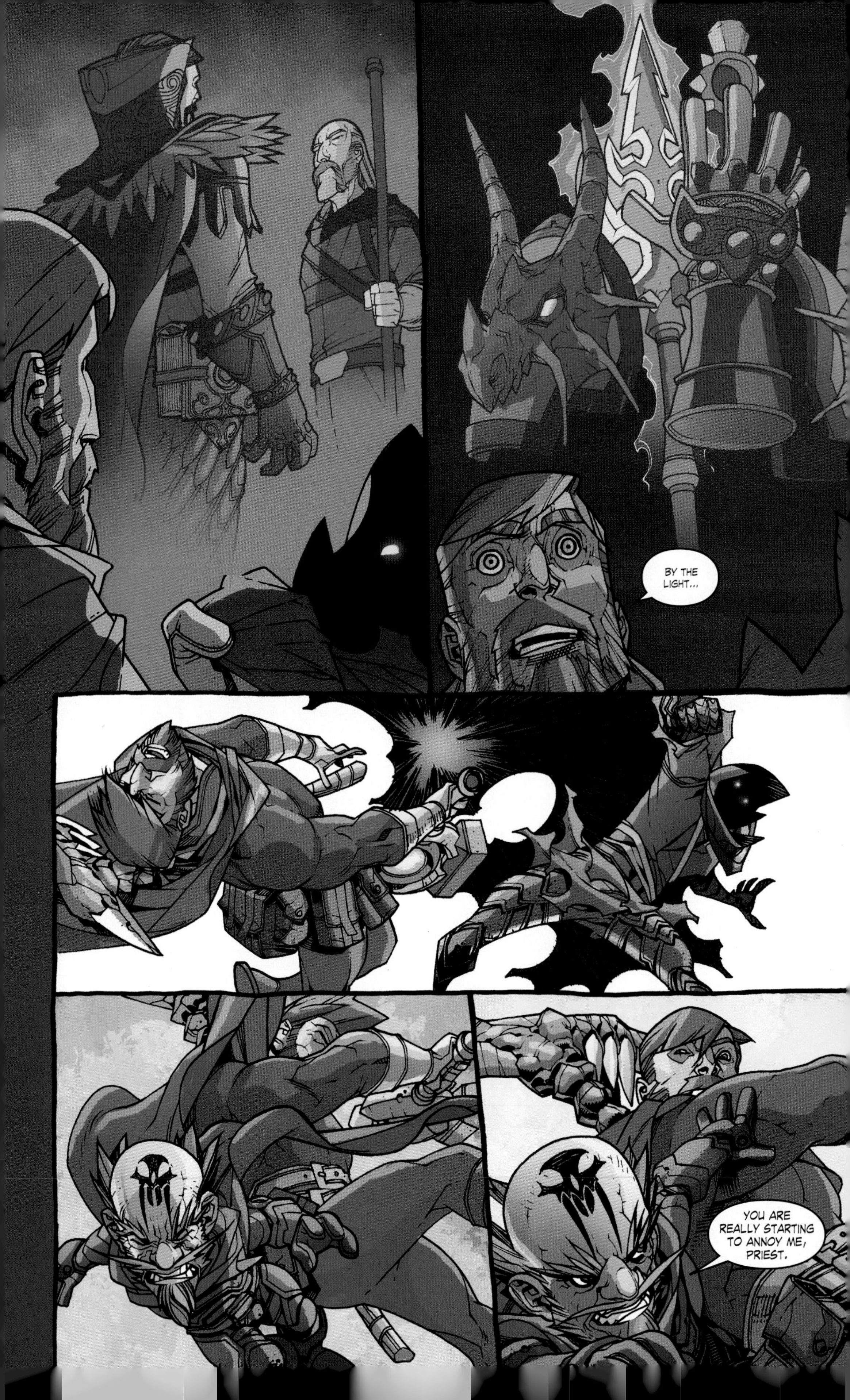
BY THE LIGHT...
YOU ARE REALLY STARTING TO ANNOY ME, PRIEST.

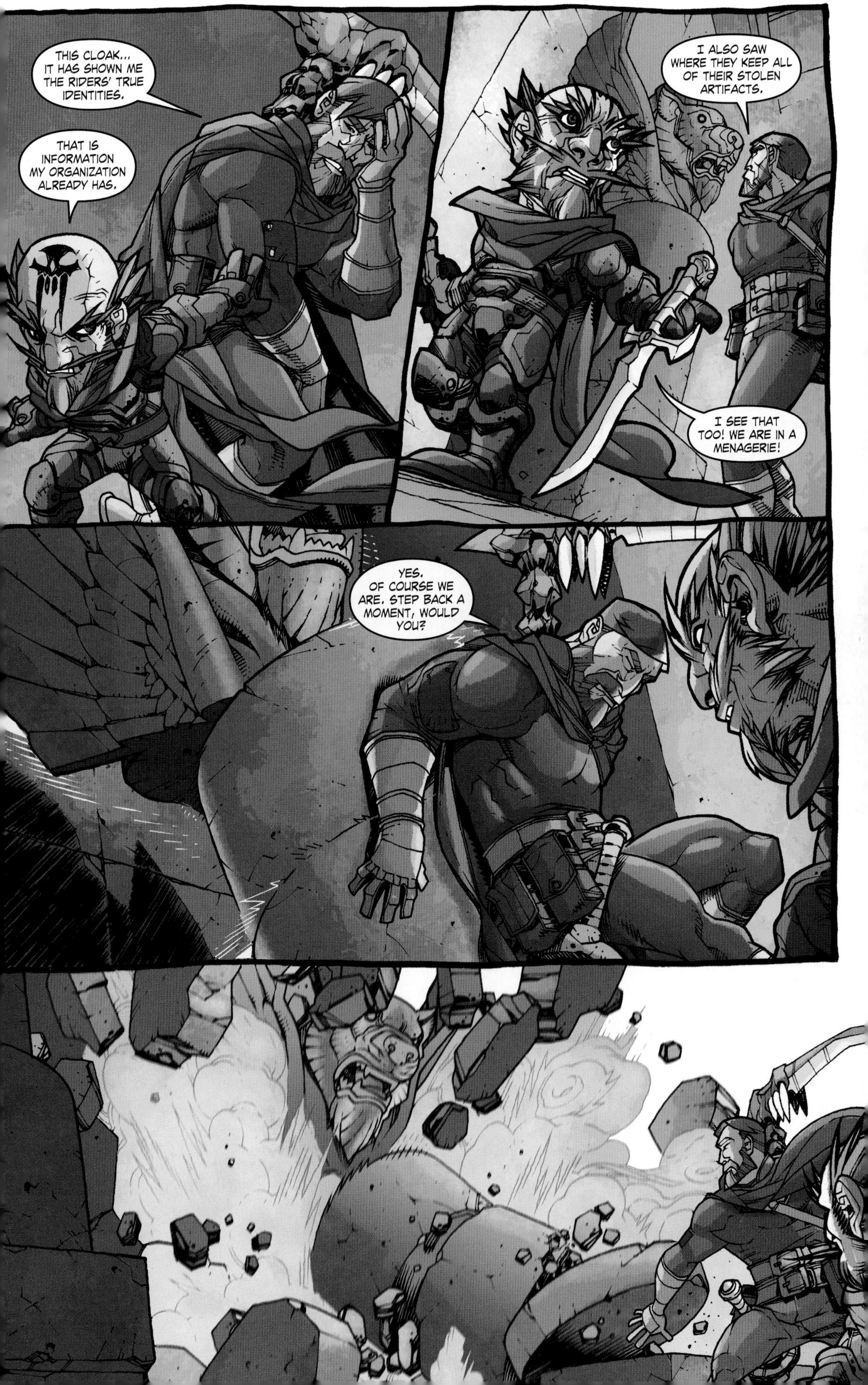
THIS CLOAK... IT HAS SHOWN ME THE RIDERS' TRUE IDENTITIES.
THAT IS INFORMATION MY ORGANIZATION ALREADY HAS.
I ALSO SAW WHERE THEY KEEP ALL OF THEIR STOLEN ARTIFACTS.
I SEE THAT TOO! WE ARE IN A MENAGERIE!
YES. OF COURSE WE ARE. STEP BACK A MOMENT, WOULD YOU?

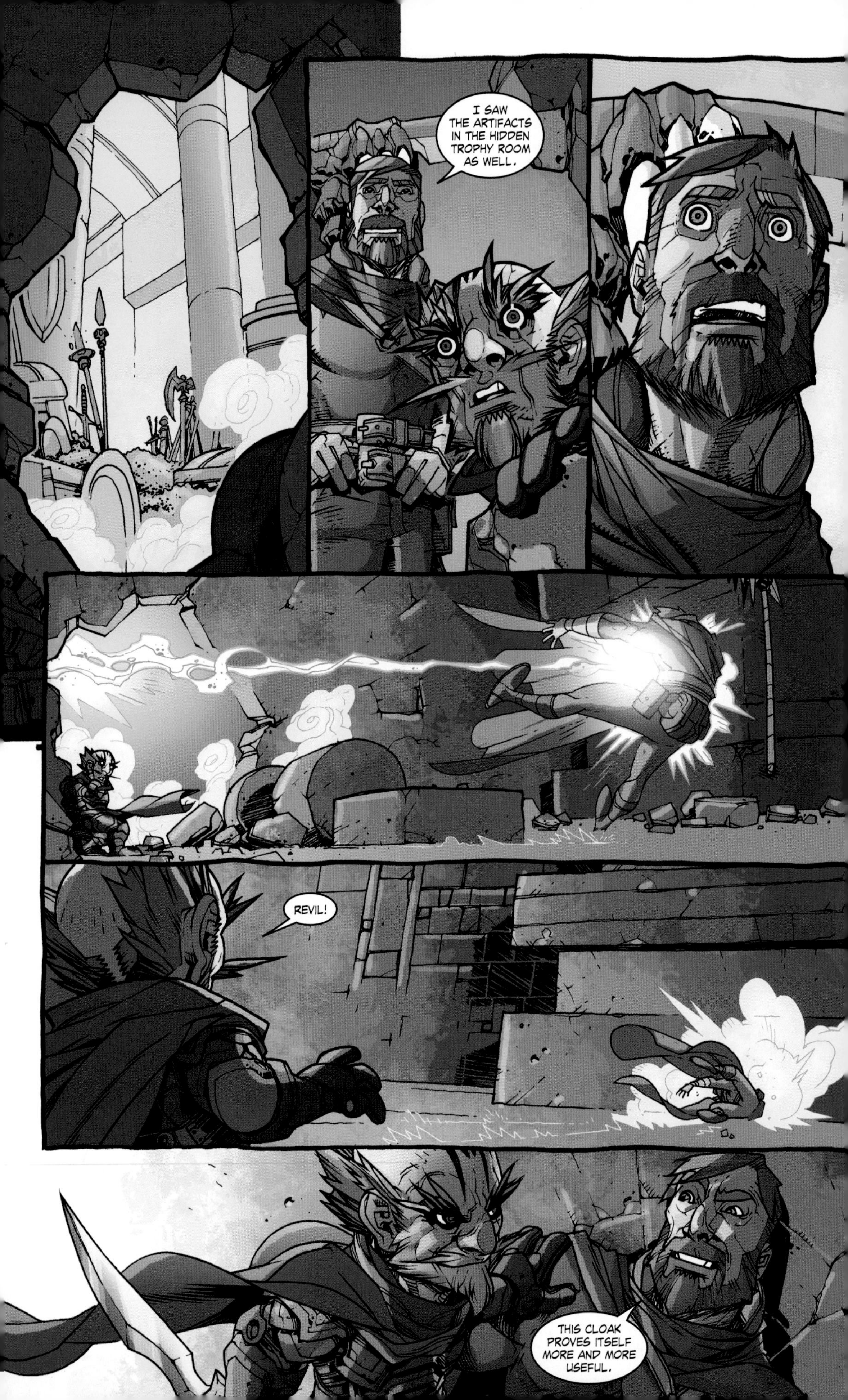
I SAW THE ARTIFACTS IN THE HIDDEN TROPHY ROOM AS WELL.
REVIL!
THIS CLOAK PROVES ITSELF MORE AND MORE USEFUL.

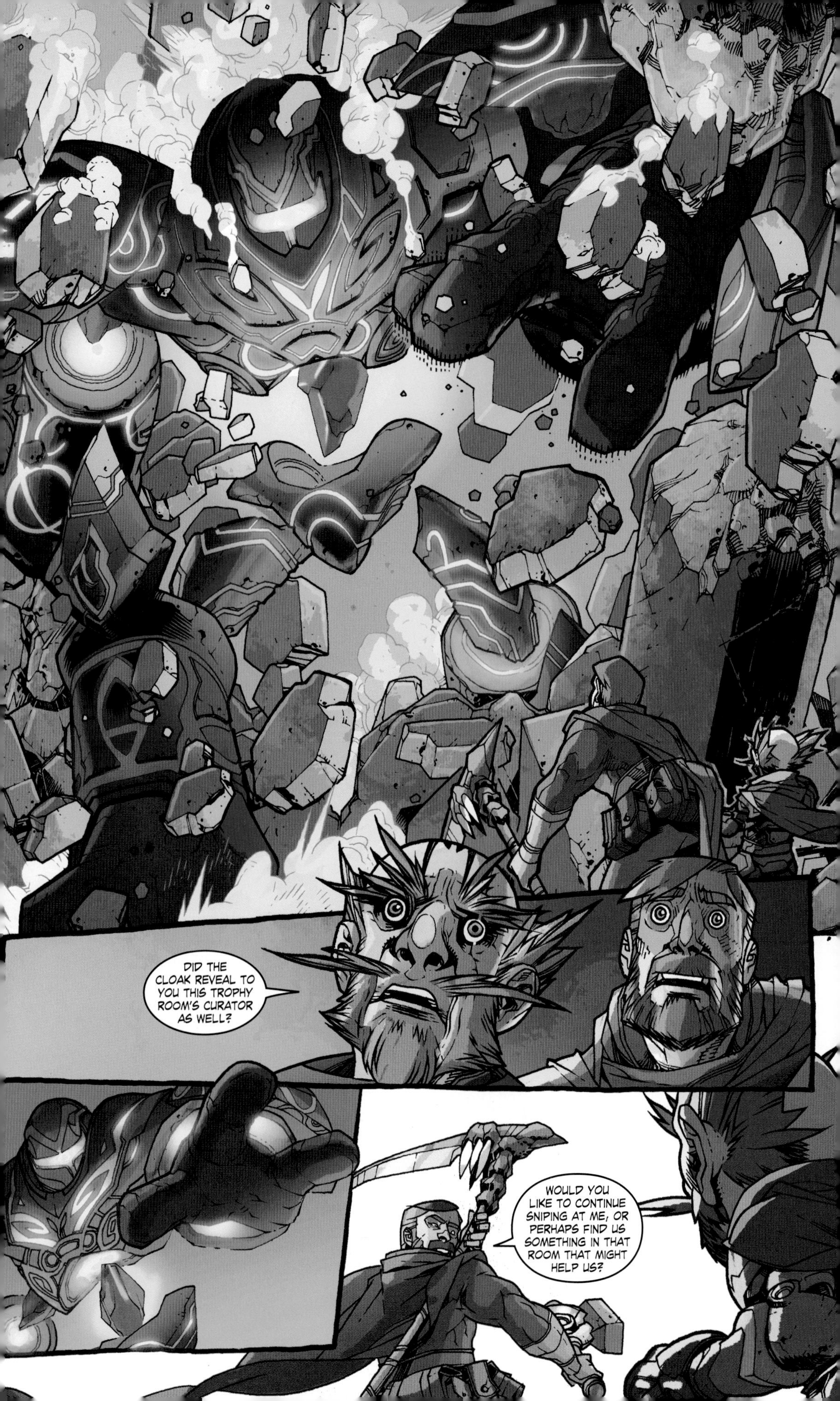
DID THE CLOAK REVEAL TO YOU THIS TROPHY ROOM'S CURATOR AS WELL?
WOULD YOU LIKE TO CONTINUE SNIPING AT ME, OR PERHAPS FIND US SOMETHING IN THAT ROOM THAT MIGHT HELP US?

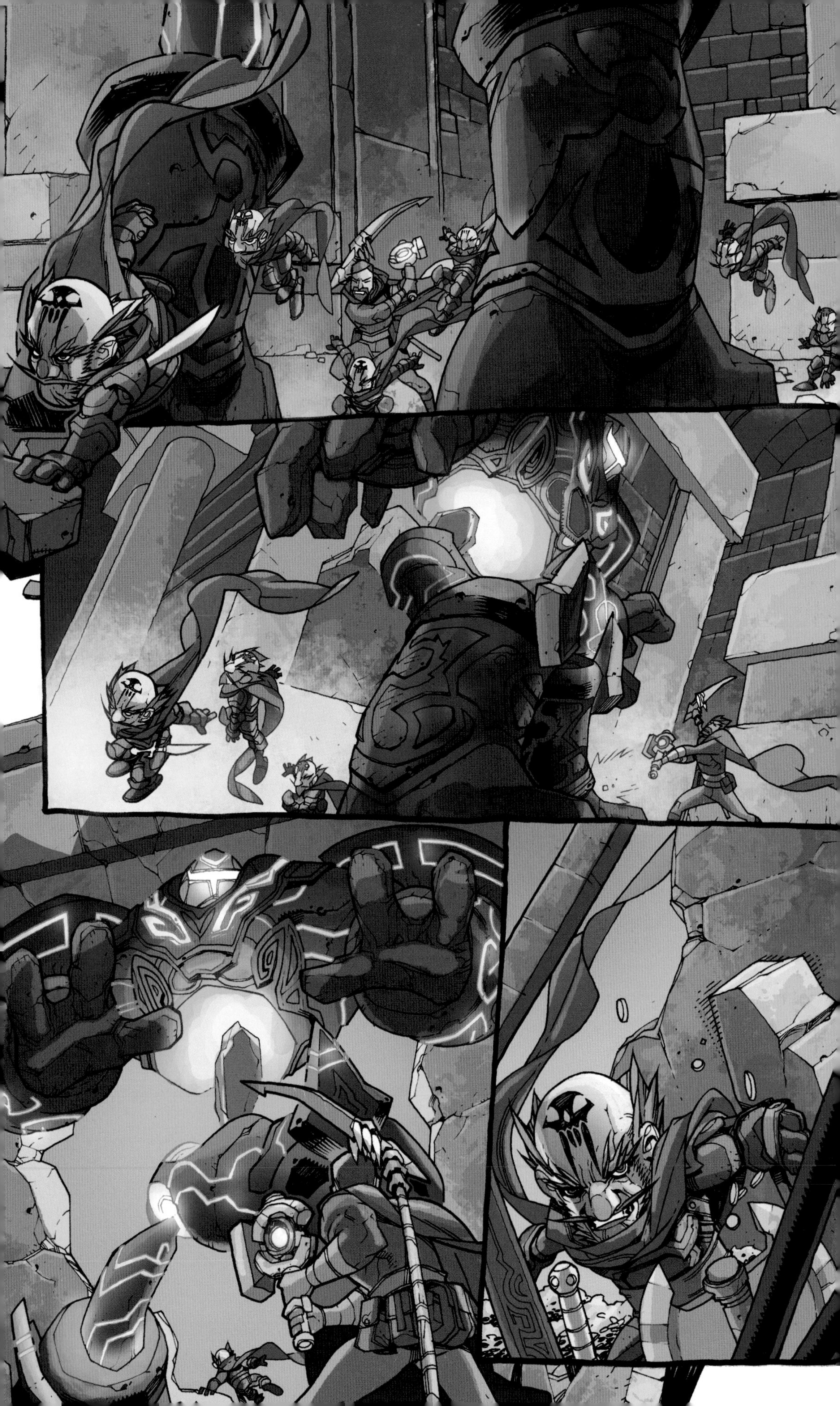

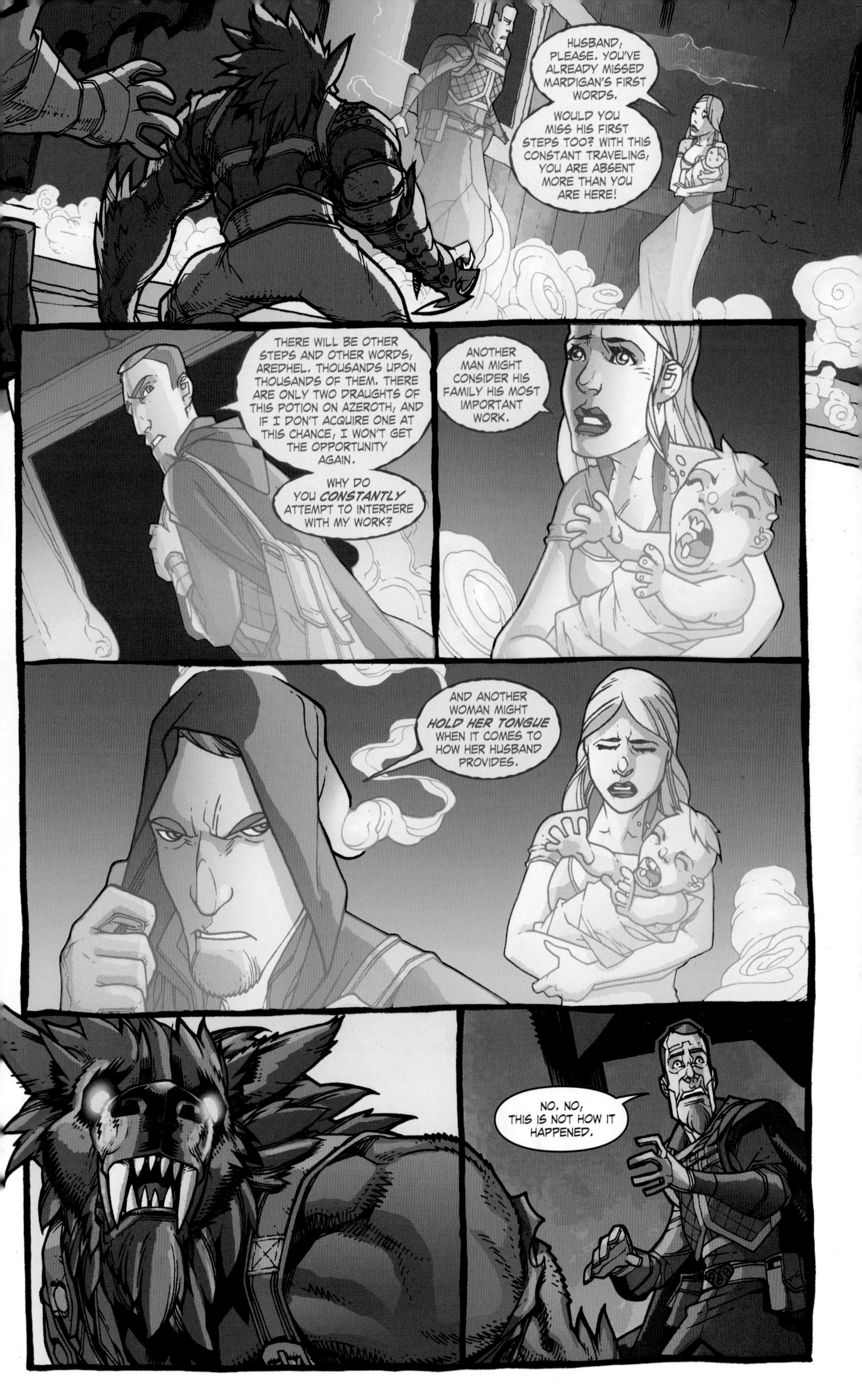
HUSBAND, PLEASE. YOU'VE ALREADY MISSED MARDIGAN'S FIRST WORDS.
WOULD YOU MISS HIS FIRST STEPS TOO? WITH THIS CONSTANT TRAVELING, YOU ARE ABSENT MORE THAN YOU ARE HERE!
THERE WILL BE OTHER STEPS AND OTHER WORDS, AREDHEL. THOUSANDS UPON THOUSANDS OF THEM. THERE ARE ONLY TWO DRAUGHTS OF THIS POTION ON AZEROTH, AND IF I DON'T ACQUIRE ONE AT THIS CHANCE, I WON'T GET THE OPPORTUNITY AGAIN.
WHY DO YOU CONSTANTLY ATTEMPT TO INTERFERE WITH MY WORK?
ANOTHER MAN MIGHT CONSIDER HIS FAMILY HIS MOST IMPORTANT WORK.
AND ANOTHER WOMAN MIGHT HOLD HER TONGUE WHEN IT COMES TO HOW HER HUSBAND PROVIDES.
NO. NO, THIS IS NOT HOW IT HAPPENED.

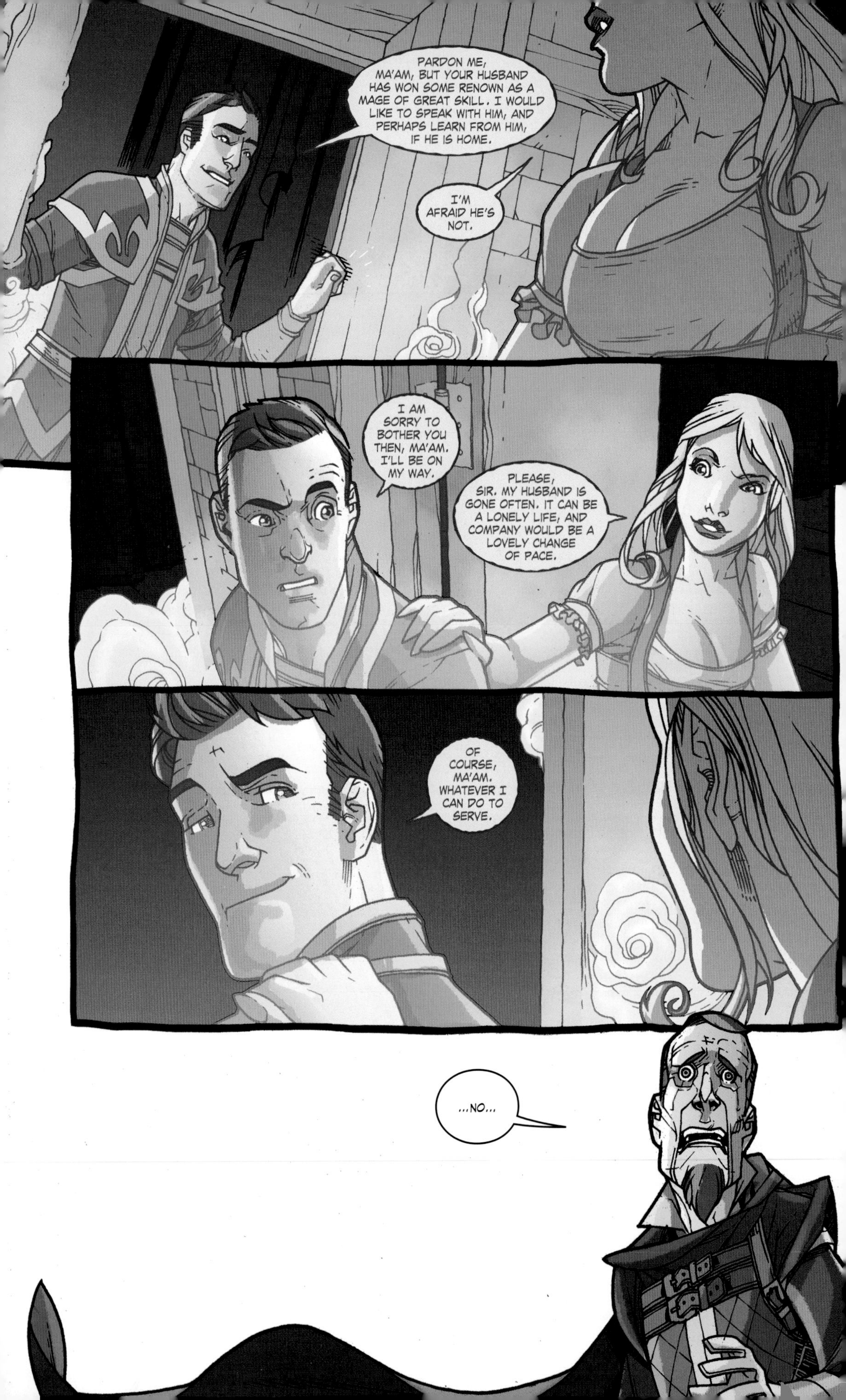
PARDON ME, MA'AM, BUT YOUR HUSBAND HAS WON SOME RENOWN AS A MAGE OF GREAT SKILL. I WOULD LIKE TO SPEAK WITH HIM, AND PERHAPS LEARN FROM HIM, IF HE IS HOME.
I'M AFRAID HE'S NOT.
I AM SORRY TO BOTHER YOU THEN, MA'AM. I'LL BE ON MY WAY.
PLEASE, SIR. MY HUSBAND IS GONE OFTEN. IT CAN BE A LONELY LIFE, AND COMPANY WOULD BE A LOVELY CHANGE OF PACE.
OF COURSE, MA'AM. WHATEVER I CAN DO TO SERVE.
...NO...

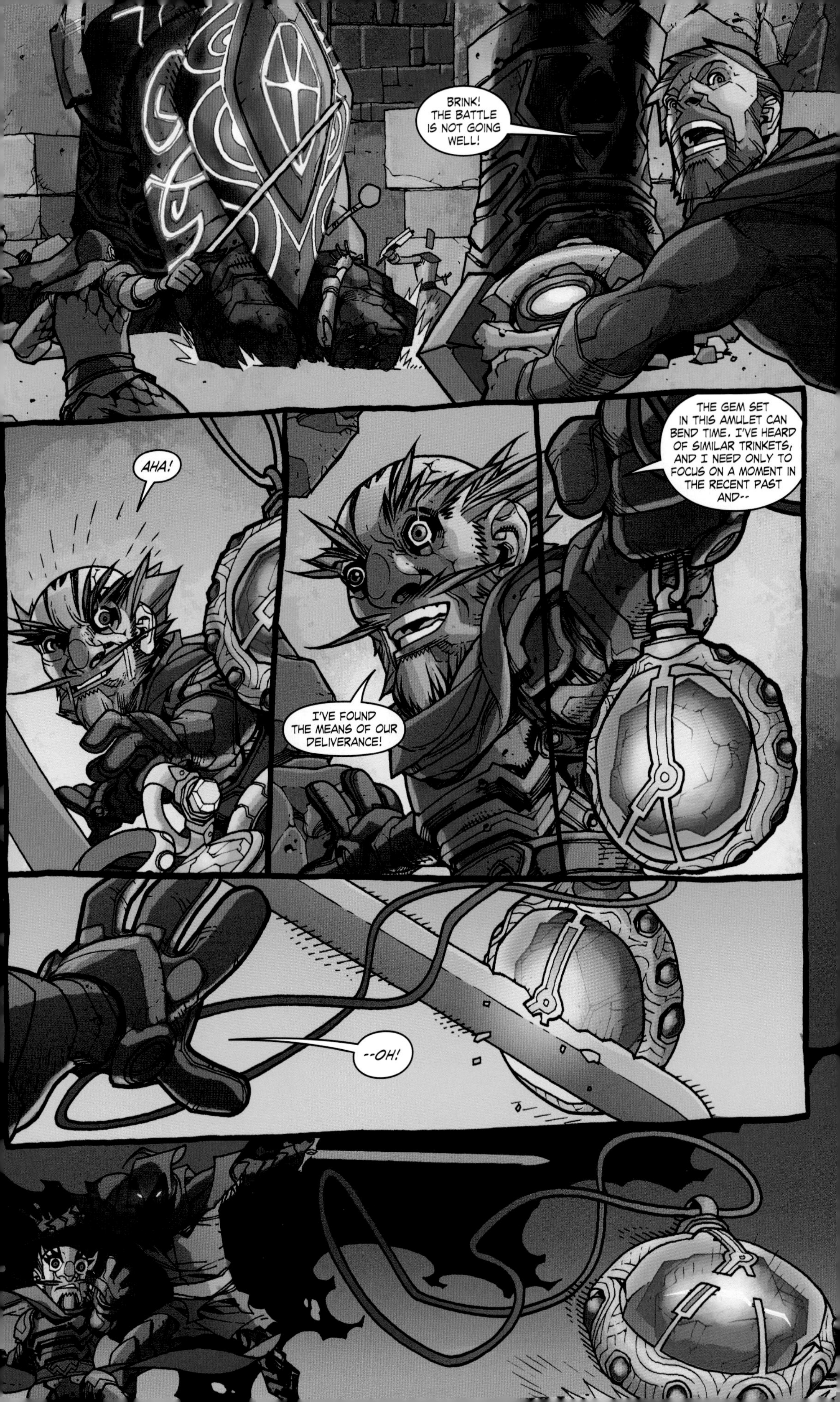
BRINK! THE BATTLE IS NOT GOING WELL!
AHA!
I'VE FOUND THE MEANS OF OUR DELIVERANCE!
THE GEM SET IN THIS AMULET CAN BEND TIME. I'VE HEARD OF SIMILAR TRINKETS, AND I NEED ONLY TO FOCUS ON A MOMENT IN THE RECENT PAST AND--
--OH!

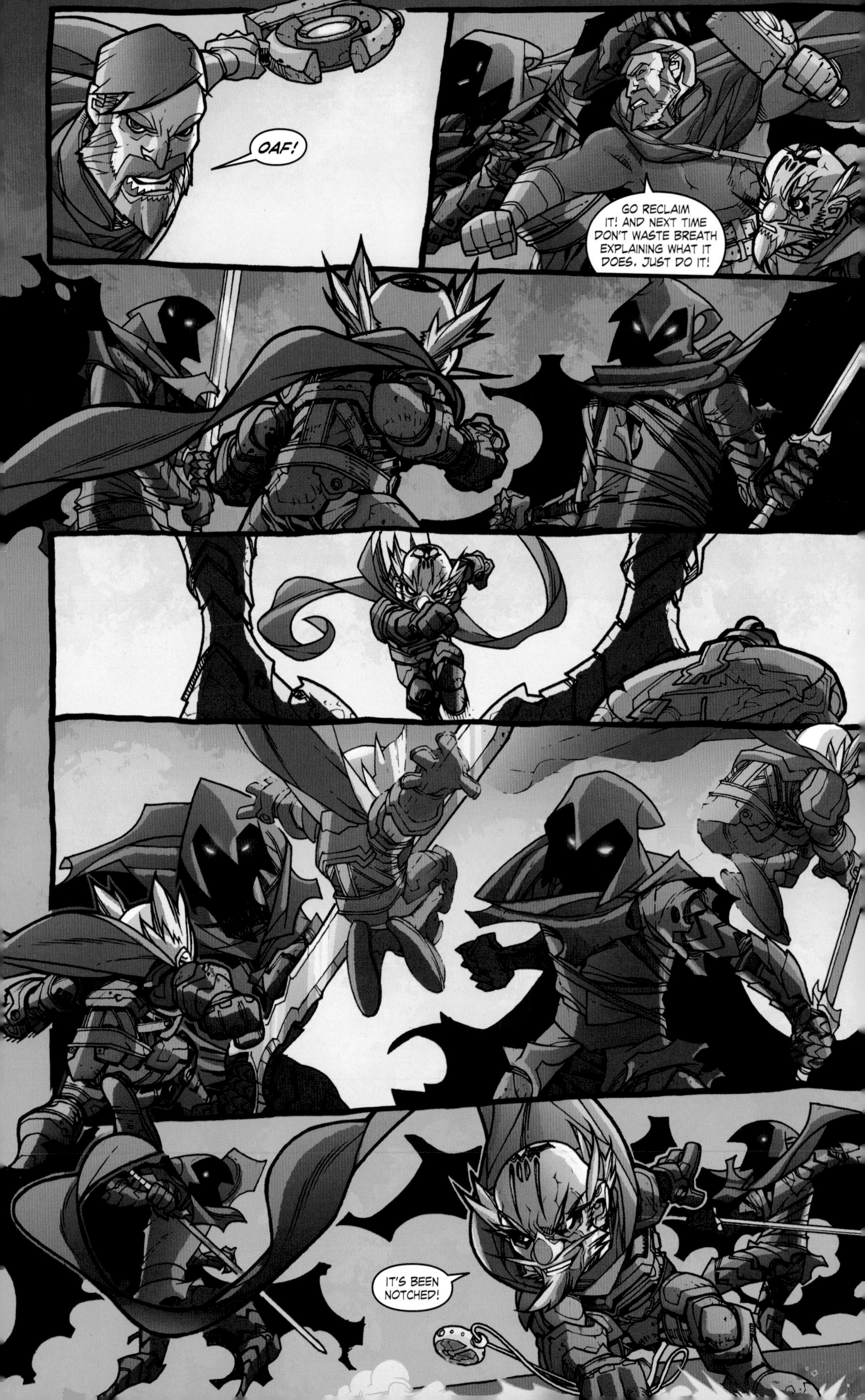
OAF!
GO RECLAIM IT! AND NEXT TIME DON'T WASTE BREATH EXPLAINING WHAT IT DOES. JUST DO IT!
IT'S BEEN NOTCHED!

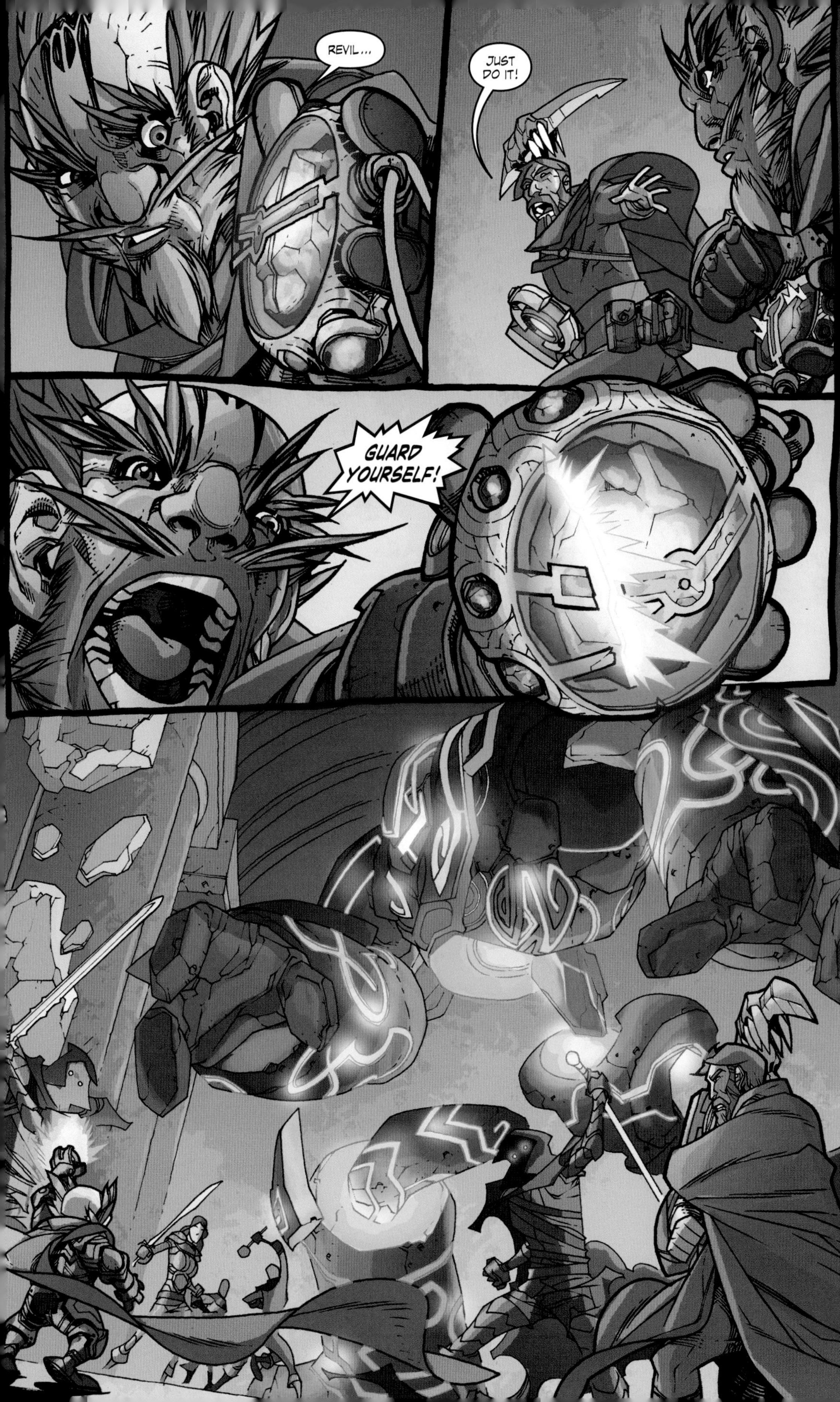
REVIL...
JUST DO IT!
GUARD YOURSELF!

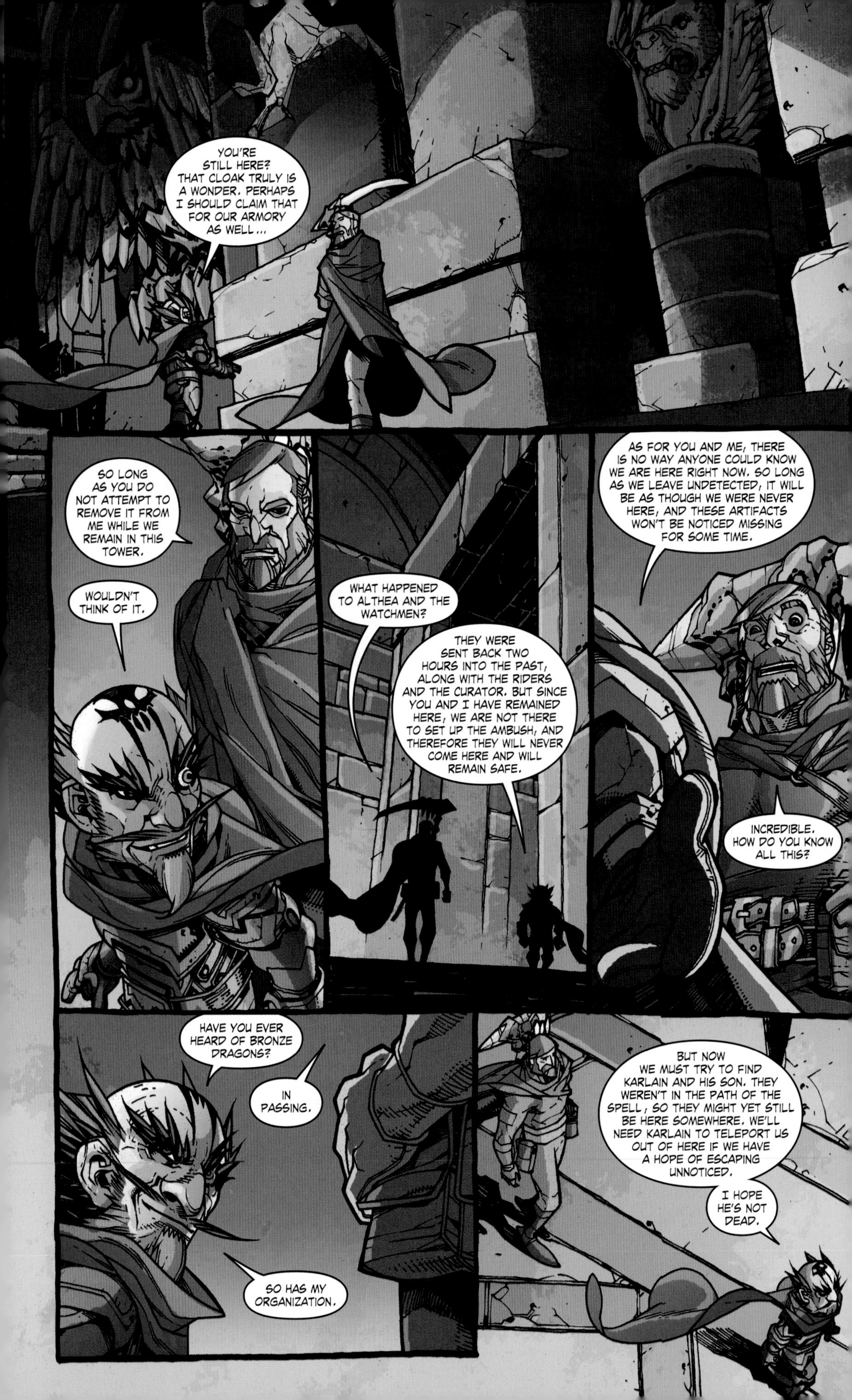
YOU'RE STILL HERE? THAT CLOAK TRULY IS A WONDER. PERHAPS I SHOULD CLAIM THAT FOR OUR ARMORY AS WELL...
SO LONG AS YOU DO NOT ATTEMPT TO REMOVE IT FROM ME WHILE WE REMAIN IN THIS TOWER.
WOULDN'T THINK OF IT.
WHAT HAPPENED TO ALTHEA AND THE WATCHMEN?
THEY WERE SENT BACK TWO HOURS INTO THE PAST, ALONG WITH THE RIDERS AND THE CURATOR. BUT SINCE YOU AND I HAVE REMAINED HERE, WE ARE NOT THERE TO SET UP THE AMBUSH, AND THEREFORE THEY WILL NEVER COME HERE AND WILL REMAIN SAFE.
AS FOR YOU AND ME, THERE IS NO WAY ANYONE COULD KNOW WE ARE HERE RIGHT NOW. SO LONG AS WE LEAVE UNDETECTED, IT WILL BE AS THOUGH WE WERE NEVER HERE, AND THESE ARTIFACTS WON'T BE NOTICED MISSING FOR SOME TIME.
INCREDIBLE. HOW DO YOU KNOW ALL THIS?
HAVE YOU EVER HEARD OF BRONZE DRAGONS?
IN PASSING.
SO HAS MY ORGANIZATION.
BUT NOW WE MUST TRY TO FIND KARLAIN AND HIS SON. THEY WEREN'T IN THE PATH OF THE SPELL, SO THEY MIGHT YET STILL BE HERE SOMEWHERE. WE'LL NEED KARLAIN TO TELEPORT US OUT OF HERE IF WE HAVE A HOPE OF ESCAPING UNNOTICED.
I HOPE HE'S NOT DEAD.

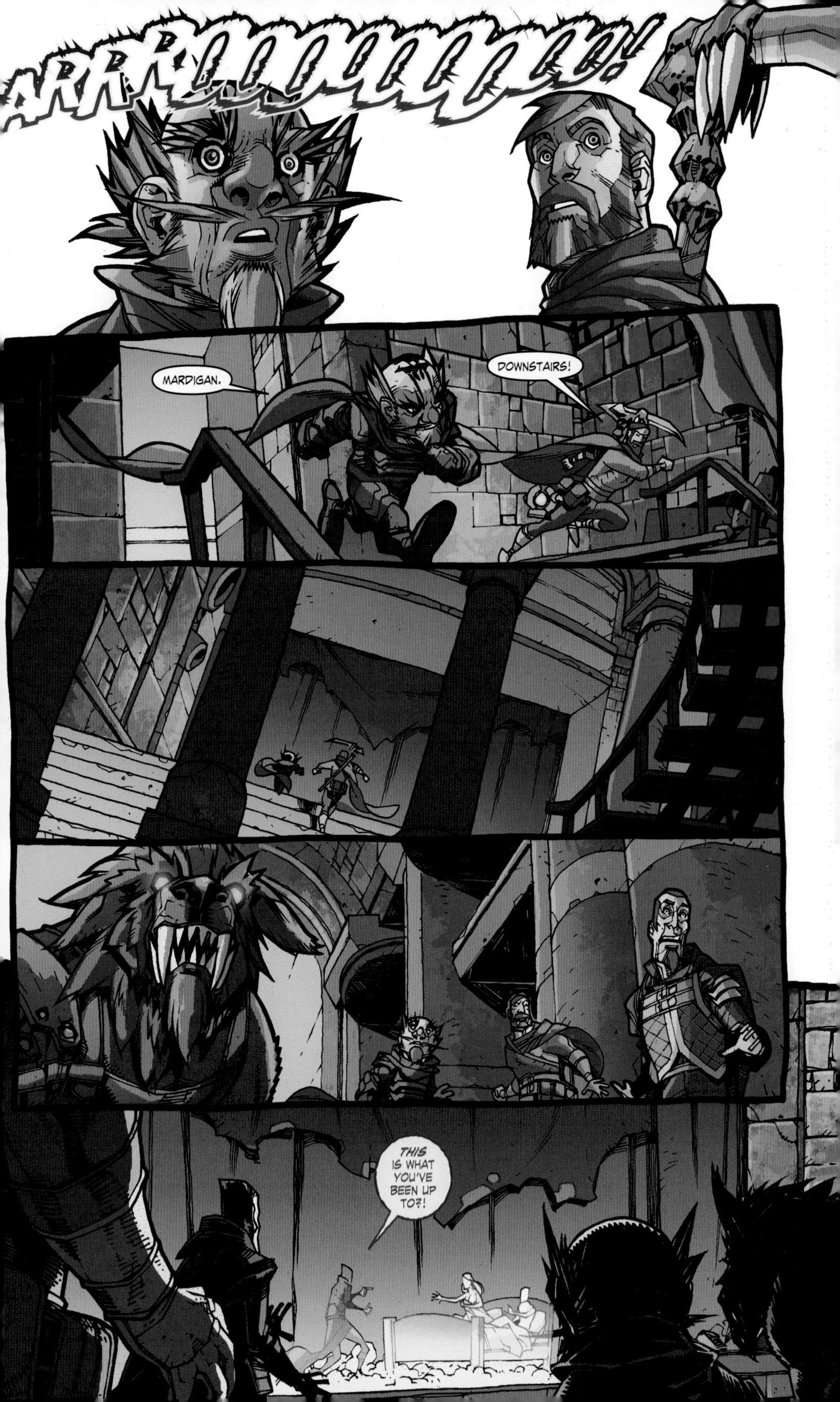

ARRROOOOOOOO!
MARDIGAN.
DOWNSTAIRS!
THIS IS WHAT YOU'VE BEEN UP TO?!

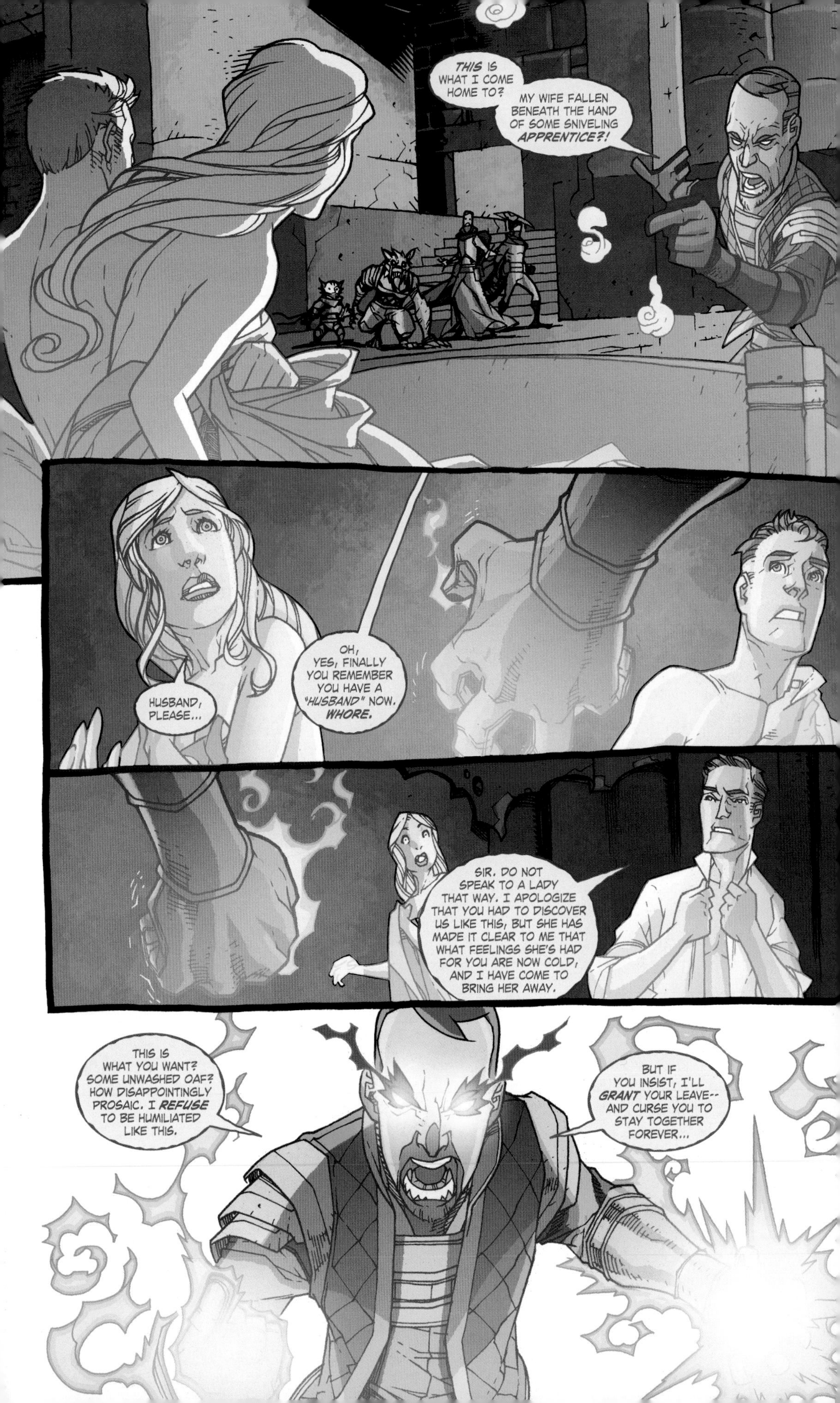

THIS IS WHAT I COME HOME TO?
MY WIFE FALLEN BENEATH THE HAND OF SOME SNIVELING APPRENTICE?!
HUSBAND, PLEASE...
OH, YES, FINALLY YOU REMEMBER YOU HAVE A "HUSBAND" NOW. WHORE.
SIR. DO NOT SPEAK TO A LADY THAT WAY. I APOLOGIZE THAT YOU HAD TO DISCOVER US LIKE THIS, BUT SHE HAS MADE IT CLEAR TO ME THAT WHAT FEELINGS SHE'S HAD FOR YOU ARE NOW COLD, AND I HAVE COME TO BRING HER AWAY.
THIS IS WHAT YOU WANT? SOME UNWASHED OAF? HOW DISAPPOINTINGLY PROSAIC. I REFUSE TO BE HUMILIATED LIKE THIS.
BUT IF YOU INSIST, I'LL GRANT YOUR LEAVE-- AND CURSE YOU TO STAY TOGETHER FOREVER...

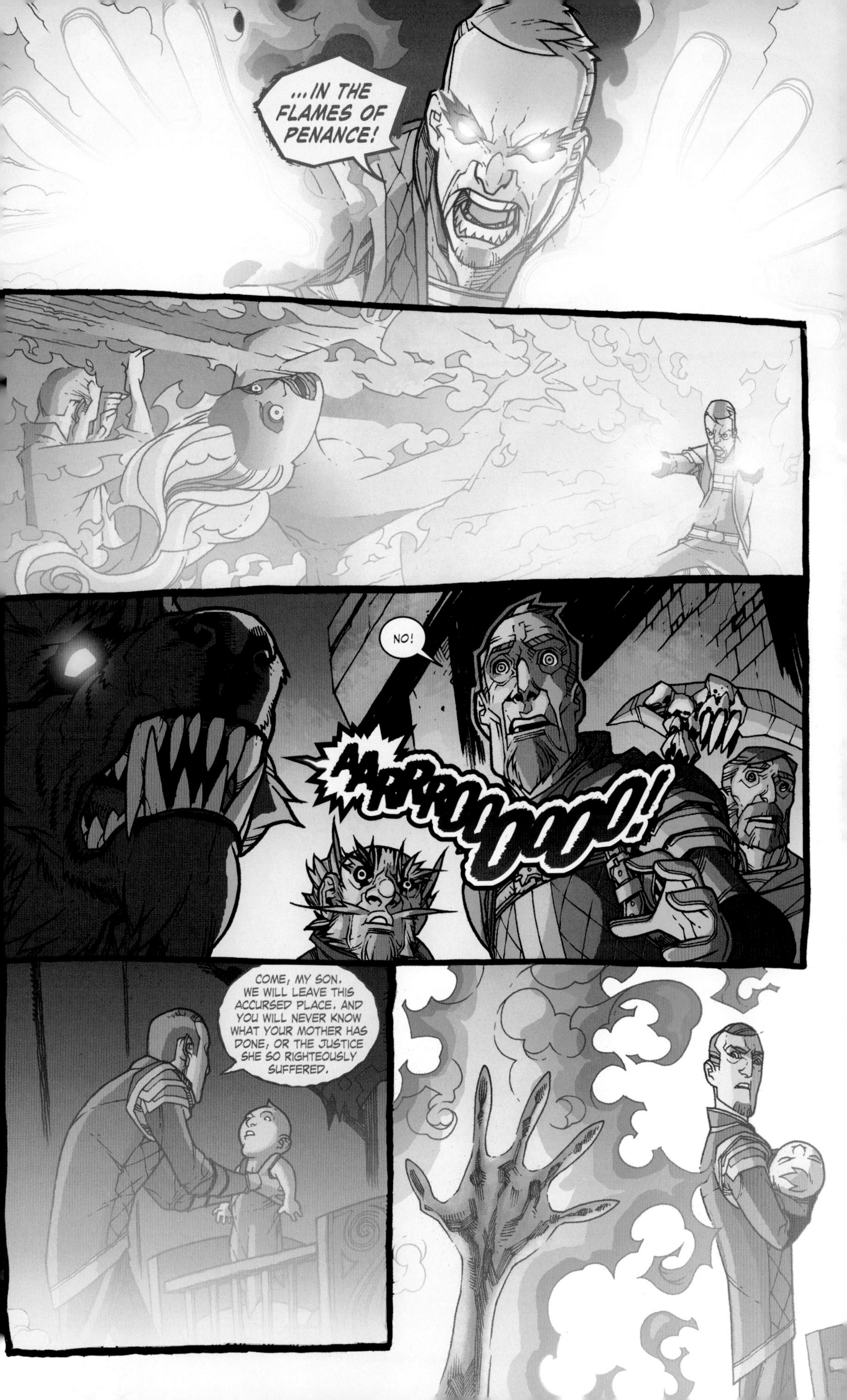
...IN THE FLAMES OF PENANCE!
NO!
AARRROOOOOO!
COME, MY SON. WE WILL LEAVE THIS ACCURSED PLACE. AND YOU WILL NEVER KNOW WHAT YOUR MOTHER HAS DONE, OR THE JUSTICE SHE SO RIGHTEOUSLY SUFFERED.

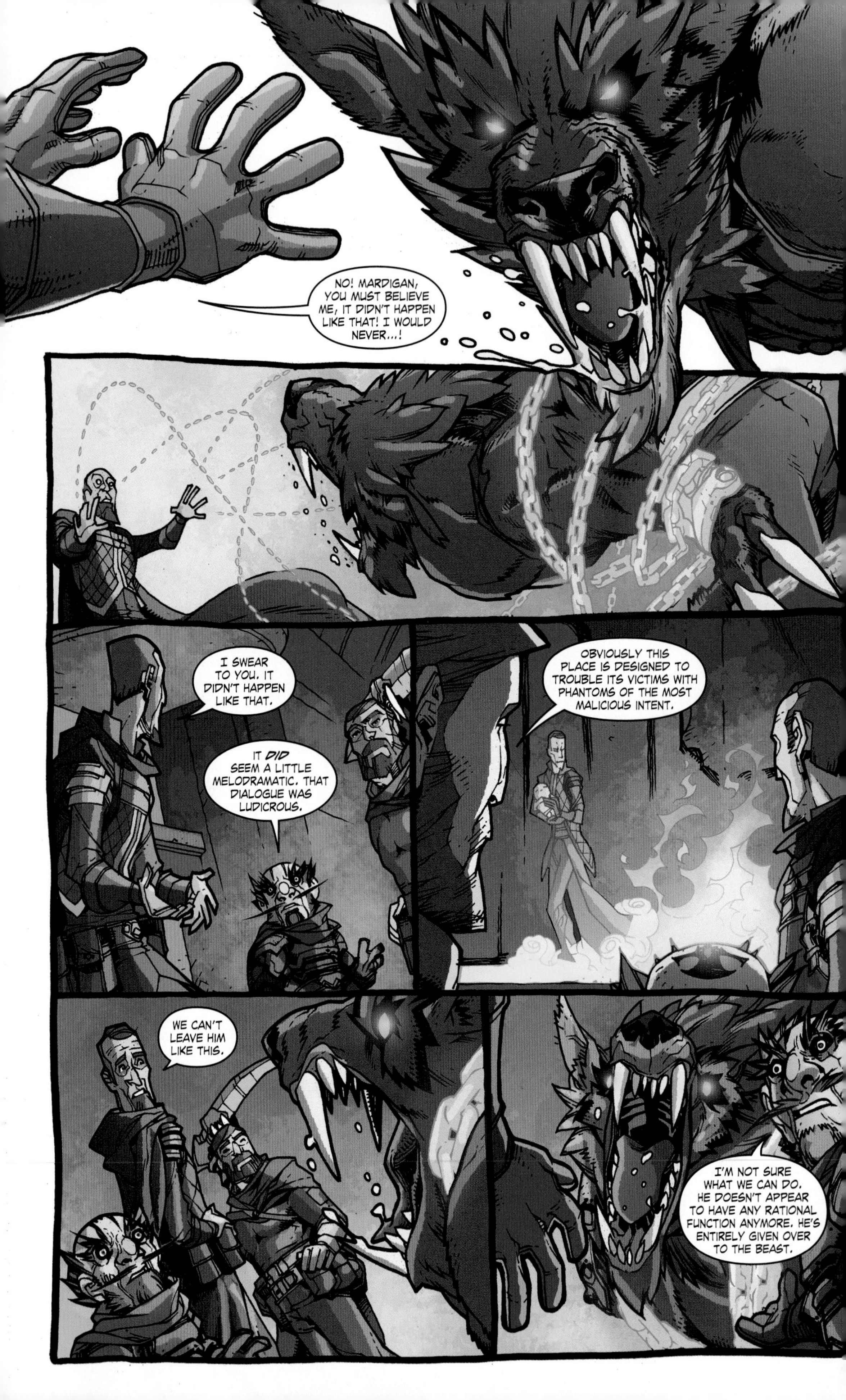

NO! MARDIGAN, YOU MUST BELIEVE ME, IT DIDN'T HAPPEN LIKE THAT! I WOULD NEVER...!
I SWEAR TO YOU. IT DIDN'T HAPPEN LIKE THAT.
IT *DID* SEEM A LITTLE MELODRAMATIC. THAT DIALOGUE WAS LUDICROUS.
OBVIOUSLY THIS PLACE IS DESIGNED TO TROUBLE ITS VICTIMS WITH PHANTOMS OF THE MOST MALICIOUS INTENT.
WE CAN'T LEAVE HIM LIKE THIS.
I'M NOT SURE WHAT WE CAN DO. HE DOESN'T APPEAR TO HAVE ANY RATIONAL FUNCTION ANYMORE. HE'S ENTIRELY GIVEN OVER TO THE BEAST.

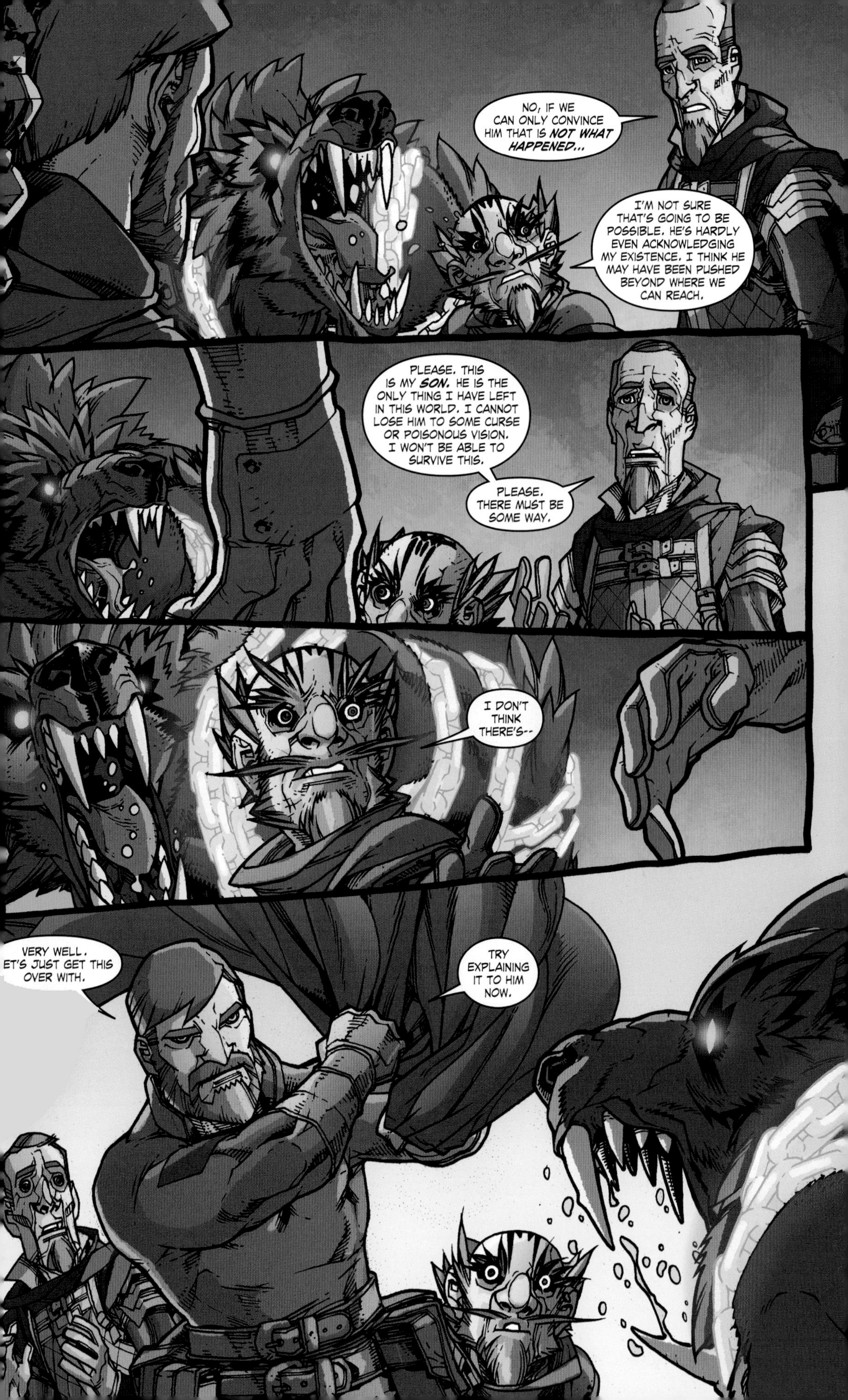
NO, IF WE CAN ONLY CONVINCE HIM THAT IS NOT WHAT HAPPENED...
I'M NOT SURE THAT'S GOING TO BE POSSIBLE. HE'S HARDLY EVEN ACKNOWLEDGING MY EXISTENCE. I THINK HE MAY HAVE BEEN PUSHED BEYOND WHERE WE CAN REACH.
PLEASE. THIS IS MY SON. HE IS THE ONLY THING I HAVE LEFT IN THIS WORLD. I CANNOT LOSE HIM TO SOME CURSE OR POISONOUS VISION. I WON'T BE ABLE TO SURVIVE THIS.
PLEASE. THERE MUST BE SOME WAY.
I DON'T THINK THERE'S--
VERY WELL. ET'S JUST GET THIS OVER WITH.
TRY EXPLAINING IT TO HIM NOW.

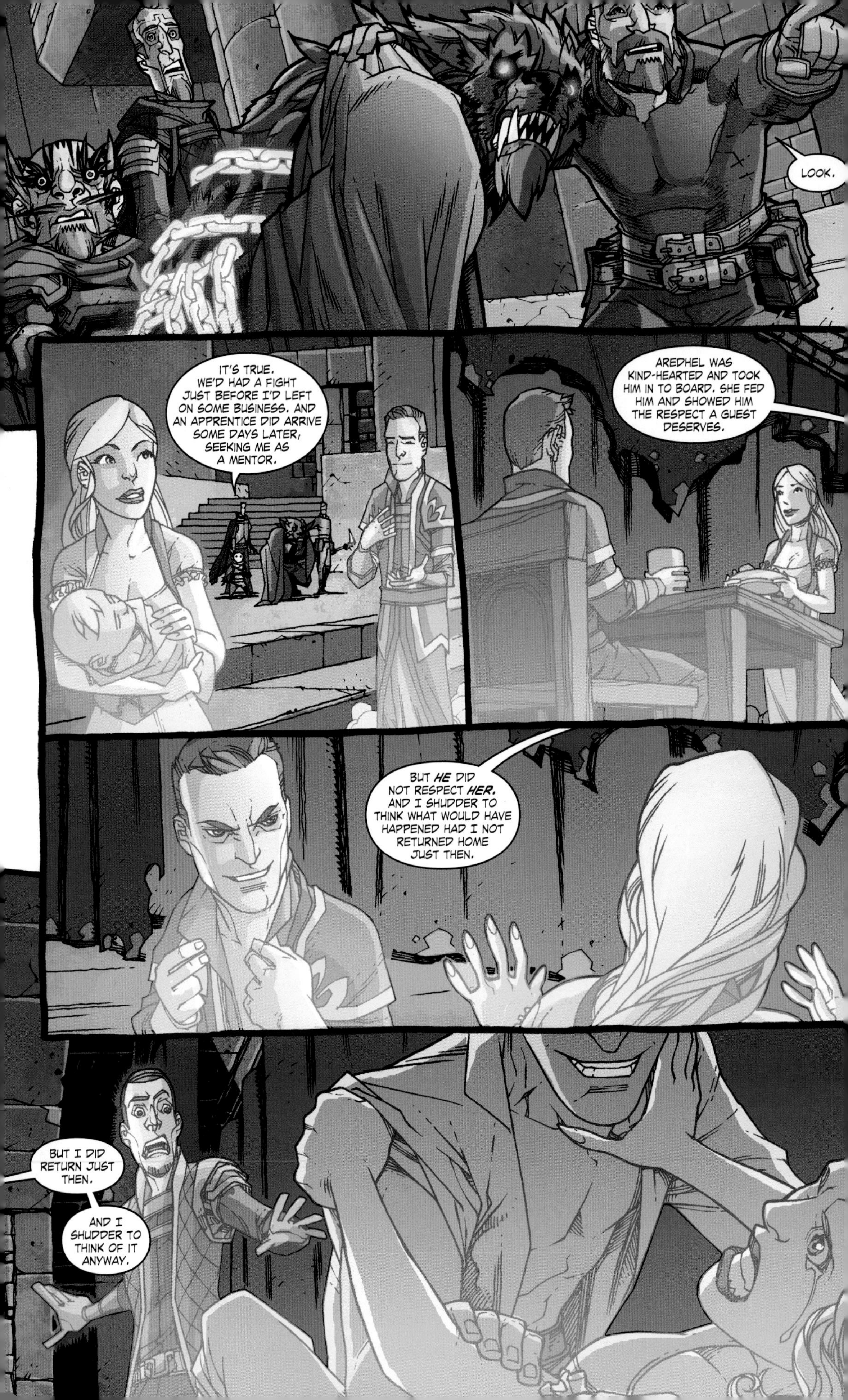
LOOK.
IT'S TRUE. WE'D HAD A FIGHT JUST BEFORE I'D LEFT ON SOME BUSINESS. AND AN APPRENTICE DID ARRIVE SOME DAYS LATER, SEEKING ME AS A MENTOR.
AREDHEL WAS KIND-HEARTED AND TOOK HIM IN TO BOARD. SHE FED HIM AND SHOWED HIM THE RESPECT A GUEST DESERVES.
BUT HE DID NOT RESPECT HER. AND I SHUDDER TO THINK WHAT WOULD HAVE HAPPENED HAD I NOT RETURNED HOME JUST THEN.
BUT I DID RETURN JUST THEN.
AND I SHUDDER TO THINK OF IT ANYWAY.

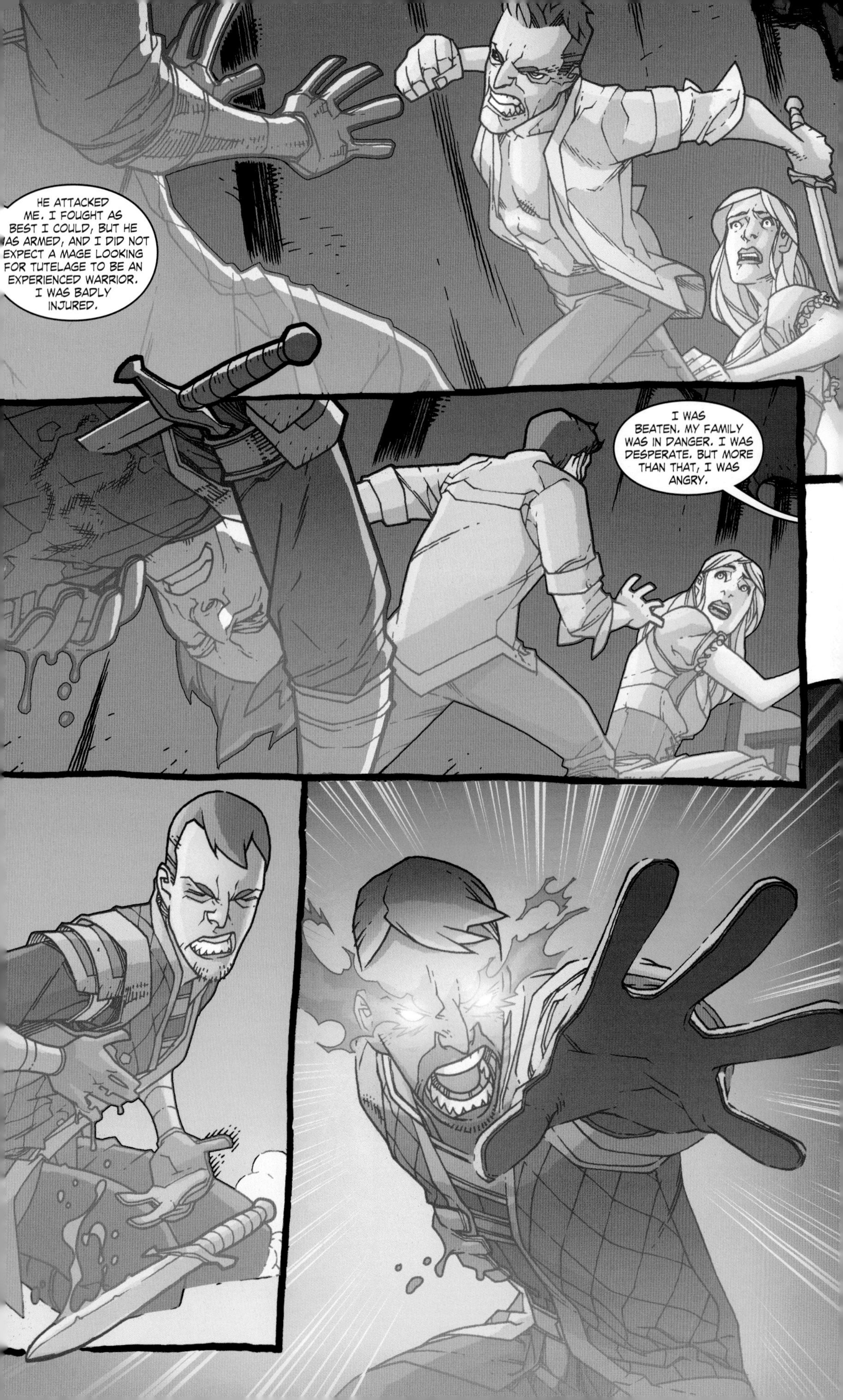
HE ATTACKED ME. I FOUGHT AS BEST I COULD, BUT HE WAS ARMED, AND I DID NOT EXPECT A MAGE LOOKING FOR TUTELAGE TO BE AN EXPERIENCED WARRIOR. I WAS BADLY INJURED.
I WAS BEATEN. MY FAMILY WAS IN DANGER. I WAS DESPERATE. BUT MORE THAN THAT, I WAS ANGRY.

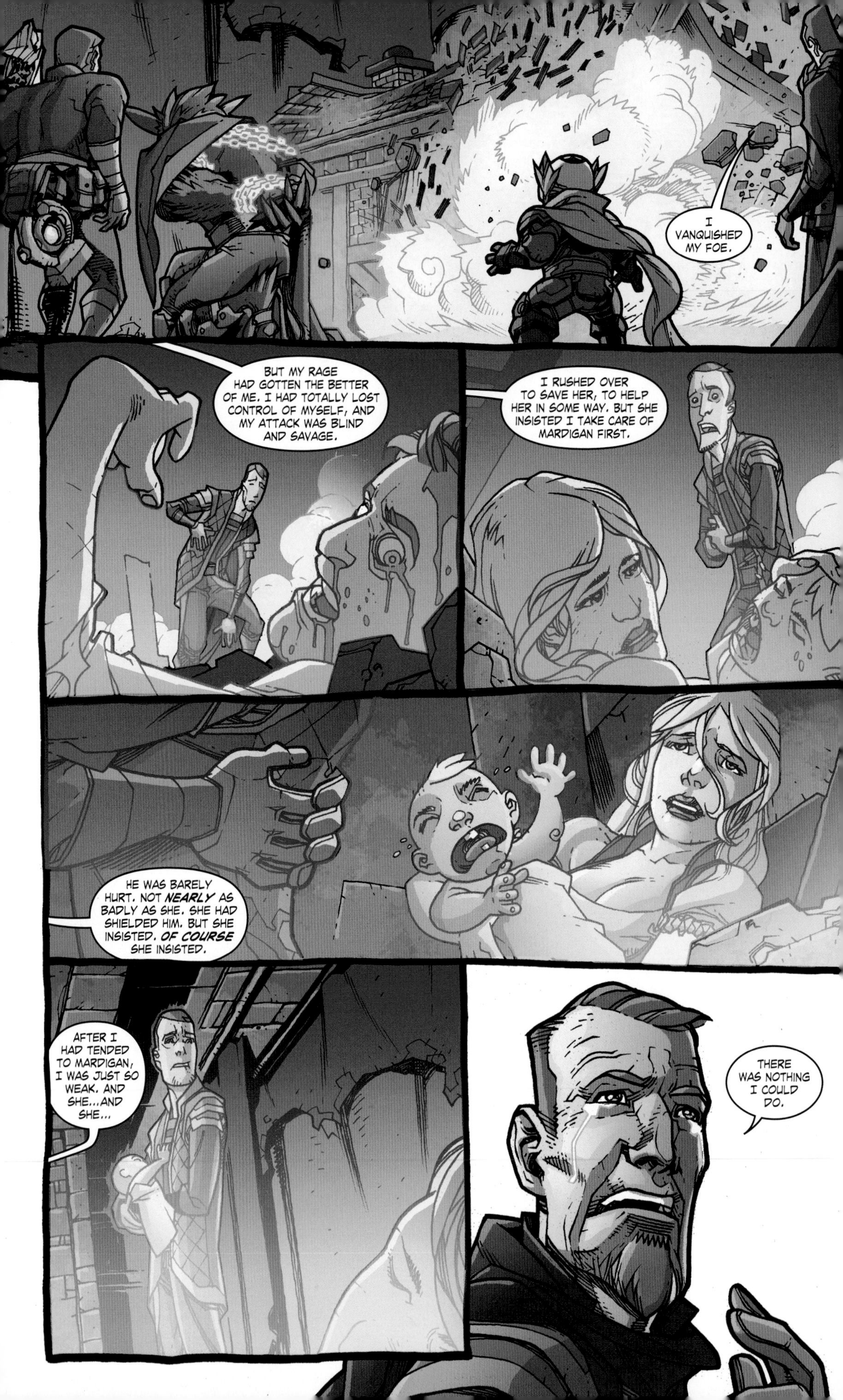
I VANQUISHED MY FOE.
BUT MY RAGE HAD GOTTEN THE BETTER OF ME. I HAD TOTALLY LOST CONTROL OF MYSELF, AND MY ATTACK WAS BLIND AND SAVAGE.
I RUSHED OVER TO SAVE HER, TO HELP HER IN SOME WAY. BUT SHE INSISTED I TAKE CARE OF MARDIGAN FIRST.
HE WAS BARELY HURT. NOT ***NEARLY*** AS BADLY AS SHE. SHE HAD SHIELDED HIM. BUT SHE INSISTED. ***OF COURSE*** SHE INSISTED.
AFTER I HAD TENDED TO MARDIGAN, I WAS JUST SO WEAK. AND SHE...AND SHE...
THERE WAS NOTHING I COULD DO.

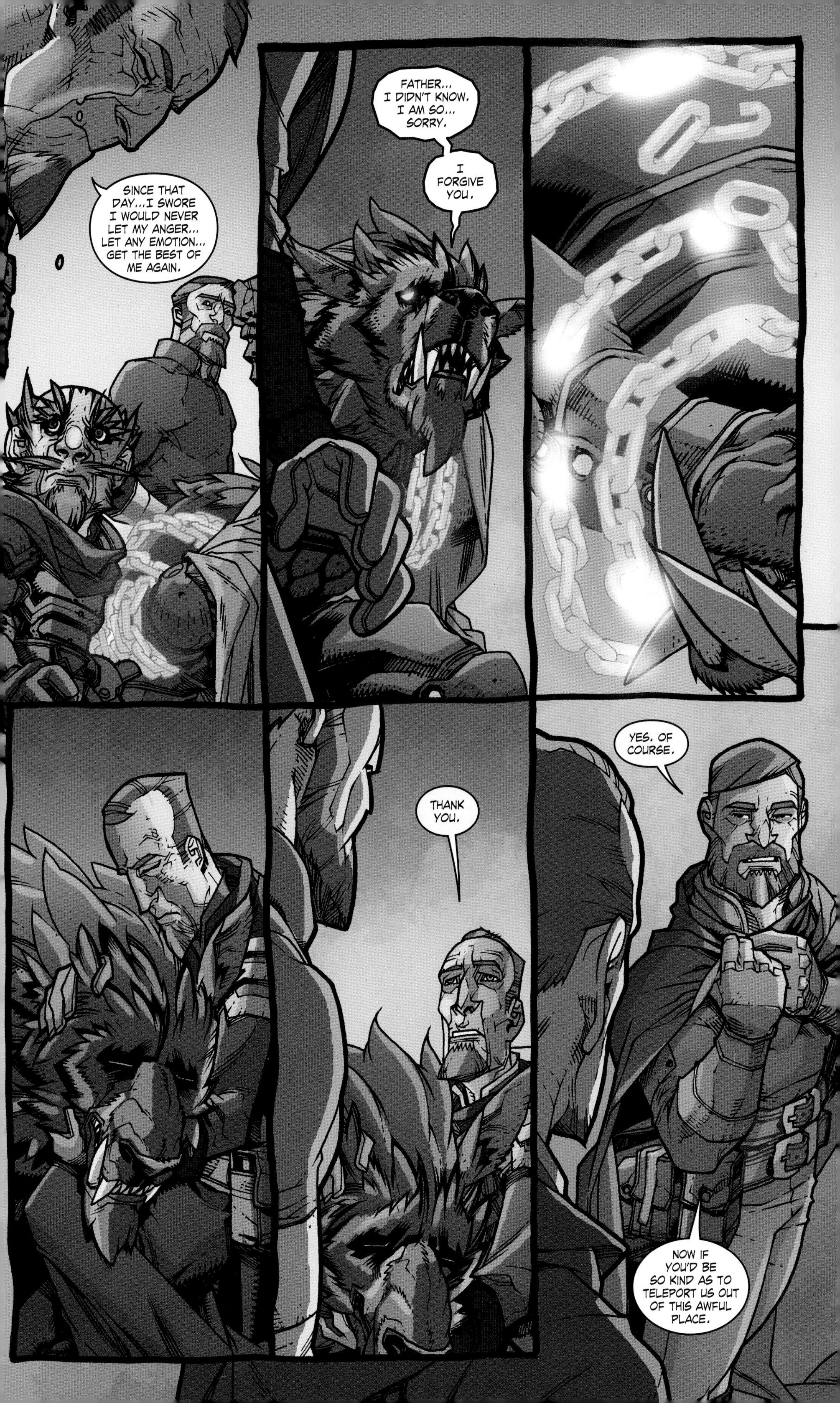

SINCE THAT DAY...I SWORE I WOULD NEVER LET MY ANGER... LET ANY EMOTION... GET THE BEST OF ME AGAIN.
FATHER... I DIDN'T KNOW. I AM SO... SORRY.
I FORGIVE YOU.
THANK YOU.
YES. OF COURSE.
NOW IF YOU'D BE SO KIND AS TO TELEPORT US OUT OF THIS AWFUL PLACE.

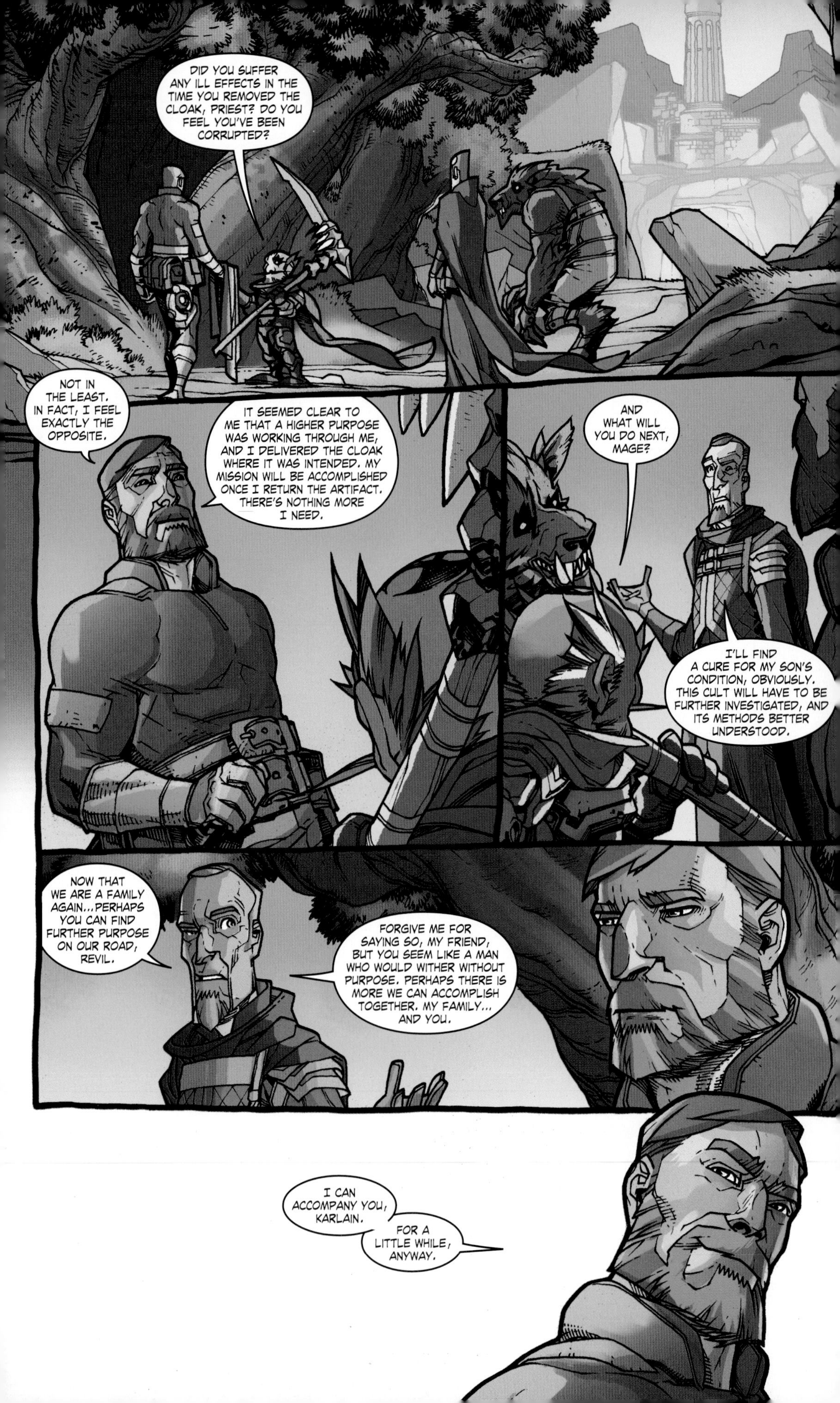
DID YOU SUFFER ANY ILL EFFECTS IN THE TIME YOU REMOVED THE CLOAK, PRIEST? DO YOU FEEL YOU'VE BEEN CORRUPTED?
NOT IN THE LEAST. IN FACT, I FEEL EXACTLY THE OPPOSITE.
IT SEEMED CLEAR TO ME THAT A HIGHER PURPOSE WAS WORKING THROUGH ME, AND I DELIVERED THE CLOAK WHERE IT WAS INTENDED. MY MISSION WILL BE ACCOMPLISHED ONCE I RETURN THE ARTIFACT. THERE'S NOTHING MORE I NEED.
AND WHAT WILL YOU DO NEXT, MAGE?
I'LL FIND A CURE FOR MY SON'S CONDITION, OBVIOUSLY. THIS CULT WILL HAVE TO BE FURTHER INVESTIGATED, AND ITS METHODS BETTER UNDERSTOOD.
NOW THAT WE ARE A FAMILY AGAIN...PERHAPS YOU CAN FIND FURTHER PURPOSE ON OUR ROAD, REVIL.
FORGIVE ME FOR SAYING SO, MY FRIEND, BUT YOU SEEM LIKE A MAN WHO WOULD WITHER WITHOUT PURPOSE. PERHAPS THERE IS MORE WE CAN ACCOMPLISH TOGETHER. MY FAMILY... AND YOU.
I CAN ACCOMPANY YOU, KARLAIN.
FOR A LITTLE WHILE, ANYWAY.

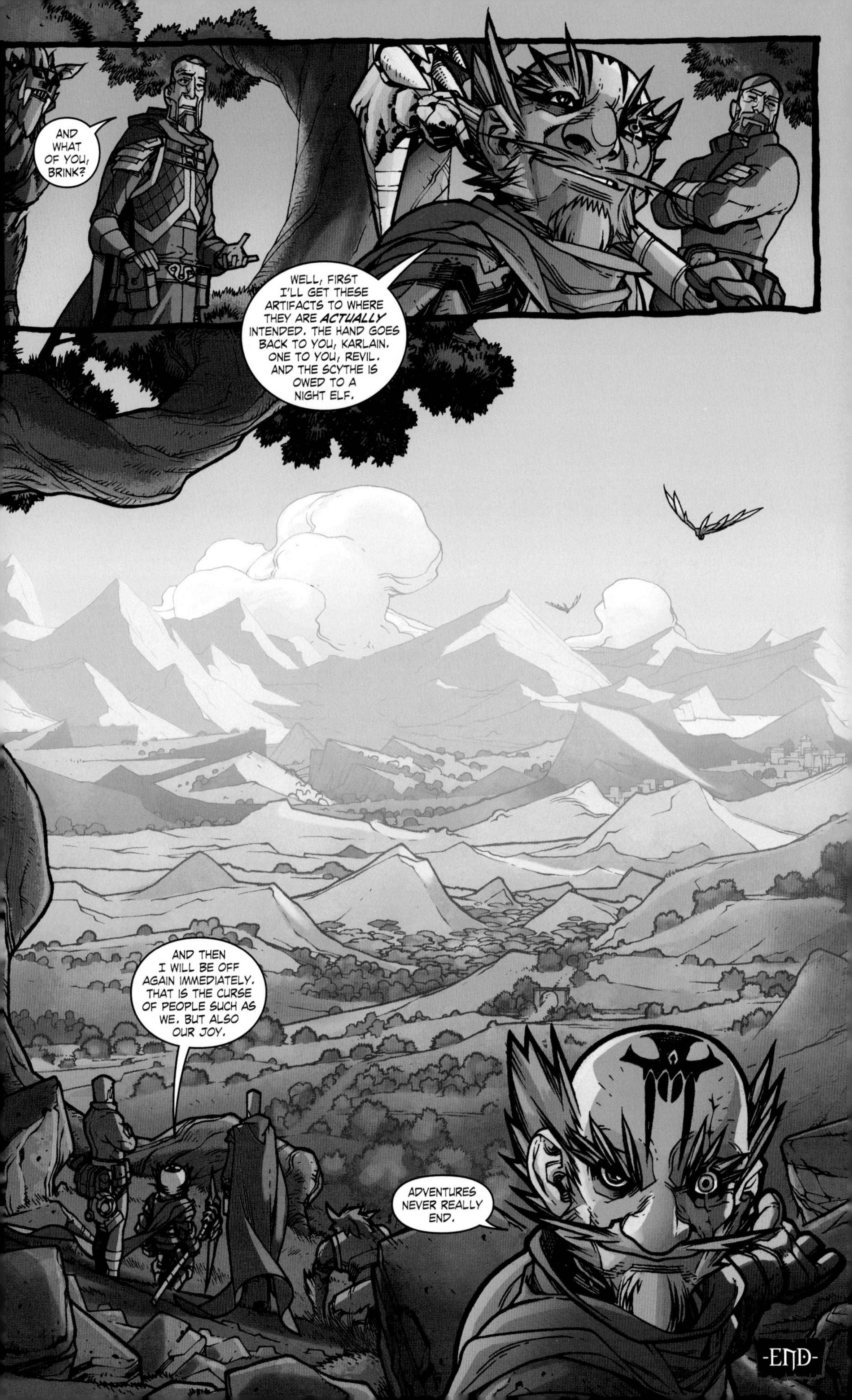
AND WHAT OF YOU, BRINK?
WELL, FIRST I'LL GET THESE ARTIFACTS TO WHERE THEY ARE ACTUALLY INTENDED. THE HAND GOES BACK TO YOU, KARLAIN. ONE TO YOU, REVIL. AND THE SCYTHE IS OWED TO A NIGHT ELF.
AND THEN I WILL BE OFF AGAIN IMMEDIATELY. THAT IS THE CURSE OF PEOPLE SUCH AS WE. BUT ALSO OUR JOY.
ADVENTURES NEVER REALLY END.
-END-

Go deeper
into the world
of the
DARK
RIDERS

Further Reading

If you'd like to read more about the characters, situations, and locations featured in this graphic novel, the sources listed below offer additional information.

- A glimpse into the lives of Karlain, Mardigan, Revil, and Brink before the events of this graphic novel can be found in Special Issue #1 of the World of Warcraft comic by Mike Costa and Pop Mhan. Additionally, Karlain's involvement in recent world events is depicted in World of Warcraft: Jaina Proudmoore: Tides of War by Christie Golden.

- The origins of the worgen have long been one of Azeroth's great mysteries. Details about these savage beasts and the mysterious artifact that created them are offered in World of Warcraft: Wolfheart by Richard A. Knaak; World of Warcraft: Curse of the Worgen by Micky Neilson, James Waugh, and Ludo Lullabi; and the short story "Lord of His Pack" by James Waugh (on www.WorldofWarcraft.com).

- Apart from the Dark Riders, other legends abound concerning Karazhan and the infamous Medivh, former Guardian of Tirisfal. More information about the haunted tower and its prior master is revealed in Warcraft: The Last Guardian by Jeff Grubb.

- Marshal Dughan, the stalwart defender of Elwynn Forest, makes an appearance in World of Warcraft: Stormrage by Richard A. Knaak, when he succumbs to the dreaded Emerald Nightmare.

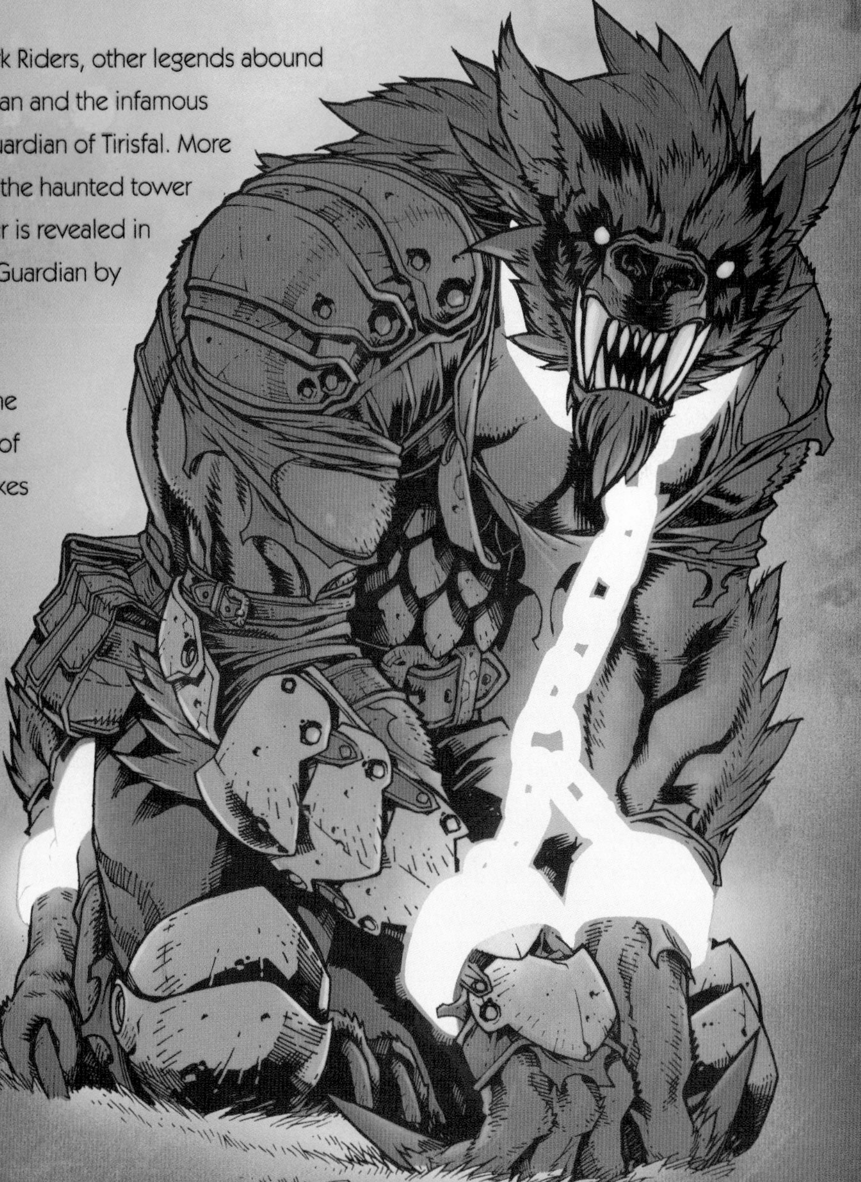

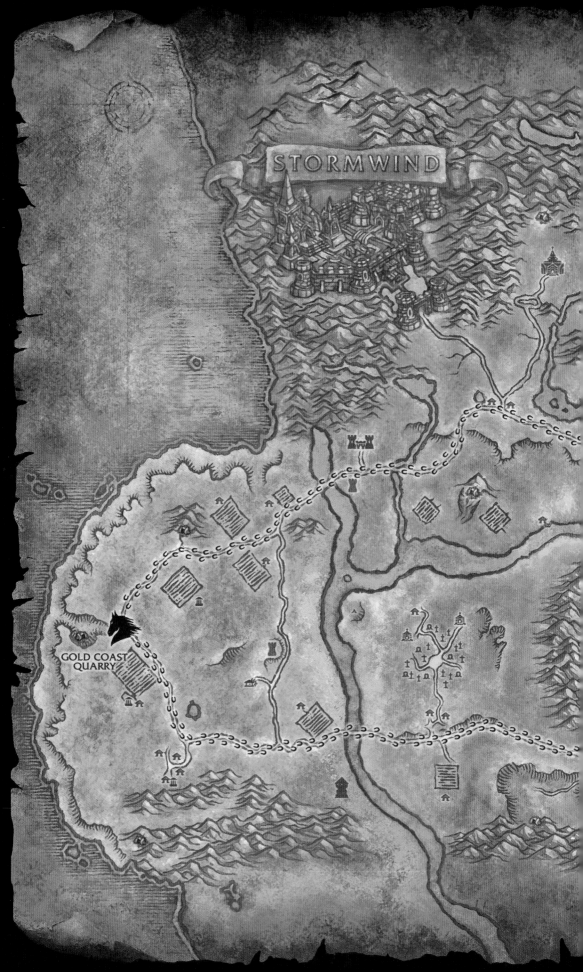

STORMWIND

GOLD COAST
QUARRY

PATH OF THE DARK RIDERS

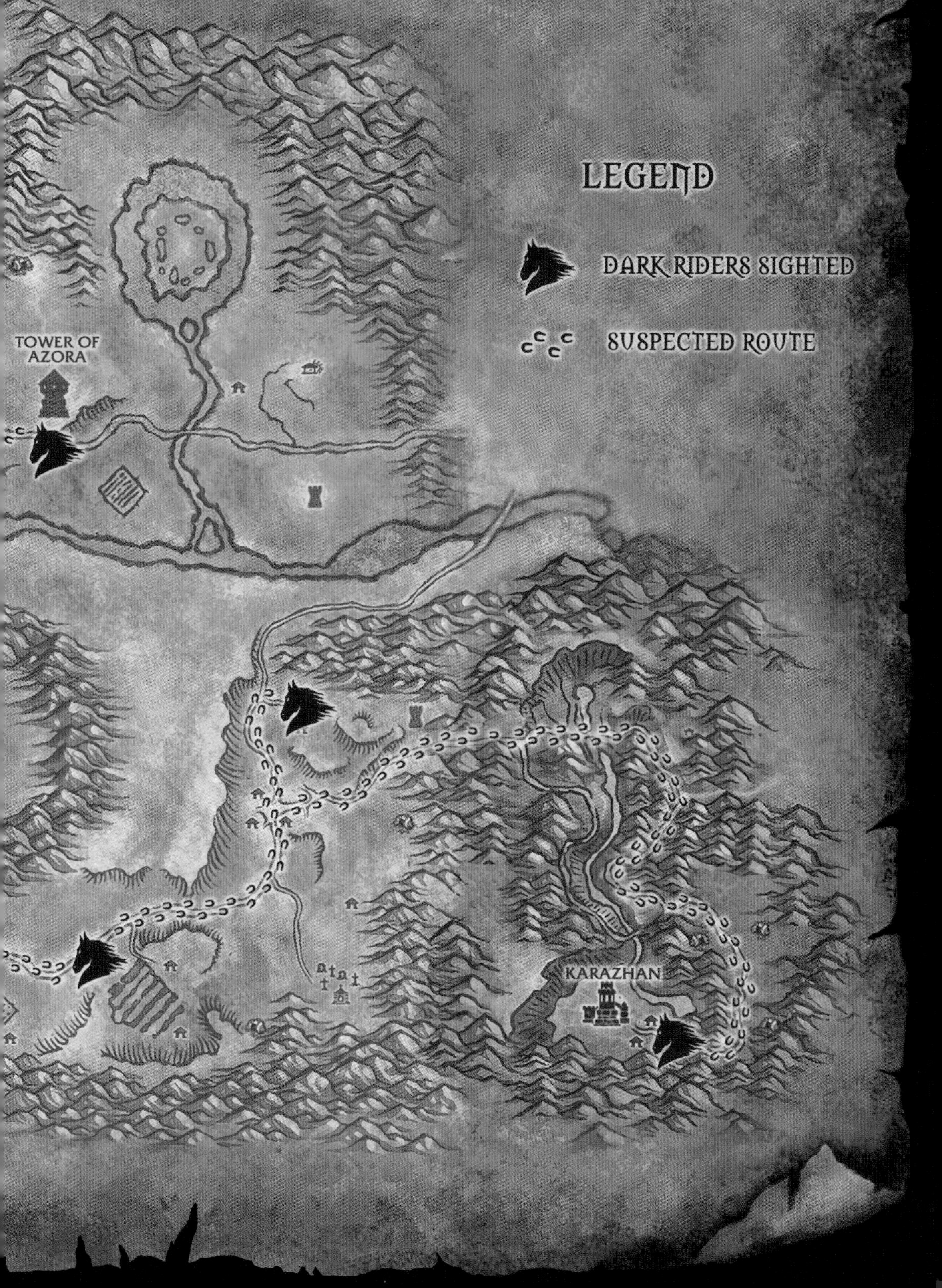
LEGEND
DARK RIDERS SIGHTED
SUSPECTED ROUTE
TOWER OF AZORA
KARAZHAN

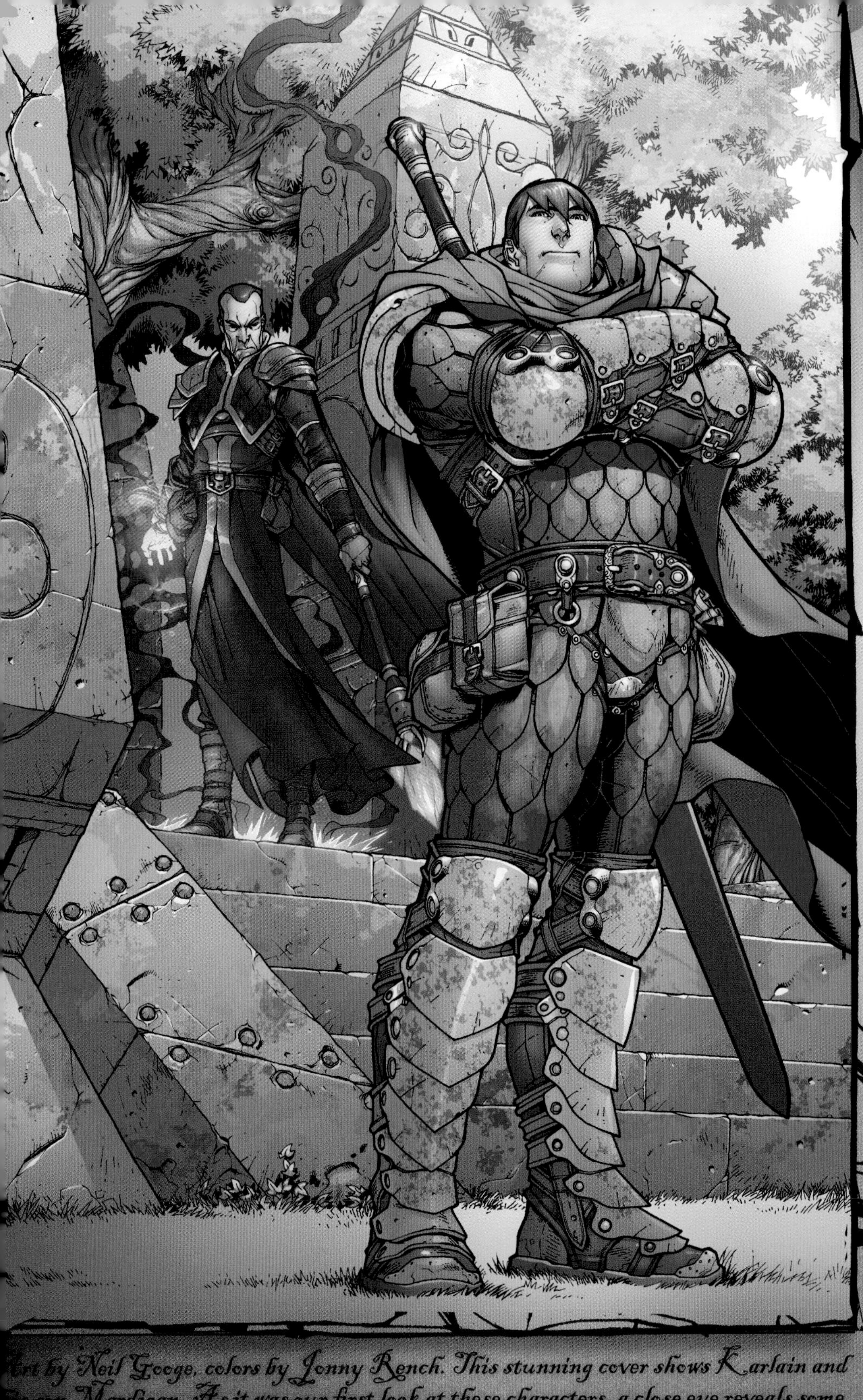

Art by Neil Googe, colors by Jonny Rench. This stunning cover shows Karlain and his son Mardigan. As it was our first look at these characters, a close eye reveals some small character design differences from the final versions.

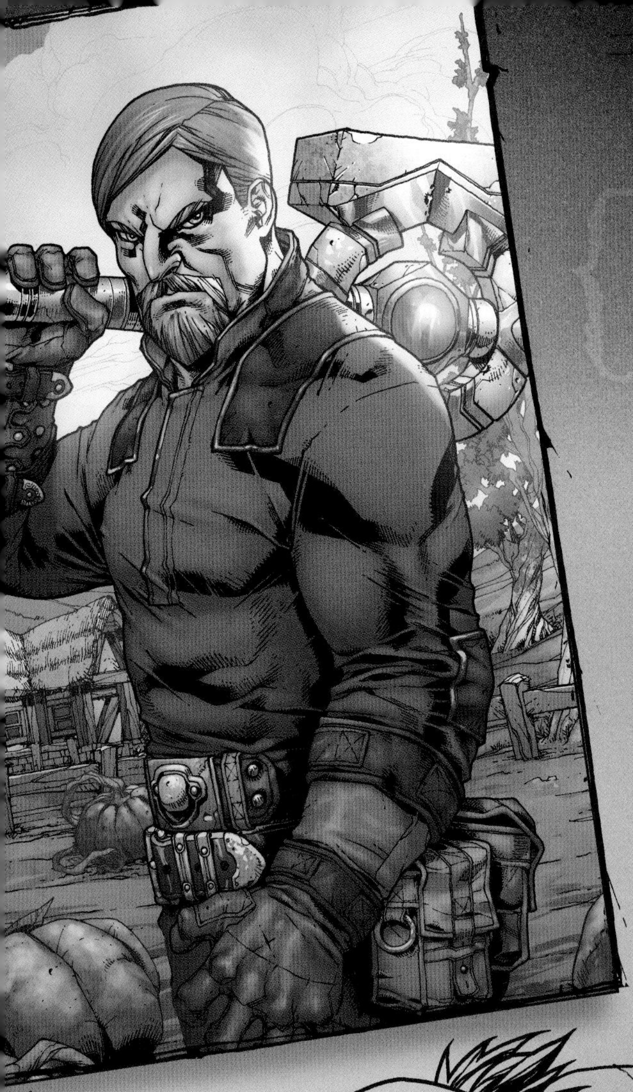

Art by Neil Googe, colors by Jonny Rench. This cover finds Revil in a serious pose, and would have been the cover to the second issue.

This stunning depiction of Brink by artist Neil Googe was to be used as a cover to a later issue. It was never colored by Jonny Rench as he tragically passed away in 2010, at the age of 28. We miss his immense artistic talent, in addition to his fantastic laugh and true friendship.

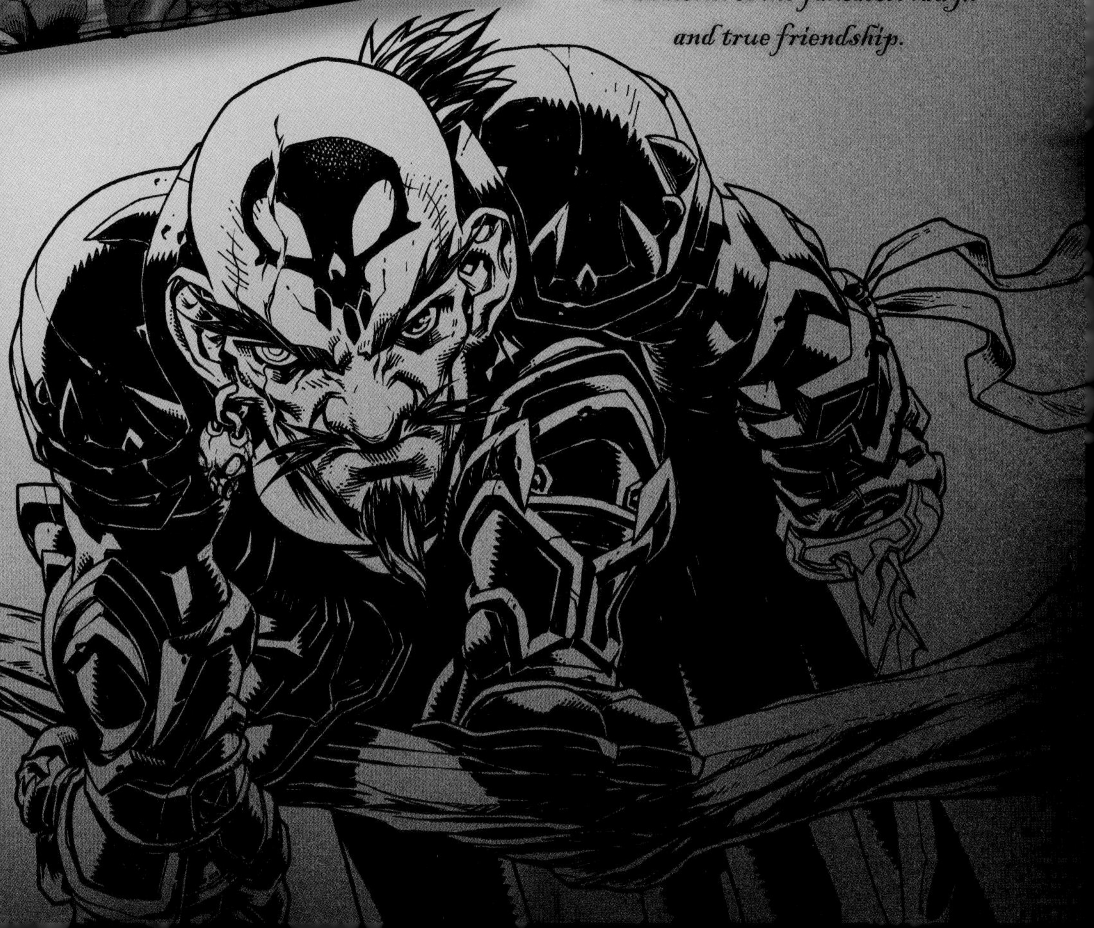

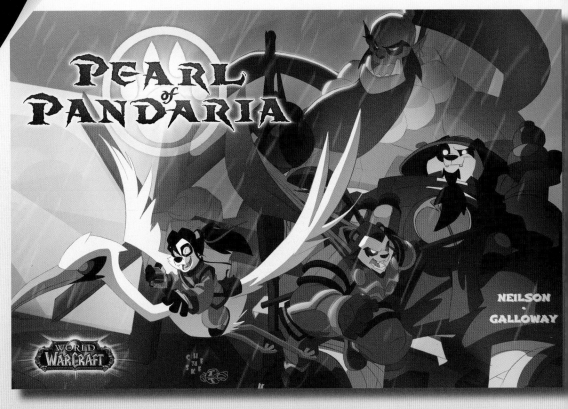

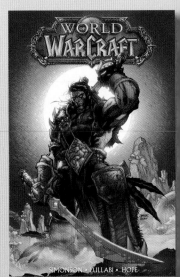